# take a hint from the heavens ...

**1986** is packed with promise. Make the most of it with the predictions, insights, clues and suggestions America's most popular astrologer, Sydney Omarr, has prepared for you!

Learn about the "geometry" of relationships—who you get along with, and why . . . pore over celebrity sun signs and personality profiles . . . discover how and why the movements of the zodiac affect men and women so differently . . . and much, much more. Whatever your desire, whatever your dilemma, let Sydney Omarr's time-tested wisdom guide you through 1986, and watch your dreams become exciting realities!

# For Expanding Your Personal Knowledge of Astrology, SIGNET Brings to You

## SYDNEY OMARR'S ASTROLOGICAL GUIDES FOR YOU IN 1986

- ☐ **ARIES** ...................................(136764—$2.75)*
- ☐ **TAURUS** ................................(136772—$2.75)*
- ☐ **GEMINI** ................................(136780—$2.75)*
- ☐ **CANCER** ...............................(136799—$2.75)*
- ☐ **LEO** ....................................(136802—$2.75)*
- ☐ **VIRGO** .................................(136810—$2.75)*
- ☐ **LIBRA** .................................(136829—$2.75)*
- ☐ **SCORPIO** ..............................(136837—$2.75)*
- ☐ **SAGITTARIUS** .........................(136845—$2.75)*
- ☐ **CAPRICORN** ...........................(136853—$2.75)*
- ☐ **AQUARIUS** ............................(136861—$2.75)*
- ☐ **PISCES** ...............................(136888—$2.75)*

*Price is $3.25 in Canada

---

**Buy them at your local bookstore or use this convenient coupon for ordering.**

**NEW AMERICAN LIBRARY**
**P.O. Box 999, Bergenfield, New Jersey 07621**

Please send me the books I have checked above. I am enclosing $__________
(please add $1.00 to this order to cover postage and handling). Send check
or money order—no cash or C.O.D.'s. Prices and numbers are subject to change
without notice.

Name__________________________________________

Address_______________________________________

City _______________ State ___________ Zip Code _________
Allow 4-6 weeks for delivery.
This offer is subject to withdrawal without notice.

# SYDNEY OMARR'S

DAY-BY-DAY ASTROLOGICAL GUIDE FOR

## *Gemini*

(MAY 21–JUNE 20)

## *1986*

A SIGNET BOOK

NEW AMERICAN LIBRARY

Copyright © 1985 by Sydney Omarr

All rights reserved

Sydney Omarr is syndicated worldwide by Los Angeles Times Syndicate.

# CONTENTS

# 1

---

# Defining Terms

## What Are Those Astrologers Talking About?

Everyone knows it is more fun to visit another country if you know a bit of the language, and it's a lot easier to find your way around, too. The same idea applies to astrology, which is still foreign territory to many people. Astrology has its very own language, but it really isn't difficult to get a handle on it as long as you understand a few important terms. What follows is a kind of "Astrological Phrase Book," a brief compendium of the most basic words and concepts in the astrological language. Once you've learned them, you'll find you know a lot more about the why of your sun sign as well as information that will help you understand other astrological factors that make you what you are. Best of all, your new language can help you enjoy and explore one of the most exciting, underdeveloped territories under the sun—modern astrology!

**Astrology Is an Ancient and Practical "Science"**
The first definition of astrology in the standard dictionary is "astronomy," and at one time in history the two studies were synonymous. The word astrology derives from Greek and literally means "the science (or study) of the stars." However, even in earliest times astrology has had much less to do with the "fixed" stars, which appear to remain in one place, than the planets, which move. (The word "planet" means wanderer.) Early man noticed that, as these heavenly bodies moved, their movements coincided with certain earthly events—mainly the changing of the seasons. Gradually, the movement

of the planets was observed to coincide with other important worldly events, such as wars, and the science of "divination" (prediction) by the planets was born. Astronomy and astrology lived happily together until the Christian church banned the latter in about 1550, condemning it as mere superstition. Astrology bounced back in the 1700s, when it came into use as an indicator of human personality, as well as a way to foretell future events. However, this so-called modern astrology is based on the same premise the ancients set down thousands of years ago: "As above, so below." Simply put, what it means is that the positions of the planets, which represent the cosmic order, are related in a significant and observable way to both human behavior and events in human life.

## The Zodiac Is a "Circle of Signs"

The zodiac ("circle of animals") is an invisible band in the sky which corresponds to the apparent yearly path of the sun, moon, and the major planets around the earth. It is the "apparent" path in the sense that it is what we *observe* from here on earth. Obviously we know that the earth and other planets revolve around the sun, but the study of astrology (and astronomy) takes earth as the reference point.

The 360-degree circle of the zodiac around the earth is divided into twelve thirty-degree segments—the twelve astrological signs. Throughout the year, as the sun appears to move, it passes through each of these segments in about thirty days. Zero degrees Aries, the vernal equinox or beginning of spring, is the beginning of the zodiac and the start of the seasonal year. It is at that point, on or about March 22, that the sun crosses or intersects with the *ecliptic*—another imaginary band that is (in the mind's eye) the extension of the earth's equator. Another major intersection of the sun's path and the ecliptic takes place at the fall equinox about September 22, the beginning of the seventh sign of the zodiac, Libra. (Equinox means equal days and nights, which is what we experience briefly in the early spring and early fall.) The zodiac "finishes" with the end of the twelfth sign Pisces, about March 21, then begins again with Aries.

Though the segments of the zodiac (the astrological signs) are *named* for the constellations of stars in the sky, they do not correspond with them. The constellations served as convenient visual markers for the ancient astrologer/priests, but the zodiac—and astrology—has always been based on the seasonal year, which never changes. The position of the constellations have changed with reference to our point of view here on earth, however, due to the slipping of the earth's axis. The constellations return a couple of degrees every year and have been doing so for centuries. That's why when the modern *astronomer* says "Aries," he is referring to a group of stars that is in a different position in the sky than the segment of the zodiac the *astrologer* calls "Aries."

**Your Sun Sign is Determined by the Month and Day You Were Born**
The twelve segments of the zodiac are the twelve astrological signs, from Aries through Pisces, and it takes the sun exactly one year to pass through all twelve signs. A person born when the sun is passing through a particular segment of the zodiac is said to be born under that sign, and it is his/her sun sign. For example, a person born October 14 is said to be born under the sign of Libra. Your sun sign is the most important component of your astrological personality, it is the "real you." However, there are nine other planets besides the sun, and at the moment of a person's birth, those planets are passing through certain segments of the zodiac, or signs, as well. You will learn about some of these lesser influences on your personality in this book later on.

**An Element Is Part of a Sign**
Obviously your sun sign is a lot more than simply a piece of the sky, or it wouldn't have any meaning. The meaning it has is based on two ancient astrological concepts, the *four elements* and the *three modes.* When these two factors are combined they form the basis of all astrological descriptions of human personality. You can't *see* an element or a quality; they are only to be under-

stood in terms of analogy, but they are fundamental to everything else in astrology, so it is important to understand them.

The four elements, defined by ancient philosophers as the basic components of everything and everybody, are *fire, earth, air,* and *water.* It is doubtful that even in earliest times this breakdown was to be taken as a physical reality: The elements are really four different ways we experience both things and people. For instance, if a thing or a person was experienced as hot rather than cold, sharp rather than dull, active rather than passive, it was said to partake of the *fire* element. And it's easy to see the connection.

Later on, during the Renaissance, the four elements were called "humors," starting a whole new way of typing people. *Fire was the humor choler*, and people who were said to have too much of it were those angry, impatient types who are subject to modern-day diseases like high blood pressure and heart attacks. *The earth element was called black bile* and could cause extreme melancholia (depression) in a person who had too much of it. *Air was the sanguine or rosy humor* and meant a lighter personality. *The water element was the humor phlegm,* and people with too much of it had rather "soggy" personalities and tended to be fat, as well. If the relationship between the elements (or humors) and the signs of the zodiac is beginning to ring a bell, it should. Here's the way the twelve signs break down into elements:

*Fire signs:* Aries, Leo, Sagittarius
*Earth signs:* Taurus, Virgo, Capricorn
*Air signs:* Gemini, Libra, Aquarius
*Water signs:* Cancer, Scorpio, Pisces

The four elements as four primal types of being exist today in the way many psychologists categorize people's thought processes. Once again, the relationship to the ways in which the twelve astrological signs really do perceive and react to the world is uncannily correct:

*The fire signs* are instant reactors who put it all together very quickly; things rarely have to be spelled out for a fire sign. These types of people also see the future possibilities inherent in the present and want to bring them about *now*. Obviously, fire signs tend to be impatient, but they have strong wills. Fire is the principle of *action*.

**The earth signs** are more pragmatic and slower to react. If they can't literally see something or touch it, they have difficulty visualizing it. They operate out of *sense perceptions* and are the realists of the zodiac—the builders who provide stability and continuity. Earth is the principle of *sustenance*.

**The air signs** see everything as connected to everything else. They are sequential thinkers for whom there must be a beginning, a middle, and an end to everything. For the most part these people operate on *logic* and act only when they can see the sense of their actions. The air signs are endlessly curious and represent the principle of *connecting and reasoning*.

**The water signs** tend to feel their way through life. What is most real to them is what their emotions tell them; they do what their emotions tell them to do as well. They are imaginative thinkers, the poets and artists of the zodiac. The water principle is that of *caring, nurturing, and protecting*.

## A Quality Is Part of a Sign

There are only four elements, but there are twelve signs. In astrological arithmetic, the *three qualities* which divide the *four elements* make up the difference. It isn't easy to grasp the concept of the elements, but the qualities (or "modes" as they are sometimes called) help a lot, because they make the elements a lot more tangible. Called *cardinal*, *fixed*, and *mutable*, the three modes can best be understood as *kinds of motion*.

*Cardinal motion is start-up movement.* It is the principle of bringing into being. Cardinal goes forward, so, the cardinal signs are *initiators*.

The four cardinal signs are those that start the four seasons:

Aries (*spring*)
Cancer (*summer*)

Libra (*fall*)
Capricorn (*Winter*)

*Fixed motion means staying in place.* Fixed things have come into being, and now simply are. The fixed signs represent stability, and are difficult to move. The four fixed signs represent the middle of each season:
Tarus (*spring*)
Leo (*summer*)
Scorpio (*fall*)
Aquarius (*winter*)

*Mutable motion means flexible motion.* Things that are mutable are changing, able to turn into something else. The mutable signs represent the *ability to adjust, and to accept change.* The four mutable signs are those that end the seasons:
Gemini (*spring*)
Virgo (*summer*)
Sagittarius (*fall*)
Pisces (*winter*)

## Elements and Qualities Together Add Up to Signs

When you put elements and qualities together you begin to get a picture of what they add up to—the twelve astrological signs. Here is how each quality modifies each element.

### *Fire element/Cardinal quality* = **Aries**

This get-up-and-go sign has all the flash and dash of fire plus an added dose of a pioneering spirit by virtue of its cardinal quality.

### *Fire element/Fixed quality* = **Leo**

Leo burns with the ardor and enthusiasms of fire, but gives off very steady heat due to its fixed quality.

### *Fire element/Mutable quality* = **Sagittarius**

Sagittarius represwents the kind of fire that spreads, igniting everything and everybody in its path—which is rather erratic because of Sagittarius's mutable quality.

### *Earth element /Cardinal quality* = **Capricorn**

Capricorn is the most active builder of the earth signs because of its cardinal quality. Capricorn's brand of reality demands that something be brought into being.

***Earth element/Fixed quality* = Taurus**
This strong sign stands and waits, holding things and people together. Taurus is the warmest and most nurturing of the earth signs, and is always "there."

***Earth element/Mutable quality* = Virgo**
Virgo's practical sense knows that all things must change. This mutable sign represents the principle of stability with flux; that is, permanence in the face of change.

***Air element/Cardinal quality* = Libra**
Libra's air nature moves forward, actively connecting people and things into partnerships via its cardinal quality of initiation.

***Air element/Fixed quality* = Aquarius**
Aquarius is the most immovable of the air signs, representing the permanance of ideas and their practical application.

***Air element/Mutable quality* = Gemini**
This very movable sign represents changing thoughts and opinions, the breaking up of static ideas so that new ones can come about.

***Water element/Cardinal quality* = Cancer**
Cancer is the most initiating of the water signs because of the cardinal quality. Though shy, Cancer generally moves quietly but effectively to the forefront.

***Water element/Fixed quality* = Scorpio**
Scorpio's powerful self-control comes from the emotional water element that is contained and compressed because of this sign's fixed quality.

***Water element/Mutable quality* = Pisces**
Pisces extreme emotionalism—as well as this sign's creativity—comes from feelings that constantly change and move into new areas, creating new outlets.

**Planets Are the Most Important Factor in Astrology**
"Planet" is probably an even more important word in the astrological language than "sign." How can that be?

*Because it is the placement of the planets in various signs which indicates personality and it is the movement of the planets through the zodiac that indicates events.* In other words, without the planets the signs would have no application to people and what happens to them.

As early man noticed that the planets moved in fairly regular patterns, he began to associate certain characteristics with each of the planets, and each planet gradually took on a "personality." In a number of different cultures, certain planets were hooked up with certain gods, because it was the gods who really controlled life on earth. The moon was virtually always a female god—like Diana or Artemis. Jupiter, always a "good guy" planet, was known as Vishnu, the preserver, to the Hindus. Before he got his Roman name of Jupiter, the Greeks knew him as Zeus, a lusty fellow who had a heart of gold. (You'll get a complete rundown on each of the planets in Chapter p, "The Planets As Stars.")

From these planetary "personalities" came the idea that each planet caused a certain kind of behavior or event by virtue of its own nature. For instance, Mars, always the war god, is still regarded by modern astrologers as an indicator of strife and conflict. When predicting events, the astrologer looks at what sign and what house Mars will be passing through at a certain point in time to see what kind of influence it is most likely to bring into a person's life.

When looking at personality, the astrologer determines which sign a person's Mars is in at the time of the person's birth to see how that individual is most likely to assert him-/herself. The sun, the most important planet makes us what we are in totality according to which sign the sun is placed in at our birth; i.e., our sun sign's Venus is the planet of relationships, and its placement in a specific sign shows how a person is likely to relate to others.

In short, planets indicate *action*, and the signs in which the planets are placed indicate *the kind of action*.

Since ancient times, astrologers have recognized seven planets. The sun (which is really a star), the moon (which is really a satellite of our own planet, earth) Mercury, Venus, Mars, Jupiter, and Saturn.

With the development of the telescope, three more planets were discovered (although there is some evidence that early astrologer/priests divined their existence). Uranus was first spotted in 1781, Neptune in 1846, and Pluto as late as 1930. Some astrologers/astronomers anticipate that there are two more to be found, so that there would be twelve planets instead of the current ten.

**A House Is an Area of Life—and a Planet's "Home"**
Just as there is a great circle in the sky called the zodiac, and it is divided into twelve equal units of *space*, there is another circle which is based on units of *time*. As we all know, the earth makes one complete rotation on its own axis every twenty-four hours. Imagine yourself standing in one place during a twenty-four-hour period and making a mark on the sky every two hours while that sky appears to pass by you as the earth turns. At the end of twenty-four hours, you will have marked off twelve different units of sky. A "house" is simply one of those pieces of sky that has passed by during your day-long vigil. Toward the end of your day of skywatching, twelve houses will have gone by, and "house one" will be coming up again.

When an astrologer draws up a natal horoscope—which is simply a map of the sky when you were born—he/she does it by drawing a picture of the sky as it appeared from the exact place of birth, at the exact time of your birth. What happens is that the twelve houses are lined up in a very specific way—a very different way than if you had been born *in another place at the same time* or *at the same time in another place.*

What is most important about the particular lineup of the houses is that each house represents a different area of human life, and how those areas are positioned *for you* has a tremendous effect on your astrological makeup. For instance, the second house is the house of income and personal possessions and has a lot to do with attitude toward money and how easy or how difficult it will be to come by in your lifetime. The seventh house is the house of partnership and offers clues about who you are likely to marry. If you know the time of your birth within one hour or so, you can add a very important dimension to your astrological self-knowledge by reading the chapter "Your House of the Sun—Your 'Piece of the Pie,' " because the house of the horoscope into which the sun falls in your horoscope usually indicates what area of life will absorb you during your lifetime.

## Your Rising Sign Is the One that Starts the First House

Your rising sign is sometimes called the ascendant, because it is the sign of the zodiac that was "ascending" on the eastern horizon at the time of your birth, no matter what time your birth occured. It is the "sunrise sign," corresponding to the nine o'clock position on the face of an ordinary clock. The astrologer's "clock" starts at this position and is read counter-clockwise around the circle of the face. If you were born around sundown, your rising sign will be the one 180 degrees *opposite* the sign you were born under. For instance, if you are an Aries born at sundown, your rising sign will be Libra. If you are an Aries born at sunrise, your rising sign is probably Aries as well.

Why is your rising sign so important? Because it starts the first house of personality, or your very individual way of presenting yourself to the world. No matter what your sun sign is, your rising sign will cover it to a greater or lesser degree (which is why it is so difficult to guess someone's Sun Sign when you first meet them). The rising sign has to do with appearances and can actually influence your physical looks.

If you don't know the time of day you were born, you can't determine your rising sign (although some astrologers can by doing what is called a "rectification," based on the events in your life so far). However, even those who do not know their rising sign can have their horoscopes read; what the astrologer does is put your sun sign on the first house, and do an analysis of what is called a solar horoscope. If you *do* know your birthtime within an hour or so, you can use the rising sign chart in this book to determine yours.

**Planets in Signs in Houses Make Up a Horoscope**
The whole basis of astrology is that anyone born in a particular moment in time partakes of the qualities of that moment in time. Actually, the same applies for things; for instance, a business that has its beginnings at a precise astrological moment also has a horoscope which can be read, and tells a lot about its potential for success or failure.

An astrologer looks at the particular moment in drawing up a horoscope—or "picture of the hour." A horoscope is basically a map of the sky, showing exactly where the planets were in relation to the signs and the houses, to each other, and from the particular reference point of your birthplace. It is also called a "natal chart" or "natal map."

Everyone's horoscope has ten planets and twelve houses. Those ten planets can be in a variety of signs, and in a variety of houses. Each planet means something different according to its own nature, how that nature operates in a particular sign, and what area of life the planet is most likely to affect by virtue of which house of the horoscope it falls into. Sound complicated? It is, and only a highly trained astrologer can interpret the many factors and put them together for you in a meaningful way. The most exciting part of astrology is the fact that *no two individuals are ever exactly alike*—not even twins, who are born a few minutes apart.

Although you can find out a lot about your astrological personality right in this book, many people like to take the next step and have a personalized horoscope drawn up for them and interpreted by a professional astrologer. There are a number of ways to find a good person to do this for you; in astrology, as in every other profession, there are variations in the level of competence. Two places you can start your search are:

National Astrological
   Society
62 West 39th St.
New York, NY 10018

American Federation of
   Astrologers
Tempe, AZ 85282

**An Aspect Is the Distance Between Planets**
Among the more sophisticated factors an astrologer looks for in your horoscope are the *aspects*. Within the 360-degree circle of the horoscope (and the zodiac), planets form certain aspects to each other by virtue of the distance between them. Some distances are considered harmonious, and some are inharmonious, in terms of how those two (or more) planets work together. It's all a matter of mathematics. The soft or harmonious aspects are the sextile (60 degrees apart) and the trine (120 degrees apart). The hard or inharmonious aspects are formed when planets are in square to each other (90 degrees apart) or in opposition, 180 degrees or exactly half a circle apart. These are only the major aspects, and there are lots and lots of minor ones between, but you can get a good picture of interplanetary relationships with only these few.

For example, if your sun sign is Aries, and at the time of your birth the planet Saturn was in the sign of Libra, or 180 degrees away from Aries, you are likely to have a more serious (Saturnine) disposition than the typical "happy" Aries. Depending on your point of view, this can be a positive note in your horoscope, because you will have greater powers of concentration than many an Aries—or a negative note, because you will be less happy-go-lucky. In another example, a person with a Capricorn sun sign may have a horoscope in which Jupiter, the planet of expansiveness, is 120 degrees away from the sun—either in the sign of Virgo or Taurus— and therefore in "trine" aspect to his/her sun. The result: a much more outgoing, giving Capricorn than the run-of-the-mill type. On the other hand, such an easy aspect could expand Capricorn's acquisitive nature too much, and make for a megalomanic (someone who craves worldly goods and power).

The ancients separated aspects into "favorable" and "unfavorable," but psychologically-thinking modern astrologers know that it is not that simple; it all depends on the total horoscope, plus the individual's reactions to the particular vibrations of the planets in that horoscope.

## A Transiting Planet Affects Your Life Now

When someone goes to an astrologer for the first time, he/she usually has *two* readings—separate, but interrelated. The first will be an interpretation of your natal chart or birth horoscope. This tells you about your given personality—the traits, problems, abilities, and advantages you are most likely to have by virtue of the placement of the planets in the sky at the time of your birth. The second reading will have to do with what you can expect in your life at the present time and the near future. Your birth horoscope always remains the same, but the planets in the sky keep changing their relationships to your birth horoscope throughout your lifetime. The astrologer will acquaint you with the current "transit"—or movements—of the planets and how you, the individual, can expect them to affect you. For instance, if an astrologer notes that Uranus, the "earthquake planet," is approaching your fourth house (the house of emotional security, the place where we really live), the astrologer might alert you to the fact that big changes are in the offing: even a total shaking of the foundations, or a pulling up of roots. This is a major transit, and many people change their residence, partners, or jobs when it occurs. Similarly, but on a less critical note, the astrologer may notice that the planet Venus is going to make a transit over the place in the zodiac occupied by Mars in your birthchart. This could indicate a firey romantic interlude or the rekindling of an old flame.

There are two important things to keep in mind about astrological predictions. The first is that your natal horoscope—your "birth imprint"—really determines how you will react to life's events. To put it even more strongly, your innate personality will really *create* the events of your life, because "character is destiny." There is no doubt that the planets create conditions, but we must take responsibility for how we cooperate with those conditions. The second thing is that *there are very few hard and fast rules*. There are guidelines, to be sure, and most of them have ancient roots; a lot of astrological prediction is based on the case history technique. However, since no two sets of conditions—

the one in the sky and the one in an individual birthchart—are ever *exactly* the same, it is virtually impossible for any astrologer to tell you specifically what is going to happen.

# 2

# Your House of the Sun

## Your "Piece of the Pie"

The prime symbol in the very symbolic language of astrology is the perfect circle; it represents the sky around us, the cosmic atmosphere into which we are all born. All astro-math is based on division of the 360-degree figure, which since ancient times has been regarded as having mystical qualities. When thinking about the houses of the horoscope, however, it helps to use a very down-to-earth analogy. Look at that circle as a great "pie in the sky," which is divided into twelve cosmic slices—each slice representing one house and a different facet of human experience.

Just as there are ten planets in everyone's horoscope, there are twelve houses. However, not all those houses may be occupied by a planet; it all depends on where the planets were in the sky at the moment of your birth. The placement of any planet in a specific house is a *very* important factor in your individual horoscope, but the most important is the placement of the sun. No matter what your sun sign, your House of the Sun has a lot to tell you about the life you've been "given" to live on this earth. As your sun sign is the prime indicator of *character and personality*, your house of the sun points to the *area of human affairs* that you are most likely to find yourself concentrating on in your lifetime.

In the sense that it helps define the boundaries of your life, your house of the sun is your "piece of the pie"—that slice of life within which you will live. Does your house of the sun totally box you in? In a way it does, but it is more productive to think of the dimensions of your house of the sun as *guidelines* about where you can most profitably focus your energies.

Here's the way it works:

- The *sun* is the most important planet in your horoscope. It is the planets that do the "acting," and the sun plays the leading role.
- Your sun sign determines *how* your sun (the real you) acts, i.e., the characteristics of the character you play.
- Your house of the sun is the "stage" on which you will play out your role.

For instance, if your sun sign is Scorpio (the great investigator) and your house of the sun is the twelfth (hidden things), you find yourself drawn to some kind of career in which you must "dig" to do your investigating. Ergo, you might make a good psychoanalyst, archeologist, or genetic researcher. Or, your greatest pleasure in life might be reading mystery novels or spy thrillers—or writing or editing them.

In order to figure out which piece of the pie you've been served, you have to know your birth-time within an hour or so. If you were born during Daylight Savings Time or War Time, you have to subtract one hour from your birth time to determine the "real sun time."

Each house is described here from three different angles:

- The matters or principles connected with it
- The people/places/things related to it
- The problems and the possibilities of having your sun in that house.

Birth time, 4 to 6 a.m.: **Sun in First House**

- *First house matters:* Exploration . . . use of the physical body . . . being on the scene . . . breaking new ground . . . independent action . . . emergencies . . . conquest . . . controversy . . . strategy . . . competition . . . being in the vanguard.

- *First house people/places/things:* Entrepreneurs . . . acrobats . . . cutting instruments . . . rock music . . . metals . . . satire . . . hardware . . . the head and face . . . opticians . . . adrenalin . . . new products . . . commodities . . . salesmen . . . fighters . . . firemen.
- *Problems and possibilities:* With your sun in the first house, your sun sign personality is quite strong. Regardless of what your sun sign is, you should be able to make clear-cut decisions and have a good sense of your own identity. If you are to gain control over your life, you are going to have to banish fear from it and develop both the moral and the physical courage that is available to you. Though your will should be strong, you will have to keep yourself from a tendency to tyrannize others. When you feel most defeated is the time your first house sun will come to your rescue. The one thing that could keep you from living out the very vivid life this house placement gives you is inflexibility and intolerance. Be willing to listen.

Birth time, 2 to 4 a.m.: **Sun in Second House**

- *Second house matters:* Calmness . . . conservation . . . ability to make grow . . . eroticism . . . collecting . . . comforting . . . administrating . . . luxury . . . stabilizing . . . building up . . . perpetuating . . . patience . . . using . . . making stronger . . . indulging.
- *Second house people/places/things:* Possessions . . . money . . . the voice . . . landscape gardeners . . . brokers and bankers . . . love/passion . . . personal adornment . . . life-sustaining skills . . . buying and selling . . . security needs . . . nurses . . . food and shelter . . . good music . . . creature comforts.
- *Problems and possibilities:* You should be able to establish yourself firmly and securely in whatever you choose to do; self-adjustment should come easily to you. Your economic life could be relatively worry-free but you must resist valuing money and

possessions for their own sake and becoming overly materialistic. You must develop the will that is given you and turn it into willpower, or you could lose self-respect. You are a good manager, but if you allow yourself to become too settled, you will fear to take the necessary risks to make your life less limited. Though things come to you fairly easily, do not let yourself over-indulge in any of them, including rich food.

Birth time midnight to 2 a.m.: **Sun in Third House**

- *Third house matters:* Connecting . . . associating . . . verbalizing . . . dexterity . . . inquisitiveness . . . distribution . . . novelty . . . thinking and reasoning . . . cause and effect . . . exchanging . . . bringing the news . . . being responsive . . . "here today, gone tomorrow."
- *Third house people/places/things:* Short journeys . . . realatives (especially siblings) . . . speech/languages . . . high school teachers . . . role-playing/entertaining . . . computers . . . graphic arts . . . handwork . . . transportation . . . the nervous system . . . handwriting . . repair men . . . gossip . . . comedy . . . ventriloquists.
- *Problems and possibilities:* You should be an excellent communicator who reports things clearly and accurately. In your desire for information, however, you could become rather superficial and a bit of a talebearer. If you don't focus your mental energies carefully, you may waste the gift of curiosity your third house sun gives you. You must also learn to live with uncertainty, and to keep your opinions flexible. If life scares you, you are likely to become very defensive and locked in to your ideas. Develop your capacity for listening as well as your talent for talking.

Birth time 10 p.m. to 12 a.m.: **Sun in Fourth House**

- *Fourth house matters:* Adaptability . . . change . . . instinctiveness . . . fluctuation . . . protecting . . .

imagination . . . softness . . . the subconscious . . . survival . . . enveloping . . . integrating . . . fertility . . . mothering.

- *Fourth house people/places/things:* Dreams . . . the past . . . roots . . . home and family . . . physical sensation . . . museums . . . caterers . . . water and other liquid . . . introverts . . . obstetrics . . . boats . . . domestics . . . imagination.
- *Problems and possibilities:* Via your fourth house sun, you are given the possibility of understanding yourself and your motivations quite thoroughly. If you handle your life in a mature way, you will establish a warm and comfortable home for you and your family. However, you must strive for real self-knowledge if you are not to become simply self-absorbed and self-centered. Your imagination is considerable, and you could be highly creative; the down side is that you could develop irrational fears that verge on paranoia. Work to see the world clearly at all times and try to conquer your tendency to play the introvert. No mater what your sun sign, the placement of that sun in the fourth house will make you instinctively avoid the limelight. Get out there and shine!

## Birth time 8 to 10 p.m.: **Sun in Fifth House**

- *Fifth house matters:* Being at the heart of things . . . pleasures . . . power . . . ambition . . . generosity/giving . . . "gilding the lily" . . . showmanship . . . stability . . . management . . . territorial rights . . . self-expression . . . autocracy . . . organization.
- *Fifth house people/places/things:* Philanthropy . . . corporations . . . impresarios . . . holidays and vacations . . . romantic love . . . children . . . gamblers . . . gold . . . circuses . . . nursery teachers . . . fashion and fashion designers . . . public life.
- *Problems and possibilities:* Even if you have a "shy" sun sign, your fifth house placement of the sun will force you into some form of self-expression that is possibly very creative. You also have a capability

for approaching life with a joyful, expectant manner; however, your pursuit of pleasure and play could become extreme. Consciously avoid any pleasure that threatens to get out of control. Your affairs of the heart could be many, but it is important to keep alert for anything that smacks of an abusive partner; it's possible you could enjoy the drama of an unhappy situation. Develop your capacity for warmly accepting others.

Birth time 6 to 8 p.m.: **Sun in Sixth House**

- *Sixth house matters:* Competence/skill . . . specialization . . . refining . . . categorizing . . . analyzing . . . obedience . . . realism . . . responsibility . . . purifying . . . invention . . . making things work . . . ministering . . . discriminating.
- *Sixth house people/places/things:* Service . . . critics . . . crafts . . . libraries . . . closets . . . public health . . . the harvest . . . small animals . . . dependents . . . dental hygienists . . . research . . . diagnosing . . . numbers work . . . chemists.
- *Problems and possibilities:* With your sun in the sixth house you have the potential of becoming a true master at something; however, if you allow yourself to get bogged down in life's details, you could possibly end up being a wage slave. No matter what your sun sign, your instincts tell you to be of service to others. While you are capable of great self-sacrifice, you must avoid the temptation to be overly humble and to assume the servant role. You are mentally very keen, and can break things and jobs down into smaller parts in order to accomplish them. Do not let the state of your own health become an obsession. With the sun is the sixth house, your basic constitution should be quite strong. Don't worry!

Birth time 4 to 6 p.m.: **Sun in Seventh House**

- *Seventh house matters:* Sharing . . . comparing . . . give-and-take . . . peacemaking . . . negotiation . . .

making things beautiful ... creating balance ... fairness ... sociability ... gratification ... advocacy ... diplomacy ... aestheticism.

- *Seventh house people/places/things:* Divorce lawyers ... love poetry ... marriage brokers ... the kidneys and lower back ... illustration ... resort managers ... public relations ... fine arts ... receptionists ... boutiques ... jugglers ... tailors ... pianos.
- Possibilities and problems: You have a great need to identify with others, and can create a wonderful rapport with them easily. However, your need for a life partner could make you overly dependent. If you have an independent sun sign, this could create a serious life conflict. With this placement, you are able to adjust to new people and new situations easily, but you must avoid a tendency not to stick with a position when you really believe in it. You have the potential of forming very warm, balanced and intimate relationships; however, if you do not handle this gift in a mature manner, you could develop a fear of intimacy, and shy away from it or become an outrageous and insincere flirt.

Birth time 2 to 4 p.m.: **Sun in Eighth House**

- *Eighth house matters:* Release of blockages ... probing ... anonymity ... procreation ... rejuvenation ... willpower ... endurance ... controlling ... investigation ... aloneness ... demolishing and rebuilding ... crisis ... elimination.
- *Eighth house people/places/things:* Puzzles ... generals ... political parties ... labor lawyers ... the healing arts ... death and dying ... taxes ... spies ... superathletes ... crime detection ... statesmen ... sex symbols ... geologists ... explorers ... mating instinct ... sanitation engineers.
- *Problems and possibilities:* A light sun sign (like Gemini or Libra), the placement of the sun in this house will add depth to your character. You will feel compelled to investigate things that are hidden or

even dangerous. While it is good to probe, you must beware of a tendency to concentrate on what is morbid. All things being equal, you will be highly sexed; however, with insufficient self-knowledge, your healthy sexual instincts could turn into obsession with the subject—or a total advoidance of it. Learn to live with your dynamic physical body and you will live with others quite happily. Also, encourage your religious or mystical feelings, which are quite real. You have the potential of totally transforming your life at one point or another.

Birth time noon to 2 p.m.: **Sun in Ninth House**

- *Ninth house matters:* Anticipating ... aspiring ... moving around ... expanding things ... speculating ... idealism ... advising ... unpredictability ... search for truth ... search for opportunity ... taking aim ... magnanimity ... excess.
- *Ninth house people/places/things* Casinos ... ambassadors ... passport offices ... luck ... international transportation ... trading/high finance ... dancers ... aristocrats ... large animals ... higher studies ... lawmaking ... profiteers ... veterinarians.
- *Problems and possibilities:* Even if you have a routine-loving sun sign (like Virgo), this placement of the sun will give you the desire and the ability to constantly renew your life, and to adapt to new patterns of behavior. You will feel strongly about one religious or ethical system or another, or at least have a very strong personal philosophy. However, you could become rather dogmatic and rigid in your opinions. Your adaptability is admirable, but a desire for the new and novel could be the "downside" of your openness to new experience. Exercise control. With certain sun signs, there may be a tendency toward inner battles between opportunity-seeking and a firm set of principles. You are a spender—of both your money and your physical resources.

Birth time 10 a.m. to 12 a.m.: **Sun in Tenth House**

- *Tenth house matters:* Realism . . . structure . . . ambition . . . rigidity . . . integrating . . . limitation . . . disciplining . . . reputation . . . social position . . . creating the useful . . . contraction . . . coolness . . . convention.
- *Tenth house people/places/things:* Figures . . . fame . . . common sense . . . property . . . correctional systems and facilities . . . ceramics . . . money lenders . . . efficiency experts . . . the bones . . . the elderly . . . sculptors . . . watches and clocks.
- *Problems and possibilities:* You have the capacity of becoming a respected member of whatever group you move in, because your public image is very important to you. If you play your cards right, you can arrive at a sense that you are fulfilling your destiny. However, if you become obsessed with power and appearances, you could end up living a shallow, meaningless life behind your strong facade. It is most important with this placement of the sun to find the right outlet for you to express yourself and get positive feedback from others. You won't be happy starving in a garret, because both money and recognition are too important to you. This position of the sun often brings fame.

Birth time 8 to 10 a.m.: **Sun in Eleventh House**

- *Eleventh house matters:* Helping . . . experimentation . . . humanitarianism . . . association . . . liberalism . . freedom . . . suddenness . . . awakenings . . . combining . . . freethinking . . . rationality . . . caring . . . breaking through . . . observing coolly . . . predicting.
- *Eleventh house people/places/things:* Paradoxes . . . stunt men . . . electricity . . . zealots . . . divorce . . . fireworks . . . the social sciences . . . reform . . . geniuses . . . aviation . . . weathermen . . . brotherly love . . . magnetism . . . groups . . . friends . . . causes.
- *Problems and possibilities:* If you are a very personal

sun sign (like Cancer), you will gain a lot of objectivity with the placement of the sun in this house. You should have very high aims and goals, and some of them will undoubtedly involve helping the less fortunate in some way or another. Though this is admirable, if you don't set yourself on a definite path in life and stick to a definite plan, you could simply drift along, with only vague ideas about where you can shine. It is important to be quite realistic with the sun in this house. Your own crowd is important to you, but you must avoid becoming such a part of the group that you lose a sense of your own individuality—which is potentially very great. Some people with the sun in the 11th house are downright wacky, but often very achieving people.

## Birth Time 6 to 8 a.m.: Sun in Twelfth House

- *Twelfth house matters:* Dissolving ... ambiguity ... disguising ... retreating ... sensualism ... enchantment ... paying dues ... healing spiritually ... insubstantiality ... confinement ... persuading ... comprehending the incomprehensible ... merging ... pretending.
- *Twelfth house people/places/things:* Makeup ... escapism ... alcohol and drugs ... drama and dramatic actors ... films ... advertising ... pastoral work ... fishing ... astrophysics ... con men ... magicians ... hospitals ... alibis ... myths ... prisons.
- *Problems and possibilities:* Yours is not an easy house of the sun to have—especially if you are a very self-expressive sun sign type like Leo. You may feel that life is confining you in some way or another; what you are really sensing is your gift of the ability to transcend self to a much higher spiritual level. You should be an expert at coping with intangibles and sensing the nuances of any situation. In a sense, you have a kind of ESP which can be developed for life success. However, the real down side of the twelfth house sun is that it

can lead to a very confused, unfocussed attitude toward life. It is essential that you give yourself a definite structure to work within if you are to free yourself from the worries and cares of life. By all means avoid any form of escapism that is dangerous.

# 3

# The Geometry of Relationships

## What Signs You Get Along with—and Why

The first thing most people want to know about their sun sign is what other signs they are compatible with. It's a natural question, and a good one to ask an astrologer, because one aspect of astrology, called "synastry" (literally, "stars together") concentrates on the subject of relationships. When practising synastry, the astrologer compares the two birth charts of the two people involved to find what connections there are between them. It is a complicated process, but it provides excellent clues about how two people will relate to each other. What chart comparison does is *describe the nature of the relationship*. Actually, to an astrologer there are no "bad" or "good" relationships; there are just a lot of different kinds and each has a special character. Of course it is true that some relationships end up on the rocks, sometimes devastating one or both parties involved. But, even in such cases, the astrologer looks at it as a "karmic" relationship—one in which people *had* to come together in order to learn some life lessons.

While comparing two complete horoscopes is the ideal way to look at a relationship, there is a very simple method of looking at two sun signs, and coming up with an overall prediction of how two people will relate to each other. This method goes back to the great circle of the zodiac and to the division of the twelve signs into four elements: fire, earth, air, and water.

Here's the lineup of signs in each element:

**Fire:** Aries, Leo, Sagittarius

**Earth:** Taurus, Virgo, Capricorn
**Air:** Gemini, Libra, Aquarius
**Water:** Cancer, Scorpio, Pisces

The general rules of thumb for element-mixing are as follows:

| Great | Good | Semi-tough or Difficult |
| --- | --- | --- |
| Fire and air | Fire and fire | Fire and water |
| Water and earth | Earth and earth | Earth and air |
| | Air and air | Fire and earth |
| | Water and water | Air and water |

Here's the way it looks mathmatically:
  If you divide the 360-degree circle of the zodiac by the twelve signs, you find that each sign is 30 degrees away from the next.
  • Signs that are 30 degrees apart—or next to each other—are semi-tough.
  • Signs that are 60 degrees (two signs) or 180 degrees (six signs) away from each other are the best combinations. (The latter, 180 degrees away from each other, makes these signs polar opposites, and in astrology polar opposites attract.)
  • Signs that are 120 degrees apart—four signs away from each other—are in the same element, and their relationship is good, but far from perfect.
  • Signs that are 90 degrees or three signs away from each other have the most difficult relationships of all. They are said to be in "square aspect" to each other.

When you look at the four elements in terms of what they signify in the physical world, you get a good idea why some elements get along more easily.

*Fire turns water into steam* (hot air).
*Water puts fire out.*
*Fire scorches earth.*

*Earth smothers fire.*
*Air fans fire and makes it brighter.*
*Fire warms up cool air.*
*Water softens up hard earth.*
*Earth makes water keep its shape.*
*Water and air do nothing (unless you add heat).*
*Air blows earth around.*

What about combinations of the same element, such as fire with fire? In effect, they tend to neutralize or cancel each other out. Or, they can simply be too much of one element for comfort.

- Two fire signs together could experience "burn out" fairly quickly.
- Two air signs might analyze each other to the death of the relationship.
- Two earth signs could depress each other a lot.
- Two water signs could make for an overly "heavy" relationship.

# 4

# Twelve Places at the Table

## A Mini Astrodrama in Which the Twelve Signs Play Themselves

No matter how accurate or colorful any description of a zodiac sign may be, it is still a description—not the real thing. A sign is simply an abstract concept until it takes form in a living, breathing human being. There are obviously as many different types of people as there are individual horoscopes, and no two are exactly alike. However, the twelve signs of the zodiac are still the best guidelines we have for sorting out human behavior into broad but meaningful categories. There are even fiction writers who use the zodiac signs as prototypes for characters they create because it makes them more realistic, i.e., more like people you are likely to meet.

What follows is fiction, but it gets closer to the truth about each zodiacal sign than a general description ever can. The twelve characters in this docudrama are obviously caricatures, because their behavior is highly exaggerated. But it is exaggeration for emphasis, and for the purpose of bringing to life the twelve signs of the zodiac, which don't really exist except as real people. Like real people, these twelve characters have foibles; but they have fine points too. As you read this drama, you may find yourself drawn to some signs and put off by others. Make mental notes of which signs you find yourself most sympathetic with and check out your findings in the parts of this book about astrological compatibility. It could prove very interesting—

and very revealing. As each sign of the zodiac has a sex or gender, they are portrayed here as male or female accordingly. But the basic behavior pattern is applicable to both sexes.

The twelve signs of the zodiac are invited to dinner at that great dining room in the sky. When they arrive, they find that their host (who shall remain signless) has slipped up, and there are only eleven places set at the table. Since it is a fancy affair, each sign is trying to be on his/her best behavior. However, the situation is a bit unsettling, so in the course of trying to resolve it, they all relapse into their natural zodiacal characteristics.

*Aries*  An energetic young man, he comes bounding into the room, almost tripping on an untied shoelace. He is dressed rather casually for the occasion, and looks as if he got dressed rather quickly. When he realizes what the situation is, there's no doubt in his mind how to handle it.

"Only eleven places? Don't worry; Pisces will probably never show anyway. But, I got here before anybody else (the doorman will prove it) so I should definitely get a seat. In fact, I should sit down *first*. No, I don't need to wash my hands or anything. I'm *starved*, so I hope you aren't having anything like the gooey mess with the French name you had before. A hamburger will do just fine. And don't serve it cold like you did the last time. Hey, there's a great-looking dish over there, ha ha! Seat me next to her, will you Cancer? Well, she looks like a nice warm type, so I think I'll go let her warm me up. By the way, I'm organizing a sky-diving club. Want to join? Seriously, if you can't afford the membership fee, I'll put it up for you, because I'd love to have you join. Oh, you're doing okay now? Glad to hear you're off the rack. Got any pretzels?"

*Taurus*  An attractive young woman with faint dimples in her roundish cheeks and a slightly unruly but pretty mass of curly hair comes sauntering into the room. She is dressed in a soft and pretty outfit that looks expensive, and has her handbag clutched tightly under her arm. She looks around the room with moderate curiosity. As the host walks up to her, she gives him a warm smile; when she speaks, her voice is low and melodious—but firm.

"Only eleven places? You mean, only eleven *chairs.* All you have to do is set another place and give me a pillow to sit on. I don't mind, as long as I'm comfortable. And I smell something wonderful, so I know the food is going to be delicious. To be honest with you, that's really why I came. I don't like to go out much, you know. What I really like is curling up in my warm and comfy bed—with someone warm and comfy, of course. (Are you busy later on?) But, now that I'm *here,* there's no way I'm not going to eat. What's for dessert? Who's that nervous-looking lady over there? Virgo? I'll go try to make her feel comfortable."

**Gemini**     It's hard to tell just how old this fellow is as he springs in the door; he could be any age, though he looks about eighteen. He is dressed in the very latest style, though nothing he has on is really extreme. His eyes dart all over the room, and he is carrying a notebook under his arm. When the host tells him about the eleven places, he is so busy listening to another conversation, he almost misses it. When he reacts, it is in a typically casual way.

"Don't worry about me; I don't need a place. I'll just float around the room, because what I really came here for is the conversation. I'm writing a book, you know—it's called *1001 Opening Conversational Gambits* and tonight I'm researching. I see you've got some really fascinating types here. How did you make up the guest list? Are they all married? Why did they come alone? What's the menu? Who's the chef? Can I see the wine list? Who's that blowsy-looking type over there? Taurus? I'll bet *she's* got a story. Where's the telephone? I've got to make a call."

**Cancer**     A sexy, voluptuous woman of indeterminate age pauses at the door; she seems shy, but conscious of the impression she is making. Her clothes are a bit unusual, and some things are from the thrift shop. However, her antique jewelry is genuine, and the whole effect is glamorous. When she discovers there are only eleven places, she is visibly upset, and there is a touch of a whine in her voice as she speaks.

"I wish I'd known; I could have stayed home with the children. They have colds, you know. If you want, I'll simply leave; but I really don't want to go home by myself; I'll get scared and have bad dreams. Upset? Yes, I am upset, and when I get upset I can't eat. Unless it's really soothing and nourishing. Did you know that a touch of heavy cream in mashed potatoes is simply heavenly? Chicken soup? I make it by the gallon. Say, you look as if you could stand a little fattening up. Well, all right. I *guess* I'll stay—unless I change my mind, of course."

**Leo**     This is a fine figure of a man—fairly tall, rather muscular, and with a thick crop of curly hair that is somewhere between blond and red. He is elegantly dressed and his gold cufflinks probably put a real drain on Fort Knox. His grand entrance is smooth and practised, and his handshake is hearty and warm. When his host tells him the news, he takes it very personally.

"Well, let me tell you, this is embarrassing! I mean, all these people here to see me, and I may have to stand? I've given bigger parties than this, and they've always gone off without a hitch. Let me handle things for you the next time. For now, just get that chair over there and squeeze someone in—Virgo won't mind. No, *here*; not *there!* While we're all waiting I guess I can entertain everyone with my tantrum act. What? No, I'm only kidding—though I am mad. I'll do my Hamlet number instead. Like my cufflinks? They match my Gold Card. I've ordered another pair with sapphires, too."

**Virgo**     A rather prim woman stands quietly at the door looking as if she would like to blend into the woodwork. She is dressed very neatly, but conservatively, with flat-heeled sensible shoes. In her handbag she carries a surgical mask to wear in case any of the other guests has a cold. Her reaction to the news that there are only eleven places is swift and shrill.

"Well, it certainly isn't *my* fault. I answered the invitation the minute I got it. I *always* do! Why didn't you check on things more carefully? If you had, this wouldn't have happened, and you wouldn't have all these people standing around thinking terrible things about you. I don't mind for myself, you understand, I don't eat much anyway; you never know what you're going to get. I'll stay in the kitchen and help the cook clean up. You can't be too careful about these things, you know. You wouldn't believe the sanitary conditions I've found in *some* kitchens. Not mentioning any names, of course. Oh, *why* did you mess things up this way; you are simply impossible. . . ."

*Intermission:* Our host walks away as Virgo continues to complain. As he checks on the guests, he discovers that Libra has just arrived. Sagittarius and Pisces are nowhere to be found, but Scorpio, Capricorn, and Aquarius are waiting to greet him. Because he looks like he's a bit uncomfortable, the host talks to Libra first.

*Libra*     A very attractive male, wearing all the right things, walks tentatively into the room, looking as if he is searching for someone. He is visibly uncomfortable alone. His gaze scans the room, quietly appraising everything and everybody in it. He seems to approve, but in his nervousness, he approaches the table, and starts rearranging one of the settings, then rearranging it again. All this is done very tactfully and gracefully. In fact, he looks as if he couldn't make an awkward gesture if he tried. His host approaches him and breaks the news. Libra's reaction is smooth and unruffled.

"Oh, how *clever* of you to arrange this little puzzle for us. It will make things so much more fun. Of course, we've got to make things absolutely fair; we wouldn't want to hurt anyone's feelings. I could leave if it would help, but . . . Oh, how nice of you to tell me I'll definitely have a place; it makes me feel a lot less awkward. I rarely go places alone, you know. Who would I like to sit next to? Well, the Capricorn lady looks like a sturdy and sensible type. But on the other hand, Scorpio is a *knockout.* Is she attached? Hmmm, Taurus looks like she'd like to chat, but oh, that Cancer! Decisions, decisions; I'll make up my mind later on. Where did you get that *great* painting?

***Scorpio*** A slim and sexy woman dressed totally in black comes slinking into the room. Her style and movement are absolutely magnetic, and every eye turns to look at her. But she gives no visible response that she is aware of it. She doesn't seem to be feeling anything at all, but when her host approaches and tells her what is going on, she is seething with quiet rage.

"Do you really think you are going to get away with this? I suspected something when I got that weird invitation. Who in the world would ever come as they are and let everybody else know what they're really like? No matter how many times you tell me it was an innocent mistake to set only eleven places, I'll never believe it. Nothing in this world is innocent. And when it comes to drawing straws, just remember you owe me one from the last time. You know, the *last* time! Who's that wimpy looking guy over there? Gemini? Maybe I'll amuse myself with him for a while. I need a new conquest; I'm getting out of practice."

***Sagittarius*** While Scorpio has been talking with the host, a tall rather rangy male has come loping into the room carrying a suitcase. He is a bit disheveled because his flight was late. He throws the suitcase in a corner and starts putting himself back together—a bit absentmindedly because he is looking around the room with a big smile and a lot of anticipation. He moves toward the host and gives a slap on his back that is almost *too* hearty.

"Only eleven places? Why worry? We'll work it out somehow. Life's too short to get uptight anyway. Had the greatest trip, and I'm turning right around tomorrow and going to the Orient so I can practice my Chinese. Say, are you serving Chinese food? I love Chinese food—and a good beer to go with it. At least I hope you're serving better wine than you did last time. You're looking a little pale . . . been partying too much lately? Ha ha, only kidding. Who's that guy over there with the flashy cufflinks? And the mouse with the sensible shoes? Think I'll see if I can loosen her up a bit. Did you hear I'm going to win the lottery again? What do you mean, how do I know? I just *know*. And I've got a great idea for an international fast food chain I'm going to bankroll with my winnings. I'm gonna call it 'The Great Gobler' and serve only turkey sandwiches. Hey, I'm thirsty. Where's the bar?"

**Aquarius**     An intellectual-looking gentleman—sort of an absentminded professor type—has been standing in the doorway quietly puffing his pipe and scrutinizing the crowd. His jacket and pants don't match, but he isn't aware of it. An even stranger—but typical—sartorial note is his electric blue tie with orange stripes. He's got his earphones with him; if things get too dull, he'll listen to some hard rock or electronic music and be in seventh heaven. When he finds out about the missing place, he gives a thoughtful answer and makes an impractical suggestion.

"Oh, well, rather than make anyone feel left out, we could cancel the whole dinner and bring the food to the local shelter for the homeless. Ah, you don't care for that idea. Too bad; I'm becoming more and more concerned about poverty in our own backyard. Of course, I'm no bleeding heart like Pisces, but fair's fair. Want to hear about a new invention I'm working on? It's an electronic stamp sorter that will revolutionize the whole philatelic world. Huh? Oh, that's stamp collecting. Glad you asked me to come alone, since I'm free as a bird now. My last attachment got so *sticky!* I've sworn off. At least off those emotional types who want you to get so involved. No, I never get lonely—I've got too many friends for that. By the way, I can just sit on the floor in the lotus position, and get some meditating in at the same time."

**Capricorn**     A rather handsome, perfectly put together woman has been quietly observing the crowd and the room, mentally putting a price tag on everything. What she has on is very expensive, but understated and in excellent taste. In her handbag she carries a petition with her name on it. She wants to run for local office, and is hoping to pick up some supporters tonight. If they are "her kind of people," that is. Her reaction to the host's situation is sober but logical.

"Well, it's obvious someone will have to go, but I

trust your judgment to decide who is most important—if you know what I mean. Your appointments are in excellent taste; I see you like Tiffany as much as I do. Who's that rather tacky looking type over there? Cancer? Where *does* she get her clothes? I have little sympathy for people who can't get their act together and run their lives successfully. She's probably a poet. Ah, well, different strokes for different folks; fantasy has no place in *my* life, you know. By the way, I have some excellent ideas about how to shape things up in the community; will you sign my petition? At dinner, are we going to discuss great books? I just bought a whole series . . . all leather-bound, of course. They look smashing in my living room."

**Pisces**     Meanwhile, a rather wispy but very pretty woman has been wandering in and out of the doorway, looking as if she isn't quite sure she is in the right place. She is dressed in a misty fabric of very pale colors; there doesn't seem to be a clear-cut edge anywhere. In fact, if you don't rub your eyes, you might think you are seeing an apparition. The host knows it's Pisces and catches her just as she's about to drift out the door again. He doesn't bother telling her about the missing place, because he knows she wouldn't understand why that was important.

"Late? Am I late? I lost my watch two weeks ago. Or was it three? Oh well, what's time anyway in the larger scheme of things? Hungry? Not really, though I can't remember the last time I ate. *Love*—it's *love* that's food for the soul, and that's what I care about nourishing. I wonder if any of these people have had any *real* soul food lately. No, don't worry, I won't try to convert anyone tonight. I'm too, too drained because of my current work. What kind? Well, it really isn't a job-job, I mean where you make money, and all. I've started a shelter for homeless animals in my apartment; I cry so much when I see a stray that I can't stand it. Who? Ho, he left some time ago. Something about there being 'other fish in the sea.' What in the world do you suppose he meant by that? By the way, I'm a little short of cash. Do you think you could lend me . . .?"

At this point, things are at a stalemate, but the situation will quickly resolve itself in one of twelve ways. Take your pick: This time *you* can choose the ending you like—and the one you think makes best astrological sense.

A. Aries gets in a fight with Leo and has to go to the emergency room.
B. Taurus gets really tired and hungry and decides to go home, cook a hamburger, and go to bed early.
C. Gemini runs out of note paper and gets laryngitis at the same time.
D. Cancer gets a call from the babysitter and is so worried she goes home to take care of her children.
E. Leo gets so irritated that no one is paying attention to the bruises Aries gave him that he leaves in a huff.
F. Virgo gets a stomach ache and decides to leave. Besides, it's time for her mineral bath.
G. Libra isn't able to make up his mind and gets a headache in the process.
H. Scorpio decides it's definitely a plot to humiliate her, and bows out less than graciously.
I. Sagittarius gets a little drunk and leaves early to get the plane.
J. Capricorn leaves as soon as she gets her petition filled up because there isn't anyone there *really* worth knowing.
K. Aquarius decides to go teach people at the shelter to use his stamp-sorting machine so they can get jobs.
L. Pisces remembers she has a date with her spiritual advisor and that she forgot to feed the animals.

# 5

# Moods of the Moon

## How to Successfully Navigate
## Its Day-by-Day Changes

Never underestimate the power of the moon. It is the closest planet to earth, and the only one whose effect on human life can actually be measured. Even the most skeptical antiastrology person has to admit that the moon rules the tides. If you stand on the beach for even a half hour or so, you can literally *see* how the moon works its magic as the water flows higher or lower, according to the time of day. There are places in the world where the tide rises as much as forty feet from its lowest to its highest point—that's *power*. If you think about the fact that humans are about 98 percent water in our chemical makeup, it's much easier to accept the fact that the moon has the same powerful effect on us as it does on the tides.

Like the "female" she symbolically is, the moon also changes her mind—or her sign—more quickly than any other planet. If you look at the day-by-day predictions in this book, which gives the position of the moon for every day, you will see that this changeable planet moves into a different sign about every two days.

As it moves from sign to sign, the moon brings a different kind of energy to the earth's atmosphere. Those who are particularly sensitive—like Cancers—feel it most strongly. But even the most stolid types are often moved by the effect of the particular sign the moon occupies on any given day, though they may not want to admit it.

Are we then slaves to the moods of the moon? Not if we understand its energies and cooperate with them. If you work *with* the moon and not against her, you can actually make life a lot easier for yourself. For instance, there are certain activities that go more smoothly when the moon is in a particular sign, just as other activities are more difficult to accomplish. Scheduling things accordingly could prevent a lot of frustration. You don't have to become a complete "lunatic" (ancient meaning, "one ruled by the moon") to benefit from its positive vibes, but simply go with the flow. Keep in mind, however, that the moon's effect will be *modified* by your sun sign, so be sure to check out your individual daily prediction. For instance, for. *any* sun sign, the days when the moon is in that sign should bring a surge of energy. Whether you handle that energy positively or negatively is up to you.

Here's a rundown of the moods of the moon and the human activities that go with them.

***When the Moon Is in Aries*** There is a very *physical* tone to this day. People may be throwing their weight around in more ways than one. Impatience, independent action, and quick tempers can sprout up all over the place. The good news is that most people will be feeling rather decisive, so some things can be completed. The bad news is that decisions may be totally unilateral; what *you* want may be exactly what someone else *doesn't* want. Similarly, people may be invading each other's territories; "keep off the grass" signs won't mean much today. Rule-breaking is the order of the day, and so are the consequences that go along with it. However, if there's a big mountain to scale, today's the day to begin the climb. If there's a formidable task that requires a lot of get-up-and-go to accomplish, today's the day to plunge in with both feet. If there's something you've been hesitating to tell someone, today you'll get the nerve to say it, but it may be difficult to be tactful. Try, anyway. On the up side, people will be feeling in the mood for some fun and frolic—practical jokes are very "moon in Aries." Even the boss may get in the spirit of things. It's a good day to:

Make a sale                    Sharpen knives  
Do heavy housework     Stop worrying  
Do some baking          Make a clean break  
Start a diet              Start an exercise class  
Buy a lottery ticket     Do something on your own  
Get a haircut           Try a new recipe  
Have your eyes checked  Throw a last-minute party

***When the Moon Is in Taurus***    Today, the amber light goes on, and people start to proceed with more caution. Rather than being adventurous, most people will feel like sticking with routine tasks. It is not a good day to try something new. In this more conservative mood, people will tend to hold on to what they have; don't try to borrow money from a friend today. Concentrate on making your own money grow, instead. Speaking of increase, this is an excellent day to "make your garden grow" in every sense of the phrase. Along with a quieter mood of the day, you may feel like pampering yourself a bit; allow yourself at least one luxury. Chocoholics, beware, however; this is a day for food binges and all forms of dietary excess. Creature comforts are a lot on everyone's mind; in fact, it may be difficult to crawl out of that comfortable bed in the morning. And more than a few people will be crawling back into it fairly early—with their favorite person. Sexual cravings are high on the list of "moon moods" today. Enjoy!

It's a good day to:

Put something off until tomorrow  Put up preserves  
Buy clothes or jewelry          Have a massage  
Get your teeth filled          Start singing lessons  
Start a savings account      Sell high on the market  
Stick to your guns            Buy a plant  
Buy candy                  Buy real estate  
Stay home and watch television  Hug somebody

***When the Moon Is in Gemini***    There's a touch more energy in the air today, and people will begin moving around a lot more. For some, there will be a lot of nervous energy and the scattery feeling that goes along with it; don't force yourself to concentrate if you can avoid it. It's a day to make connections—call, write, or bump into both new and old friends. Wits are generally sharp today, and people could be cracking jokes all around you. On the other hand, they may also be spilling some secrets. Gossip is easy to start today, and it could spread like wildfire. Mind your mouth! Anything requiring manual dexterity can easily get done today; even those who are usually clumsy may find they have nimble fingers. The tendency today is to do things quickly, if a bit superficially. If there are a couple of things that require a once-over-lightly treatment, get them out of the way now. If you haven't been invited to a party, give your own—or at least plan to get together with some buddies for a little socializing; the time is definitely right.

It's a good day to:

| | |
|---|---|
| Get your hair cut | Use your hands |
| Join a club | Pay bills |
| Have a tooth pulled | Eat out |
| Sign up for a new course | Take a walk/drive |
| Send a letter | Call your brother/sister |
| Try something new | Tell a fib |
| Learn a language | Do two things at once |

***When the Moon Is in Cancer***     In Cancer, the moon is in her very own sign—and you'll know it. All those "moon" characteristics—like changeableness, sensitivity, and the desire for security—will be heightened. Cancers, of course, will feel it most strongly; and the other water signs, Scorpio and Pisces, may be even moodier than usual. The general tendency today is to do things that make you feel comfortable and feel good. For some, that means eating a lot of food; for others, it could be hitting the bottle a bit. People tend to feel a bit sorry for themselves during the transit of the moon through Cancer. When two people who live together are both feeling that way, the result can be a rather touchy day—and evening. As much as you want the comfort of others, you are better off on your own and working off those anxious feelings by yourself. Not for safety, but for comfort's sake, the best place to go today is no farther than your own backyard. You'll probably be feeling very stay-at-home anyway. However, it's an excellent day for memories. Reminisce with somebody you love, or get out that old photo album by yourself. You might find yourself shedding a tear or two, but it's all in a good cause.

It's a good day to:

| | |
|---|---|
| Bake something delicious | Hug your children |
| Buy something old | Take care of somebody |
| Put up preserves | Go without makeup |
| Buy property | Call your mother |
| Start a habit | Buy something for the house |
| Plant something | Entertain at home |
| Pamper yourself | Give your hair a treatment |

***When the Moon Is in Leo***    Today, everyone feels like "coming out of the woodwork." Just as Cancer moon makes you want to hide, Leo moon makes you want to get out there and be seen. Nothing but the best will do on this day, so it could be a rather expensive one. Most people will be more generous than usual—both with their money and their affections; many a new romance has started under a Leo moon. Leo is also one of the more playful signs, so a lot of you will be in the mood for fun and games. Eating out is very Leo moon—and so is picking up the check. Today, you may have to fight for it. However, the boss may be a lot stricter than usual, and even those with nobody to "boss" will try to push somebody around. If you've got children, today you will appreciate them very much—no matter what they do. Most people find themselves reaching for the newest thing in the closet under this transit of the moon. If they don't have anything new to wear, they'll probably go out and buy it—on credit. No matter what time of the year it is, you'll be looking for a little sunshine or at least a warm place. On the beaches or by the fireplaces are where most people would like to be today—wishing life were one long vacation.

It's a good day to:

| | |
|---|---|
| Borrow money | Buy jewelry |
| Get a new hairstyle | Invest in the market |
| Start building something | Do something creative |

Follow a hunch
Steal the spotlight
Be brave
Be waited on

Prepare a gourmet meal
Dress up
Kiss somebody new

**When the Moon Is in Virgo**     Now it's back to work, and back to reality. There's a sharp distinction between the Virgo moon mood and what precedes it, so you may shock yourself. Perhaps by deciding it's really time to get organized and then actually *doing* it. On the home front it's a great day to rearrange all those sloppy closets and cupboards. On the job, you couldn't pick a better time to wrestle with that nasty detail work you've been avoiding. However, all is not good news under Virgo moon. For one thing, by contrast to Leo moon's generosity, people will be positively stingy today—both with their money and their love. Even the best of situations could deteriorate today when one or the other of the involved parties decides to point out the other's flaws. Your best course under the Virgo moon is to check that impulse to criticize. People can become highly self-critical during this transit, too. One extreme example of the going-over some people can give themselves during a Virgo moon is to develop mysterious maladies or to discover aches and pains they never felt before. Not to worry; they'll be all better by the time the moon moves into the next sign. Virgo moon is also inspection time, so the boss may be particularly sensitive to messy desks today and sloppiness in general. Keep things buttoned up and tidy for best results.

It's a good time to:

Start a diet
Get a physical
Bake bread
Quit smoking
Buy a pet
Try to do without something
Buy health food

Start a new job
Sew or mend something
Read a good book
Get a complete makeover
Call your maiden aunt
Feel like a martyr
Do a puzzle

**When the Moon Is in Libra**     Now it's time to kiss and make up. Any relationships that suffered from the ragged nerves of Virgo moon time can be nicely patched up today. Pleasantries should be easy for one and all. In fact, even people who are normally rather gruff should smile a bit more today. Libra moon is one of the most social of moon periods; meeting and greeting should be prevalent activities. Most people will want to put their best foot forward, too, so the impulse to dress up and look your best may come upon you. You may feel rather self-indulgent as well; hard work is not as compatible with the Libra moon period as rest and relaxation are. It's definitely a time of togetherness, so even habitual loners may be looking for company. Most people will feel they need people—possibly one special person. Romance blossoms under the Libra moon in its purest form. It's not so much sex people want now as romantic love and companionship. No one's actually made a count, but it's a fair bet that more flowers get sent under the Libra moon than at any other time. Physical beauty is also highly important, so Libra moon is a great one under which to get yourself a whole new look or to redo anything that needs it. Something that's off-balance will bother you more at this time.

It's a good day to:

| | |
|---|---|
| Be tactful | Forgive and forget |
| Redecorate | Add color to your life |
| Give a party | Luxuriate |
| Fall in love | Sign up for a dance class |
| Join a singing group | Buy a stereo |
| Buy something beautiful | Buy a down comforter |
| Try a new makeup | Learn about wine |

***When the Moon Is in Scorpio*** Things could easily get heavy today, and the tendency will be to go to extremes. Haters will hate more; lovers will love more passionately and physically. The sex drive is stimulated in many people during this transit of the moon. With all those intense emotions flying around, it's not surprising that people easily get hot under the collar—and/or imagine that somebody is out to get them. However, there is an up side to the Scorpio moon, and that is the extra jot of will power it gives the most weak-willed people. If you've got to dig in your heels and clench your teeth to get something done, today's the day you will be able to do it. People *endure* a lot under the Scorpio moon. The only problem is that they may develop some resentment toward those they believe should be enduring with them. However, the tendency is to keep silent. In spite of the intense emotionalism of the Scorpio moon, there isn't a lot of outright complaining. People will let the pressure build up inside of them and then burst out into violent rages. If your temper isn't good under the best of circumstances, control it during the Scorpio moon, by all means. It's also a time when people tend to feel a bit claustrophobic; a good walk in the fresh air can work wonders at this time.

It's a good day to:

See a psychiatrist
Buy a house
Open a secret bank account
Make a firm decision
Do your taxes
Throw away what you
   don't need
Do some strenuous exercise

Have good sex
Face up to a crisis
Read a good mystery
Take body-building
Get a prescription filled
Buy life insurance
Change your life

***When the Moon Is in Sagittarius***    Things definitely lighten up when the moon moves into Sagittarius—and people loosen up, too. In fact, one danger under this moon is getting too relaxed—with your diet, your money, or your generous spirits. Moderation is not the mood of the day, so you may have to force it on yourself. It is not a good time to try to stop smoking—or to stop doing anything self-indulgent. There's definitely a "live and let live" attitude in the air when the moon is in Sagittarius, so bad relations should be easily improved. A spirit of good will is pervasive, as well as a light-hearted attitude. One thing that means is that even normally conservative people will be willing to take chances; those for whom a more liberal outlook is a natural state of affairs could really go too far out on a limb. If you gamble, bet *only* what you can afford to lose today. The place everyone will want to be today is outdoors. In fact, more than one person will simply disappear from the scene to do something either adventurous or relaxing. It's an excellent day to think big, but you may find the follow-through a bit difficult. The big picture is what's easiest to see right now; leave the fine brush strokes for another time. Enjoy the spirit of fun and generosity that should be in the air.

It's a good day to:

Make a long-distance call
Plan a trip
Buy a dog (or a horse)
Contribute to a wildlife-
   foundation
Try a new approach
Sell anything to anybody
Try your luck/feel lucky
Go to church
Enjoy a hobby
Learn a new language
Do something charitable
Borrow money
Run away from it all
Get a bigger place

***When the Moon Is in Capricorn***     In sharp contrast to the "easy come, easy go" feeling of the Sagittarius moon, the moon in Capricorn brings on a much more serious mood. You could call it the "workaholic's moon," and even those whose work style is less intense will find themselves wanting to get a lot done. It's important to *accomplish something* when the moon is in Capricorn, if you are to feel comfortable. Most people want to tread only on solid ground at this time, so there could be a bit of distrust in the air. No one wants to waste time— and least of all on things or people from whom they are not likely to derive some kind of benefit. Another curious facet of the Capricorn moon mood is a tendency to feel older and more serious; some lighter types dislike the feeling so much they will go out of their way to look young. It's the kind of day that matronly secretary in the office is likely to appear in something rather frilly. People can really handle things under the Capricorn moon too; endurance is *very* Capricorn. That means those who exercise will work out harder and longer; those who normally do not push themselves will do at least a little self-prodding. A good image is paramount to many people when the moon is in this sign, and the tendency is for people to be quite status conscious. Self-control is the order of the day, in every respect.

It's a good day to:

Start a new job
Buy antiques
Make a list
Keep your money

Buy anything for investment
Wear anything with a
 good label on it
Bet on a favorite
Go to the chiropractor
Buy insurance
Go to the dentist
Start a diet
Work late
Ask for repayment of a
 debt
Clean house

***When the Moon Is in Aquarius***   When the moon moves into the sign of Aquarius from the sign of Capricorn, it's as if somebody took the cork out of the bottle. Suddenly, the rather repressed mood bursts into a desire for change—a *need* for change. This is one of those days when people tend to make rash moves like quit a dull job, call it quits with a clinging person, throw out everything in their closet and start all over again. Reaching this point is easy to do under the Aquarian moon. However, it's usually very positive. What's important at this time is to try something new, not just get rid of something old. Some people decide to experiment with a new recipe, a new lover, or a new hair style. It's the kind of day when a woman with long hair will decide to get a crew cut. On the relationship side, the mood now is one of brotherly love and friendship rather than highly charged sexual encounters. Wanting to be with friends and feeling like part of a group is what's important now. No one is a stranger under the Aquarian moon, and talking to people on the street is very common. The thing to be careful of under this moon is doing something irreparable—like finally telling the boss what you really think of him. He/she could easily decide that it's time for a change of personnel.

It's a good day to:

Do something kinky
Try a new food
Do something friendly
Start flying lessons
Do something impulsive
Join a club
Make a speculative
 investment
Buy/wear something crazy
Color your hair
Contribute to a charity
Move to a new place
Buy a television/stereo
Make a new friend
Be fair

***When the Moon Is in Pisces***   This is a time when people wear their hearts on their sleeves and feel *very* vulnerable. There's a lot of ultrasensitivity under the Pisces moon, and a lot of crying on shoulders—if you can find one that isn't already occupied. Mixed in with the emotionalism is a real feeling of empathy with others; now's the time people feel that everyone is in the same boat. However, it may be a bit difficult to keep things afloat today, because there isn't a lot of firm direction from anyone or anything. It's confusion time, and even the clearest of messages can get a little garbled. Indecisiveness will spread like the plague, so don't expect to get any clear-cut answers today. Creative people get more creative under the Pisces moon, and anyone could feel just a bit poetic. Romantic relationships are heavenly under the Pisces moon as long as they don't get out of control. Keeping certain other things under control—like drinking and other forms of escapism—is a wise precaution, too. The most satisfying and least dangerous escape is to hold hands with someone you love while you watch a real tearjerker movie. Lots of people call in sick under the Pisces moon, and there's a good reason: Most people don't like to cry in public.

It's a good day to:

| | |
|---|---|
| Put on weight | Write a poem |
| Fall in love | Take in a stray dog or cat |
| Develop ESP | Visit the sick |
| Find God | See a therapist |
| Buy flowers or perfume | Stay home and read |
| Swear off something | Pamper yourself |
| Get hooked on something | Buy a camera |

# 6

# Venus and Mars

## Love and Sex
## Peace and War
## Cooperating and Competing

Next to your sun sign, your moon sign, and your rising sign, the positions of Venus and Mars in your horoscope are probably the most important indicators of your personal psychology. This is because Venus shows your affectional nature and Mars shows your sexual nature. To put it another way, *Venus shows your wants and needs in romantic love while Mars shows your sexual style and your manner of expressing it.*

In a broader sense, Venus and Mars are the principles of peace and war. Venus wants to cooperate and relate to others, to share life experiences. Mars is totally concerned with self and getting what you want. Everybody's got a Venus and Mars in their horoscope because every human being has to both live with others and assert him-/herself. It's all a matter of degree. If you want to, you can think of Venus as the "higher" side of human relationships; Mars the "lower." However, you've got to keep in mind that—like all other opposites in the universe—both *cooperating* and *competing* are necessary if the world is to continue going round.

Because Venus has to do with the need to share, the sign in which it is placed will tell a lot about how you attract people you want to share with. It will also show what attracts you to others. Beyond the love arena, the position of Venus in your horoscope shows your attitudes toward money and personal possessions, creature comforts, and things of beauty. Venus is "feminine" in nature, and women tend to relate to their Venus sign more than men. But for *both* sexes, it is an available energy.

**The good side of Venus is:**
*Sharing, beautifying, peacemaking*
**The bad side is:**
*acquisitiveness, self-indulgence, laziness*

Because the position of Mars shows how you go about getting what you want, it will tell a lot about your personal drive—how *much* you want what you want. It is the desire principle, and will indicate just how passionate your passions are. Ambition, assertiveness, and anger are just a few steps away from each other, so Mars will also reveal what makes you angry or what gets you going. The planet Mars is "masculine" in nature—highly so—and men will find it easier to get in touch with their Mars energy. However, every woman's got a Mars too, and sooner or later a woman's Mars energy will present itself.

**The "good" side of Mars is:**
*Dynamic energy, courage, sexual drive*
**The "bad" side is:**
*manipulation, cowardice, sexual abuse*

No matter what area of life you are relating these planets to, it is useful to think of them in sexual terms, and of our human sexual organs. Venus is open and receptive; Mars thrusts forward and penetrates. Because we normally attract someone or are attracted to someone before we get sexually involved, Venus energy precedes Mars energy. In other words, Venus shows how *receptive* you are; Mars shows how *active* you are. Venus also has a lot to do with our ideas and images of romance, our romantic fantasies, while Mars is an indicator of sexual fantasies—which may or may not be acted out, depending on the individual's degree of inhibition.

Just as some combinations of people can coexist in constant harmony while others are in constant conflict,

Venus and Mars in an individual person can work well together, or at cross-purposes. When your Venus doesn't get along well with your Mars, you've got a problem. Sometimes a sexual problem, but always an inner conflict. How can you tell if your Venus and Mars are "friends" or "foes"? First, by looking up the positions of your personal Mars and Venus in the charts provided at the end of this chapter, reading the descriptions of those planets in the signs they fall in for you. But, just to make things a bit clearer, here's a rundown of easy Mars/Venus relationships and difficult ones. (By the way, you can also apply this principle in comparing your Venus/Mars positions to those of someone else, as well.)

Venus and Mars are "at war" when:

- One is in a fire sign, and one is in an earth sign. Here you've got a conflict between the practical and the experimental sides of yourself.
- One is in a fire sign and one is in a water sign. One part of you says "let's do it"; the other side says, "I might get hurt," so you might be stalled.
- One is in an earth sign and one is in an air sign. Air likes to think about things a little; earth needs to know it will work. Once again, it may hold you back.
- One is in an air sign and one is in a water sign. Yours is a conflict between the mental relationship and the emotional one; you may find it hard to decide what you want.

Venus and Mars are on good terms when:

- One is in a fire sign, one is in an air sign.
- One is in an earth sign and one is in a water sign.
- Both are in the same element.

## Venus and Mars in The Signs

### Venus in Aries (fire element)

While this position of Venus in a man or a woman indicates the kind of person who falls in love impulsively, both sexes want to be conquered, when they have Venus in Aries. They may be outrageously flirtatious, but can lead others on a merry chase before they give in. There is a tendency to look for trouble when Venus is in ths position; actually, it is excitement Venus in Aries people crave. Their personal likes and dislikes will be quite clearly defined, and they will be vocal about them. In matters of taste, there is less refinement than when Venus is in a softer sign. Both the males and the females may play up their sexuality in the way they dress; they like very loud things like rock music and bright colors. There is also an impish charm in these people and a tendency to play love games. The *real* goal is to be swept away by a romantic lover who lives up to a mediaeval code of chivalry and/or chastity.

### Mars in Aries (fire element)

This is a highly competitive position for Mars; people with Mars in Aries leave no doubt about the fact that they want it, and they want it *now*—whatever "it" is. Mars in Aries can cut through a lot of life's red tape. When it comes to courtship, Mars in Aries people are equally able to disregard the small talk and get right down to business. However, this position of Mars often makes for a rather selfish lover—one who is so concerned with getting that he/she doesn't do an awful lot of giving. Mars in Aries people are likely to turn off as quickly as they turn on. Passion burns brightly, but is often short-lived. They are highly independent and likely to leave if a romantic partner gets too possessive or demanding. Mars in Aries is also always ready for a fight, so relationships are a bit stormy.

### Venus in Taurus (earth element)

This is a highly sensual position for Venus to be in. People with Venus in Taurus are turned on by sweet words and soft music—and any form of touching. They like all kinds of nice and beautiful things, and will be attracted by someone who dresses well and has expensive taste. Venus in Taurus people can be a little self-indulgent, but in the main their desire is to make the object of their affection comfortable. And they will do it in very tangible ways; Venus in Taurus people of both sexes like to do things for others. When someone with Venus in Taurus is attracted, he/she is loyal. Love does not come in a flash, as it does with Venus in Aries people, but when it comes, it usually stays. At least as far as the person with Venus in Taurus is concerned. These people are generally so devoted that a breakup is extremely unsettling. You can always make a Venus in Taurus person happy with candy or flowers. The best kind of love feels good, tastes good, looks good, and smells good.

### Mars in Taurus (earth element)

This Mars can express itself as ambition with a definite direction—or as controlled sexuality. Mars in Taurus people of both sexes can appear rather lazy, but actually their slow movements are usually on a deliberate course. Some people with Mars in Taurus are really looking for a safe position in a job or with a partner. Their manner of sexuality is highly sensual though they may be slow to get aroused. When a Mars in Taurus person enters into an affair, however, there is usually the intention to make it a long and serious one. These people are certainly capable of quick affairs, but they generally prefer a comfortable relationship where they do not constantly have to keep proving their love. There is a certain giving quality to Mars in Taurus, and the men are exceptionally considerate lovers. The women are fairly passive, but passionate and giving when they get going.

### Venus in Gemini

Venus in Gemini people of both sexes tend to be turned on more by *talk* than by physical stimulation. Relationships have to have a mental dimension in order for them to get involved. In fact, Venus in Gemini people are likely to make better friends than lovers. When their affections *are* engaged, the connection is likely to be a little tenuous, and the Venus in Gemini's feelings may not run as deep as his/her partner's. Fickleness is a reality with these people— they like a lot of changes, and that goes for people as well as environments. Job-hopping is a trait of Venus in Gemini, and so is a constant changing of the guard in their romantic lives. However, Venus in Gemini people make wonderful romantic partners, because they are really *interested* in the people they get involved with. Never tell a Venus in Gemini person to "shut up and make love"; he/she will be very likely to shut the door on the relationship.

### Mars in Gemini

Mars in Gemini people assert themselves rather erratically; there isn't a lot of staying power, in jobs or in relationships. The "alternating current" of Mars in Gemini energy makes for a rather on again, off again sexual life. People with Mars in this position are capable of having a number of purely mental relationships in between their sexual ones. These are the kind of people who talk their way into things, including a job and someone's bed. Their approach is a bit on the delicate side, and one may wonder when the Mars in Gemini person is really going to get started. However, once their passion is aroused, Mars in Gemini people like a lot of variety; sex can get quite original with these people. The tendency to bore easily goes both for their attitudes toward their sexual partners and the manner in which they have sex. Both sexes are real charmers, however, and sometimes get their way in a rather devious manner.

### Venus in Cancer (water element)

The overriding thing that people with Venus in Cancer want is *security,* really the emotional kind, but since a secure home base goes along with their needs, the material kind is important too. Venus in Cancer people can be highly traditional in their romantic values—home, mother, and apple pie are symbols of the things that turn these people on. If you want to engage the emotions of a Venus in Cancer person, all you have to do is look as if you *need* somebody—preferably a mother. Venus in Cancer people need to be needed, but sometimes can go overboard by totally taking over the other person's life. With Venus in this sign, people respond strongly to all kinds of romantic things, from the card that says "I love you" to a little token of affection for no special occasion. However, Venus in Cancer people are highly self-protective, so you first have to break down their natural reserve and fear of getting hurt. Once you do, you won't find a more faithful lover. Except perhaps Taurus.

### Mars in Cancer (water element)

Mars in Cancer people can sneak up on you when they've decided they want you; their approach is a bit sideways, like the locomotion of the crab that is the Cancer symbol. They are soft and subtle lovers and said by some to be among the best sexual partners in the zodiac. However, as sensitive and understanding as they tend to be in the sexual area, they can be overly possessive with people they love, and even turn rather cruel when they are rejected. Cancer is a water sign, and it is as if that water starts boiling—invisibly—then the lid totally pops off when the explosion comes. Mars in Cancer people tend to be a little blind to their sexual/ambition drive and can even pretend to themselves that it doesn't exist. For this reason, they make formidable enemies, because while they look as if they are asking for peace they are really preparing for battle.

### Venus in Leo (fire element)

There's a pretty simple way to get a Venus in Leo person to like you. Give him/her a lot of attention—*positive* attention. Venus in Leo people do want love, but they want admiration and adulation to come along with it. A bit like Venus in Aries, Venus in Leo wants a *courtly* lover—someone who will swear absolute loyalty. When it's a Leo sun sign person who also has Venus in Leo, you've got the absolute monarch of them all. Venus in Leo also goes only for the best, and is attracted to what looks expensive or rewarding—in both jobs and people. Venus in Leo expects you to dress and look your best, no matter what the circumstances. It is not a "casual" Venus. Demonstrations of love are very important, too. Words are great, of course, and so is a lot of hugging and the rest of the physical love spectrum. However, candy—or some other tangible token of affection—is expected. Venus in Leo has fierce pride, so if you even slip once and appear not to *respect* this person, he/she is likely to brush you off—with a very grand gesture of course.

### Mars in Leo (fire element)

Speaking of grand gestures, Mars in Leo wrote the book. This kind of person is the one who will lavish the object of his/her affection with all kinds of luxurious things. Mars in Leo is a real showy person and expects to be appreciated for it. Both the males and the females are aggressive about going after what they want, and once they are happily ensconced—with a lover or a job—they are loyal and steady. However, the down side of the Mars in Leo position is a violent temper: a *really* violent temper. Both sexes can get quite physical in expressing anger. This is the position of the female who throws plates and the man who slaps his faithless lover on the cheek. Mars in Leo is unrelentingly honest—and will expect you to be too. One devious move, and it's over

### Venus in Virgo (earth element)

Venus in Virgo wants a love that *works*. Pure sex or romance may appeal to Virgo's desire for the unadulterated, but there's got to be an element of the practical in it too. People with Venus in Virgo often actually fall in love with their jobs faster than they do with people. When Venus is in the sign, you often find the dedicated, loyal, "number two" person who spends a lifetime catering to the needs of a powerful boss. He/she is likely to be just a little bit in love with that boss too. As for sex, the Venus in Virgo person has a very healthy attitude toward it—possibly too healthy in the sense that it is sometimes regarded as an excellent form of exercise. Venus in Virgo people are not really cold—in fact, when they love someone they can't do enough for them, particularly in attending to their physical comfort. The problem is that this position of Venus makes a person overly analytical in determining what he/she wants. If the Venus in Virgo person keeps his/her mouth shut, and doesn't openly criticize, there is a much better possibility that he/she will make good, solid relationships.

### Mars in Virgo (earth element)

Virgo's inventive sexuality is one of the best-kept secrets in the zodiac; Mars in Virgo turns out some of the most experimental and skillful lovers of all. That is, if you can attract one of these people in the first place. Mars in Virgo people are far from promiscuous; in fact, their standards are likely to be a bit too high. They are constantly questioning their *own* desires and drives, picking them apart instead of acting upon them. Mars in Virgo is ideal for success in just about any job or profession. With any sun sign, it adds to the ability to cooly analyze problems and solve them with a reasonable amount of dispatch. When it comes to romantic involvement, this is not one of the more "romantic" Mars positions (unless the sun sign is Libra). You may feel as if your Mars in Virgo lover is checking you over first for anything that might turn him/her off. This is the sign that usually says "let's shower together" before he/she says "let's go to bed."

### Venus in Libra (air element)
First off, remember that when the planet Venus is in Libra, it's in its "home sign." When it comes to beauty, harmony, and balance, Venus in Libra people want it all. When Venus is in Libra, the most attractive things in life are the *nicest*—people, places, jobs, clothes, you name it. Venus in Libra people want it nice, but they also want it *easy*. In fact, this sometimes "cold" position of Venus can make for a person who marries for status or money. If you look comfortable in every sense of the word, you've got a shot at attracting that Venus in Libra person who catches your eye. And he/she will, because this position of Venus usually confers a great-looking body. Even if the Venus in Libra person loves or marries for convenience, he/she gives an awful lot in return. Once you've engaged his/her love the Venus in Libra person considers you the best, the most beautiful/handsome, and the brightest person in the universe and will treat you accordingly.

### Mars in Libra (air element)
This position of Mars often makes for a passive/aggressive type of individual—a specific psychological pattern. The Mars in Libra person rarely goes directly after what he/she wants, but more or less lingers in front of it, waiting for the other person to make the right move. Mars in Libra people don't get hired as quickly as other types because they don't seem to *care* enough about whether or not they get the job. When it

comes to love, Mars in Libra can be quite frustrating. You really don't know what's going on here—does or doesn't he/she want to get involved? This is also a rather "refined" position for brash Mars. Mars in Libra people usually have excellent manners, and never appear to get ruffled. They will just sit and smile while you rant and rave. Suddenly, however, they can turn on their heel and walk out the door. The technique Mars in Libra people use to go about making their subtle conquests is *talk*—but it can easily fool you because it seems so casual.

### Venus in Scorpio (water element)

A lot of people with sun sign Scorpio have Venus in Scorpio too; (one's Venus sign is often one's sun sign because Venus is so close to the sun in the solar system). These double-whammy Scorpios are extraordinarily intense in all their emotional needs, but anyone with Venus in Scorpio is going to be touched by the madness of this intense sign. The curious paradox is that Venus in Scorpio people are either totally *turned on* by someone or something—or totally *turned off*. There are very few halfway deals in their lives. Venus in Scorpio can also be highly manipulative, adjusting his/her emotions to suit other needs—like money. When Venus is in Scorpio, people are attracted to what seems mysterious, dangerous, or hard-to-get. They love puzzles, and can be a bit of a puzzle themselves to prospective romantic partners. When they do get involved, however, they have a great deal of staying power—emotionally at least. They can fairly easily separate their physical *actions* from their mental states, however.

### Mars in Scorpio (water element)

People with Mars in Scorpio have a very strong "energy field" surrounding them; you can almost see it and feel it. What they want, they want passionately—and will seek in no uncertain terms. They are equally positive about what they *don't* want—so you will know whether you've got a shot with them right away. No waiting with *this* aggressive sign. The legendary super-sexuality of Scorpio is real with Mars in Scorpio people. However, they may use their sexual power to control other people and situations. And, if they are rejected against their will (which doesn't happen too often) they are capable of the worst kind of venomous reactions. Jealous lovers who are violent to their former partners are a parody of the Mars in Scorpio type of intensity. One way Mars in Scorpio people can hurt or simply tease others is by withholding their love—and their physical passion. They have great powers of self-control.

### Venus in Sagittarius (fire element)

People with Venus in the restless, mobile sign of the Centaur often get the reputation for being fickle, and there is more than a grain of truth in that label. But the reason a Venus in Sagittarius person may move around or not become committed is that he/she is so vulnerable to deceit and dishonesty. As the saying goes, "once burned, twice shy," and openhearted, friendly Sagittarius is likely to get burned very early in life. When Venus in Sagittarius people do get involved, they are absolutely delightful to love. Broadminded, unpossessive, full of fun, they really want to enjoy romance. Sagittarius is also a very intellectual sign, so in order to get Venus in Sagittarius people to stick with you for a while, you've got to keep them interested. Sex is great, but sex with talk is even greater for these people. Venus in Sagittarius is also highly idealistic, so you've got to be a higher type to appeal to someone with Venus in this sign. Love is gallantry and honor and all those things that are so hard to find in life.

### Mars in Sagittarius (fire element)

Sagittarius is a sign that thinks in global terms, so when Mars is in the sign of Sagittarius, you find a person who wants it all—and often has to be satisfied with nothing. People with Mars in Sagittarius assert themselves bluntly and get right to the point. However, they tend to be so optimistic in their expectations that they may just as quickly decide they have made a mistake. Better luck next love. Mars in Sagittarius doesn't deliberately hurt people; this sign is kind to all—both animals and humans. Their sexual nature can also be rather "animalistic" because this is a lusty sign, and so fond of all outdoor sports that they often want to do it anywhere, anytime. One way Mars in Sagittarius people get to your heart is through your sense of humor; they really know how to make people laugh. It is a powerful weapon in their professional lives too; it's hard to fire someone who is such a delight to have around—even if he/she isn't around that much. The big problem with Mars in Sagittarius people is that they sometimes don't want to take responsibility for their own actions, and lay things on other people. Even if Mars in Sagittarius is the one to break things up, he/she will somehow or other get you to believe that it's *your* fault.

### Venus in Capricorn (earth element)

Appearances count a lot to Venus in Capricorn people—in every sense of the word. In order to appeal to them, you've got to look solid and substantial—and fairly rich as well. Because there is a natural reserve to Capricorn, people with Venus in this sign will dislike public displays of affection; the cooler you are in your approach, the better. Their public image and their private one are not too far apart, either. Not that Venus in Capricorn isn't normal; he/she can be quite passionate in bed. But very, very *serious*, too. If you mistake this sign's sober approach to life for coldness, you will not be the first person who has. Once again, like those with Venus in Virgo, Venus in Capricorn is attracted to *practical* people—people who can really work for them in one way or another. While some do actually consciously go after a financially comfortable marital situation, what the vast majority will settle for is someone who is willing to help handle a lot of the more serious aspects of life. Male or female, Venus in Capricorn people want you to be *useful.* Unfortunately, some people with Venus in this sign have such a low sense of self-worth, that they will try to buy love—or sell it—because they don't feel anyone will accept them for what they are.

### Mars in Capricorn (earth element)

Mars in Capricorn people always want to know the rules before they enter the game; they assert themselves with extreme caution. However, when they *know* what they want, they have incredible powers to help them get it. One is patience; Mars in Capricorn can wait very well. Another thing they have going for them is self-control; their timing is excellent because they can hold themselves back when they want to. All this makes for a rather sexually confusing type, and sometimes one who is sexually confused. Mars in Capricorn people can go without sex for amazing lengths of time if nothing seems worth the effort. When they do go for it, their approach can be extremely lusty and earthy, as befits the earth element of Capricorn. Even more than someone with Mars in Scorpio, the person with Mars in Capricorn can be a user. In love or business, he/she can easily fake it to get the carrot on the end of the stick. Then, before you know it, the person who seemed so hot for you has now turned stone cold. Sad, but true.

### Venus in Aquarius (air element)

The best way to attract someone with Venus in Aquarius is to be a bit unconventional; these people love anyone or anything that is off-beat. However, you may find that you are considered a specimen rather than a romantic partner—or at least that's how it's likely to feel. People with Venus in Aquarius seem to have a real problem with deep involvement; often they really *want* it, but somehow or other their deepest wells of emotion are very difficult to tap.

Their habitual reaction to love is often "easy come, easy go." Are they cruel people? Generally not, and often Venus in Aquarius people suffer a lot from their difficulty with feeling. They will rarely tell you, however, because there is a real need for distance there. And distance is what they seek in one-on-one relationships. If you become possessive with, or jealous of a person with Venus in Aquarius, you will lose him/her very quickly. As with some of the other mental signs like Gemini and Libra, you have got to keep the affair or the marriage *interesting* in one way or another. This is a Venus position that often likes kinky sex, porno movies, and other forms of artificial stimulation. However, they usually don't care enough about sex-for-the-sake-of-sex to be unfaithful.

### *Mars in Aquarius (air element)*

When Mars is in this erratic sign, people tend to go through periods of feast and famine, largely because they can fluctuate between being extremely assertive and sure about what they want or totally inactive. During the latter periods you could actually call the Mars in Aquarius person lazy. In love, the Mars in Aquarius person tends to go after the unusual or difficult; involvements with people who are already attached are quite common. In many cases it is because the Mars in Aquarius person really is terribly afraid of deep involvement. There is a detachment about Mars in Aquarius people that sometimes works against permanent attachment to people or professional situations. Mars in Aquarius really prefers to go it alone. Perhaps the reason is that they always want to be free to experiment with the new. In sex, the Mars in Aquarius person is hung up on technique; he/she likes intelligent sex, and sometimes wants to prove how clever he/she is via this rather bizarre route.

### *Venus in Pisces (water element)*

For people with Venus in Pisces, what's attractive is often bound up with some kind of sacrifice. This is the position of Venus that leads to martyrdom of all kinds. Some Venus in Pisces people find it impossible to get involved with anything or anyone normal and healthy; their instinctive need is to care for the lame and needy. Therefore, many Venus in Pisces people are rather easily taken advantage of by unscrupulous types who use them or take them for all they're worth. By the same token, Venus in Pisces people can put a real *drain* on the object of their affections—demanding more and more proofs of undying love, soulful demonstrations, sometimes even more tangible support. However, in the broadest, most universal sense of the word, Pisces is the "best" position for Venus as it represents the principle of *true love*. True love is totally unselfish, totally self-sacrificing. Though few normal mortals are capable of such "divine" love, Venus in Pisces people come closest to being able to make it. On the more mundane side, people wth Venus in Pisces are attracted by all kinds of sentimental and often impractical things. They will love you most if you spend your last penny on a bouquet of violets rather than bread for the table. So what? You'll just live on love.

### Mars in Pisces (water element)

Mars in Pisces people can easily lose their way; the sign of Pisces is not stable enough for the aggressive energy of Mars, so Mars in Pisces people tend to scatter their energies in too many places. On the other hand, they are the most subtle and devious people in the zodiac when it comes to going after what they really *do* want. Their come-on is usually to be rather weak and helpless. Both the males and the females snare you by making you think they really *need* you. There's a lot of poetry to Mars in Pisces people, so the start of an affair is likely to be all moonlight and roses. However, you may find that once you are entangled, you can't get yourself out when you want out. Mars in Pisces people have a way of snarling you up in their webs of erratic energy. Just when they've agreed that you should go, they'll become helpless again and make you feel you have to stay. However, Mars in Pisces people do offer a very wonderful kind of love—soft, sensitive, and caring. The object of their desires is often someone similar or someone involved with art or music in some way. However, Pisces types are best off hooking up with a strong partner—someone who can keep their Mars energy on a straight and even course. The best part of Mars in Pisces people is that they are rarely, if ever, cold.

| | Aries | Taurus | Gemini | Cancer | Leo | Virgo |
|---|---|---|---|---|---|---|
| **1910** | 5/7-6/3 | 6/4-6/29 | 6/30-7/24 | 7/25-8/18 | 8/19-9/12 | 9/13-10/6 |
| **1911** | 2/28-3/23 | 3/24-4/17 | 4/18-5/12 | 5/13-6/8 | 6/9-7/7 | 7/8-11/8 |
| **1912** | 4/13-5/6 | 5/7-5/31 | 6/1-6/24 | 6/24-7/18 | 7/19-8/12 | 8/13-9/5 |
| **1913** | 2/3-3/6<br>5/2-5/30 | 3/7-5/1<br>5/31-7/7 | 7/8-8/5 | 8/6-8/31 | 9/1-9/26 | 9/27-10/20 |
| **1914** | 3/14-4/6 | 4/7-5/1 | 5/2-5/25 | 5/26-6/19 | 6/20-7/15 | 7/16-8/10 |
| **1915** | 4/27-5/21 | 5/22-6/15 | 6/16-7/10 | 7/11-8/3 | 8/4-8/28 | 8/29-9/21 |
| **1916** | 2/14-3/9 | 3/10-4/5 | 4/6-5/5 | 5/6-9/8 | 9/9-10/7 | 10/8-11/2 |
| **1917** | 3/29-4/21 | 4/22-5/15 | 5/16-6/9 | 6/10-7/3 | 7/4-7/28 | 7/29-8/21 |
| **1918** | 5/7-6/2 | 6/3-6/28 | 6/29-7/24 | 7/25-8/18 | 8/19-9/11 | 9/12-10/5 |
| **1919** | 2/27-3/22 | 3/23-4/16 | 4/17-5/12 | 5/13-6/7 | 6/8-7/7 | 7/8-11/8 |
| **1920** | 4/12-5/6 | 5/7-5/30 | 5/31-6/23 | 6/24-7/18 | 7/19-8/11 | 8/12-9/4 |
| **1921** | 2/3-3/6<br>4/26-6/1 | 3/7-4/25<br>6/2-7/7 | 7/8-8/5 | 8/6-8/31 | 9/1-9/25 | 9/26-10/20 |
| **1922** | 3/13-4/6 | 4/7-4/30 | 5/1-5/25 | 5/26-6/19 | 6/20-7/14 | 7/15-8/9 |
| **1923** | 4/27-5/21 | 5/22-6/14 | 6/15-7/9 | 7/10-8/3 | 8/4-8/27 | 8/28-9/20 |
| **1924** | 2/13-3/8 | 3/9-4/4 | 4/5-5/5 | 5/6-9/8 | 9/9-10/7 | 10/8-11/12 |
| **1925** | 3/28-4/20 | 4/21-5/15 | 5/16-6/8 | 6/9-7/3 | 7/4-7/27 | 7/28-8/21 |
| **1926** | 5/7-6/2 | 6/3-6/28 | 6/29-7/23 | 7/24-8/17 | 8/18-9/11 | 9/12-10/5 |
| **1927** | 2/27-3/22 | 3/23-4/16 | 4/17-5/11 | 5/12-6/7 | 6/8-7/7 | 7/8-11/9 |
| **1928** | 4/12-5/5 | 5/6-5/29 | 5/30-6/23 | 6/24-7/17 | 7/18-8/11 | 8/12-9/4 |
| **1929** | 2/3-3/7<br>4/20-6/2 | 3/8-4/19<br>6/3-7/7 | 7/8-8/4 | 8/5-8/30 | 8/31-9/25 | 9/26-10/19 |
| **1930** | 3/13-4/5 | 4/6-4/30 | 5/1-5/24 | 5/25-6/18 | 6/19-7/14 | 7/15-8/9 |
| **1931** | 4/26-5/20 | 5/21-6/13 | 6/14-7/8 | 7/9-8/2 | 8/3-8/26 | 8/27-9/19 |

VENUS SIGN 1910–1975

| Libra | Scorpio | Sagittarius | Capricorn | Aquarius | Pisces |
|---|---|---|---|---|---|
| 10/7-10/30 | 10/31-11/23 | 11/24-12/17 | 12/18-12/31 | 1/1-1/15 | 1/16-1/28 |
| | | | | 1/29-4/4 | 4/5-5/6 |
| 11/19-12/8 | 12/9-12/31 | | 1/1-1/10 | 1/11-2/2 | 2/3-2/27 |
| 9/6-9/30 | 1/1-1/4 | 1/5-1/29 | 1/30-2/23 | 2/24-3/18 | 3/19-4/12 |
| | 10/1-10/24 | 10/25-11/17 | 11/18-12/12 | 12/13-12/31 | |
| 10/21-11/13 | 11/14-12/7 | 12/8-12/31 | | 1/1-1/6 | 1/7-2/2 |
| | | | | | |
| 8/11-9/6 | 9/7-10/9 | 10/10-12/5 | 1/1-1/24 | 1/25-2/17 | 2/18-3/13 |
| | 12-6/12-30 | 12/31 | | | |
| 9/22-10/15 | 10/16-11/8 | 1/1-2/6 | 2/7-3/6 | 3/7-4/1 | 4/2-4/26 |
| | | 11/9-12/2 | 12/3-12/26 | 12/27-12/31 | |
| 11/3-11/27 | 11/28-12/21 | 12/22-12/31 | | 1/1-1/19 | 1/20-2/13 |
| 8/22-9/16 | 9/17-10/11 | 1/1-1/14 | 1/15-2/7 | 2/8-3/4 | 3/5-3/28 |
| | | 10/12-11/6 | 11/7-12/5 | 12/6-12/31 | |
| 10/6-10/29 | 10/30-11/22 | 11/23-12/16 | 12/17-12/31 | 1/1-4/5 | 4/6-5/6 |
| 11/9-12/8 | 12/9-12/31 | | 1/1-1/9 | 1/10-2/2 | 2/3-2/26 |
| 9/5-9/30 | 1/1-1/3 | 1/4-1/28 | 1/29-2/22 | 2/23-3/18 | 3/19-4/11 |
| | 9/31-10/23 | 10/24-11/17 | 11/18-12/11 | 12/12-12/31 | |
| 10/21-11/13 | 11/14-12/7 | 12/8-12/31 | | 1/1-1/6 | 1/7-2/2 |
| 8/10-9/6 | 9/7-10/10 | 10/11-11/28 | 1/1-1/24 | 1/25-2/16 | 2/17-3/12 |
| | 11/29-12/31 | | | | |
| 9/21-10/14 | 1/1 | 1/2-2/6 | 2/7-3/5 | 3/6-3/31 | 4/1-4/26 |
| | 10/15-11/7 | 11/8-12/1 | 12/2-12/25 | 12/26-12/31 | |
| 11/3-11/26 | 11/27-12/21 | 12/22-12/31 | | 1/1-1/19 | 1/20-2/12 |
| 8/22-9/15 | 9/16-10/11 | 1/1-1/14 | 1/15-2/7 | 2/8-3/3 | 3/4-3/27 |
| | | 10-12/11-6 | 11/7-12/5 | 12/6-12/31 | |
| 10/6-10/29 | 10/30-11/22 | 11/23-12/16 | 12/17-12/31 | 1/1-4/5 | 4/6-5/6 |
| 11/10-12/8 | 12/9-12/31 | 1/1-1/7 | 1/8 | 1/9-2/1 | 2/2-2/26 |
| 9/5-9/28 | 1/1-1/3 | 1/4-1/28 | 1/29-2/22 | 2/23-3/17 | 3/18-4/11 |
| | 9/29-10/23 | 10/24-11/16 | 11/17-12/11 | 12/12-12/31 | |
| 10/20-11/12 | 11/13-12/6 | 12/7-12/30 | 12/31 | 1/1-1/5 | 1/6-2/2 |
| | | | | | |
| 8/10-9/6 | 9/7-10/11 | 10/12-11/21 | 1/1-1/23 | 1/24-2/16 | 2/17-3/12 |
| | 11/22-12/31 | | | | |
| 9/20-10/13 | 1/1-1/3 | 1/4-2/6 | 2/7-3/4 | 3/5-3/31 | 4/1-4/25 |
| | 10/14-11/6 | 11/7-11/30 | 12/1-12/24 | 12/25-12/31 | |

| | Aries | Taurus | Gemini | Cancer | Leo | Virgo |
|---|---|---|---|---|---|---|
| **1932** | 2/12-3/8 | 3/9-4/3 | 4/4-5/5<br>7/13-7/27 | 5/6-7/12<br>7/28-9/8 | 9/9-10/6 | 10/7-11/1 |
| **1933** | 3/27-4/19 | 4/20-5/28 | 5/29-6/8 | 6/9-7/2 | 7/3-7/26 | 7/27-8/20 |
| **1934** | 5/6-6/1 | 6/2-6/27 | 6/28-7/22 | 7/23-8/16 | 8/17-9/10 | 9/11-10/4 |
| **1935** | 2/26-3/21 | 3/22-4/15 | 4/16-5/10 | 5/11-6/6 | 6/7-7/6 | 7/7-11/8 |
| **1936** | 4/11-5/4 | 5/5-5/28 | 5/29-6/22 | 6/23-7/16 | 7/17-8/10 | 8/11-9/4 |
| **1937** | 2/2-3/8<br>4/14-6/3 | 3/9-4/17<br>6/4-7/6 | 7/7-8/3 | 8/4-8/29 | 8/30-9/24 | 9/25-10/18 |
| **1938** | 3/12-4/4 | 4/5-4/28 | 4/29-5/23 | 5/24-6/18 | 6/19-7/13 | 7/14-8/8 |
| **1939** | 4-25/5/19 | 5/20-6/13 | 6/14-7/8 | 7/9-8/1 | 8/2-8/25 | 8/26-9/19 |
| **1940** | 2/12-3/7 | 3/8-4/3 | 4/4-5/5<br>7/5-7/31 | 5/6-7/4<br>8/1-9/8 | 9/9-10/5 | 10/6-10/31 |
| **1941** | 3/27-4/19 | 4/20-5/13 | 5/14-6/6 | 6/7-6/1 | 7/2-7/26 | 7/27-8/20 |
| **1942** | 5/6-6/1 | 6/2-6/26 | 6/27-7/22 | 7/23-8/16 | 8/17-9/9 | 9/10-10/3 |
| **1943** | 2/25-3/20 | 3/21-4/14 | 4/15-5/10 | 5/11-6/6 | 6/7-7/6 | 7/7-11/8 |
| **1944** | 4-10/5-3 | 5/4-5/28 | 5/29-6/21 | 6/22-7/16 | 7/17-8/9 | 8/10-9/2 |
| **1945** | 2/2-3/10<br>4/7-6/3 | 3/11-4/6<br>6/4-7/6 | 7/7-8/3 | 8/4-8/29 | 8/30-9/23 | 9/24-10/18 |
| **1946** | 3/11-4/4 | 4/5-4/28 | 4/29-5/23 | 5/24-6/17 | 6/18-7/12 | 7/13-8/8 |
| **1947** | 4/25-5/19 | 5/20-6/12 | 6/13-7/7 | 7/8-8/1 | 8/2-8/25 | 8/26-9/18 |
| **1948** | 2/11-3/7 | 3/8-4/3 | 4/4-5/6<br>6/29-8/2 | 5/7-6/28<br>8/3-9/7 | 9/8-10/5 | 10/6-10/31 |
| **1949** | 3/26-4/19 | 4/20-5/13 | 5/14-6/6 | 6/7-6/30 | 7/1-7/25 | 7/26-8/19 |
| **1950** | 5/5-5/31 | 6/1-6/26 | 6/27-7/21 | 7/22-8/15 | 8/16-9/9 | 9/10-10/3 |
| **1951** | 2/25-3/21 | 3/22-4/15 | 4/16-5/10 | 5/11-6/6 | 6/7-7/7 | 7/8-11/9 |
| **1952** | 4/10-5/4 | 5/5-5/28 | 5/29-6/21 | 6/22-7/16 | 7/17-8/9 | 8/10-9/3 |
| **1953** | 2/2-3/13<br>4/1-6/5 | 3/4-3/31<br>6/6-7/7 | 7/8-8/3 | 8/4-8/29 | 8/30-9/24 | 9/25-10/18 |

## VENUS SIGN 1910–1975

| Libra | Scorpio | Sagittarius | Capricorn | Aquarius | Pisces |
|---|---|---|---|---|---|
| 11/2-11/25 | 11/26-12/20 | 12/21-12/31 | | 1/1-1/18 | 1/19-2/11 |
| 8/21-9/14 | 9/15-10/10 | 1/1-1/13 | 1/14-2/6 | 2/7-3/2 | 3/3-3/26 |
| | | 10/11-11/5 | 11/6-12/4 | 12/5-12/31 | |
| 10/5-10/28 | 10/29-11/21 | 11/22-12/15 | 12/16-12/31 | 1/1-4/5 | 4/6-5/5 |
| 11/9-12/7 | 12/8-12/31 | | 1/1-1/7 | 1/8-1/31 | 2/1-2/25 |
| 9/5-9/27 | 1/1-1/2 | 1/3-1/27 | 1/28-2/21 | 2/22-3/16 | 3/17-4/10 |
| | 9/28-10/22 | 10/23-11/15 | 11/16-12/10 | 12/11-12/31 | |
| 10/19-11/11 | 11/12-12/5 | 12/6-12/29 | 12/30-12/31 | 1/1-1/5 | 1/6-2/1 |
| 8/9-9/6 | 9/7-10/13 | 10/14-11/14 | 1/1-1/22 | 1/23-2/15 | 2/16-3/11 |
| | 11/15-12/31 | | | | |
| 9/20-10/13 | 1/1-1/3 | 1/4-2/5 | 2/6-3/4 | 3/5-3/30 | 3/31-4/24 |
| | 10/14-11/6 | 11/7-11/30 | 12/1-12/24 | 12/25-12/31 | |
| 11/1-11/25 | 11/26-12/19 | 12/20-12/31 | | 1/1-1/18 | 1/19-2/11 |
| 8/21-9/14 | 9/15-10/9 | 1/1-1/12 | 1/13-2/5 | 2/6-3/1 | 3/2-3/26 |
| | | 10/10-11/5 | 11/6-12/4 | 12/5-12/31 | |
| 10/4-10/27 | 10/28-11/20 | 11/21-12/14 | 12/15-12/31 | 1/1-4/4 | 4/6-5/5 |
| 11/9-12/7 | 12/8-12/31 | | 1/1-1/7 | 1/8-1/31 | 2/1-2/24 |
| 9/3-9/27 | 1/1-1/2 | 1/3-1/27 | 1/28-2/20 | 2/21-3/16 | 3/17-4/9 |
| | 9/28-10/21 | 10/22-11/15 | 11/16-12/10 | 12/11-12/31 | |
| 10/19-11/11 | 11/12-12/5 | 12/6-12/29 | 12/30-12/31 | 1/1-1/4 | 1/5-2/1 |
| 8/9-9/6 | 9/7-10/15 | 10/16-11/7 | 1/1-1/21 | 1/22-2/14 | 2/15-3/10 |
| | 11/8-12/31 | | | | |
| 9/19-10/12 | 1/1-1/4 | 1/5-2/5 | 2/6-3/4 | 3/5-3/29 | 3/30-4/24 |
| | 10/13-11/5 | 11/6-11/29 | 11/30-12/23 | 12/24-12/31 | |
| 11/1-1/25 | 11/26-12/19 | 12/20-12/31 | | 1/1-1/17 | 1/18-2/10 |
| 8/20-9/14 | 9/15-10/9 | 1/1-1/12 | 1/13-2/5 | 2/6-3/1 | 3/2-3/25 |
| | | 10/10-11/5 | 11/6-12/5 | 12/6-12/31 | |
| 10/4-10/27 | 10/28-11/20 | 11/21-12/13 | 12/14-12/31 | 1/1-4/5 | 4/6-5/4 |
| 11/10-12/7 | 12/8-12/31 | | 1/1-1/7 | 1/8-1/31 | 2/1-2/24 |
| 9/4-9/27 | 1/1-1/2 | 1/3-1/27 | 1/28-2/20 | 2/21-3/16 | 3/17-4/9 |
| | 9/28-10/21 | 10/22-11/15 | 11/16-12/10 | 12/11-12/31 | |
| 10/19-11/11 | 11/12-12/5 | 12/6-12/29 | 12/30-12/31 | 1/1-1/5 | 1/6-2/1 |

| | Aries | Taurus | Gemini | Cancer | Leo | Virgo |
|---|---|---|---|---|---|---|
| 1954 | 3/12-4/4 | 4/5-4/28 | 4/29-5/23 | 5/24-6/17 | 6/18-7/13 | 7/14-8/8 |
| 1955 | 4/25-5/19 | 5/20-6/13 | 6/14-7/7 | 7/8-8/1 | 8/2-8/25 | 8/26-9/18 |
| 1956 | 2/12-3/7 | 3/8-4/4 | 4/5-5/7<br>6:24-8/4 | 5/8-6/23<br>8/5-9/8 | 9/9-10/5 | 10/6-10/31 |
| 1957 | 3-26/4-19 | 4/20-5/13 | 5/14-6/6 | 6/7-7/1 | 7/2-7/26 | 7/27-8/19 |
| 1958 | 5-6/5-31 | 6/1-6/26 | 6/27-7/22 | 7/23-8/15 | 8/16-9/9 | 9/10-10/3 |
| 1959 | 2-25/3-20 | 3/21-4/14 | 4/15-5/10 | 5/11-6/6 | 6/7-7/8<br>9/21-9/24 | 7/9-9/20<br>9/25-11/9 |
| 1960 | 4-10/5-3 | 5/4-5/28 | 5/29-6/21 | 6/22-7/15 | 7/16-8/9 | 8/10-9/2 |
| 1961 | 2-3/6-5 | 6/6-7/7 | 7/8-8/3 | 8/4-8/29 | 8/30-9/23 | 9/24-10/17 |
| 1962 | 3/11-4/3 | 4/4-4/28 | 4/29-5/22 | 5/23-6/17 | 6/18-7/12 | 7/13-8/8 |
| 1963 | 4/24-5/18 | 5/19-6/12 | 6/13-7/7 | 7/8-7/31 | 8/1-8/25 | 8/26-9/18 |
| 1964 | 2/11-3/7 | 3/8-4/4 | 4/5-5/9<br>6/18-8/5 | 5/10-6/17<br>8/6-9/8 | 9/9-10/5 | 10/6-10/31 |
| 1965 | 3/26-4/18 | 4/19-5/12 | 5/13-6/6 | 6/7-6/30 | 7/1-7/25 | 7/26-8/19 |
| 1966 | 5/6-6/31 | 6/1-6/26 | 6/27-7/21 | 7/22-8/15 | 8/16-9/8 | 9/9-10/2 |
| 1967 | 2/24-3/20 | 3/21-4/14 | 4/15-5/10 | 5/11-6/6 | 6/7-7/8<br>9/10-10/1 | 7/9-9/9<br>10/2-11/9 |
| 1968 | 4/9-5/3 | 5/4-5/27 | 5/28-6/20 | 6/21-7/15 | 7/16-8/8 | 8/9-9/2 |
| 1969 | 2/3-6/6 | 6/7-7/6 | 7/7-8/3 | 8/4-8/28 | 8/29-9/22 | 9/23-10/17 |
| 1970 | 3/11-4/3 | 4/4-4/27 | 4/28-5/22 | 5/23-6/16 | 6/17-7/12 | 7/13-8/8 |
| 1971 | 4/24-5/18 | 5/19-6/12 | 6/13-7/6 | 7/7-7/31 | 8/1-8/24 | 8/25-9/17 |
| 1972 | 2/11-3/7 | 3/8-4/3 | 4/4-5/10<br>6/12-8/6 | 5/11-6/11<br>8/7-9/8 | 9/9-10/5 | 10/6-10/30 |
| 1973 | 3/25-4/18 | 4/18-5/12 | 5/13-6/5 | 6/6-6/29 | 7/1-7/25 | 7/26-8/19 |
| 1974 | | | | | | |
| | 5/5-5/31 | 6/1-6/25 | 6/26-7/21 | 7/22-8/14 | 8/15-9/8 | 9/9-10/2 |
| 1975 | 2/24-3/20 | 3/21-4/13 | 4/14-5/9 | 5/10-6/6 | 6/7-7/9<br>9/3-10/4 | 7/10-9/2<br>10/5-11/9 |

| Libra | Scorpio | Sagittarius | Capricorn | Aquarius | Pisces |
| --- | --- | --- | --- | --- | --- |
| 8/9-9/6 | 9/7-10/22 | 10/23-10/27 | 1/1-1/22 | 1/23-2/15 | 2/16-3/11 |
| | 10/28-12/31 | | | | |
| 9/19-10/13 | 1/1-1/6 | 1/7-2/5 | 2/6-3/4 | 3/5-3/30 | 3/31-4/24 |
| | 10/14-11/5 | 11/6-11/30 | 12/1-12/24 | 12/25-12/31 | |
| 11/1-11/25 | 11/26-12/19 | 12/20-12/31 | | 1/1-1/17 | 1/18-2/11 |
| | | | | | |
| 8/20-9/14 | 9/15-10/9 | 1/1-1/12 | 1/13-2/5 | 2/6-3/1 | 3/2-3/25 |
| | | 10/10-11/5 | 11/6-12/16 | 12/7-12/31 | |
| 10/4-10/27 | 10/28-11/20 | 11/21-12/14 | 12/15-12/31 | 1/1-4/6 | 4/7-5/5 |
| 11/10-12/7 | 12/8-12/31 | | 1/1-1/7 | 1/8-1/31 | 2/1-2/24 |
| | | | | | |
| 9/3-9/26 | 1/1-1/2 | 1/3-1/27 | 1/28-2/20 | 2/21-3/15 | 3/16-4/9 |
| | 9/27-10/21 | 10/22-11/15 | 11/16-12/10 | 12/11-12/31 | |
| 10/18-11/11 | 11/12-12/4 | 12/5-12/28 | 12/29-12/31 | 1/1-1/5 | 1/6-2/2 |
| 8/9-9/6 | 9/7-12/31 | | 1/1-1/21 | 1/22-2/14 | 2/15-3/10 |
| 9/19-10/12 | 1/1-1/6 | 1/7-2/5 | 2/6-3/4 | 3/5-3/29 | 3/30-4/23 |
| | 10/13-11/5 | 11/6-11/29 | 11/30-12/23 | 12/24-12/31 | |
| 11/1-11/24 | 11/25-12/19 | 12/20-12/31 | | 1/1-1/16 | 1/17-2/10 |
| | | | | | |
| 8/20-9/13 | 9/14-10/9 | 1/1-1/12 | 1/13-2/5 | 2/6-3/1 | 3/2-3/25 |
| | | 10/10-11/5 | 11/6-12/7 | 12/8-12/31 | |
| 10/3-10/26 | 10/27-11/19 | 11/20-12/13 | 2/7-2/25 | 1/1-2/6 | 4/7-5/5 |
| | | | 12/14-12/31 | 2/26-4/6 | |
| 11/10-12/7 | 12/8-12/23 | | 1/1-1/6 | 1/7-1/30 | 1/31-2/23 |
| | | | | | |
| 9/3-9/26 | 1/1 | 1/2-1/26 | 1/27-2/20 | 2/21-3/15 | 3/16-4/8 |
| | 9/27-10/21 | 10/22-11/14 | 11/15-12/9 | 12/10-12/31 | |
| 10/18-11/10 | 11/11-12/4 | 12/5-12/28 | 12/29-12/31 | 1/1-1/4 | 1/5-2/2 |
| 8/9-9/7 | 9/8-12/31 | | 1/1-1/21 | 1/22-2/14 | 2/15-3/10 |
| 9/18-10/11 | 1/1-1/7 | 1/8-2/5 | 2/6-3/4 | 3/5-3/29 | 3/30-4/23 |
| | 10/12-11/5 | 11/6-11/29 | 11/30-12/23 | 12/24-12/31 | |
| | 11/25-12/18 | 12/19-12/31 | | 1/1-1/16 | 1/17-2/10 |
| 10/31-11/24 | | | | | |
| 8/20-9/13 | | 1/1-1/12 | 1/13-2/4 | 2/5-2/28 | 3/1-3/24 |
| | | 10/9-11/5 | 11/6-12/7 | 12/8-12/31 | |
| | | | 1/30-2/28 | 1/1-1/29 | |
| 10/3-10/26 | 10/27-11/19 | 11/20-12/13 | 12/14-12/31 | 3/1-4/6 | 4/7-5/4 |
| | | | 1/1-1/6 | 1/7-1/30 | 1/31-2/23 |
| 11/10-12/7 | 12/8-12/31 | | | | |

## MARS SIGN 1910–1975

| | Jan. | Feb. | Mar. | Apr. | May | June | July | Aug. | Sept. | Oct. | Nov. | Dec. |
|---|---|---|---|---|---|---|---|---|---|---|---|---|
| 1910 | AR | TA | GE | GE | CA | CA | LE | VI | VI | LI | SC | SC |
| 1911 | SA | CP | AQ | AQ | PI | AR | TA | TA | GE | GE | GE | TA |
| 1912 | TA | GE | GE | CA | CA | LE | LE | VI | LI | LI | SC | SA |
| 1913 | CP | CP | AQ | PI | AR | AR | TA | GE | CA | CA | CA | CA |
| 1914 | CA | CA | CA | CA | LE | LE | VI | LI | LI | SC | SA | SA |
| 1915 | CP | AQ | PI | PI | AR | TA | GE | GE | CA | LE | LE | LE |
| 1916 | LE | LE | LE | LE | LE | VI | VI | LI | SC | SC | SA | CP |
| 1917 | AQ | AQ | PI | AR | TA | GE | GE | CA | LE | LE | VI | VI |
| 1918 | LI | LI | VI | VI | VI | VI | LI | LI | SC | SA | CP | CP |
| 1919 | AQ | PI | AR | TA | GE | CA | CA | LE | VI | VI | VI | LI |
| 1920 | LI | SC | SC | SC | LI | LI | SC | SC | SA | SA | CP | AQ |
| 1921 | PI | AR | AR | TA | GE | GE | CA | LE | LE | VI | LI | LI |
| 1922 | SC | SC | SA | SA | SA | SA | SA | SA | CP | CP | AQ | AQ |
| 1923 | PI | AR | TA | TA | GE | CA | CA | LE | VI | VI | LI | SC |
| 1924 | SC | SA | CP | CP | AQ | AQ | PI | PI | AQ | AQ | PI | PI |
| 1925 | AR | TA | TA | GE | CA | CA | LE | VI | VI | LI | SC | SC |
| 1926 | SA | CP | CP | AQ | PI | AR | AR | TA | TA | TA | TA | TA |
| 1927 | TA | TA | GE | GE | CA | LE | LE | VI | LI | LI | SC | SA |
| 1928 | SA | SA | AQ | PI | PI | AR | TA | GE | GE | CA | CA | CA |

MARS SIGN 1910–1975

| Year | Jan. | Feb. | Mar. | Apr. | May | June | July | Aug. | Sept. | Oct. | Nov. | Dec. |
|------|------|------|------|------|-----|------|------|------|-------|------|------|------|
| 1929 | GE | GE | CA | CA | LE | LE | VI | VI | LI | SC | SC | SA |
| 1930 | CP | AQ | AQ | PI | AR | TA | GE | GE | CA | CA | LE | LE |
| 1931 | LE | LE | CA | LE | LE | VI | VI | LI | LI | SC | SA | CP |
| 1932 | CP | AQ | PI | AR | TA | TA | GE | CA | CA | LE | VI | VI |
| 1933 | VI | VI | VI | VI | VI | VI | LI | LI | SC | SA | SA | CP |
| 1934 | AQ | PI | AR | AR | TA | GE | GE | CA | LE | LE | VI | LI |
| 1935 | LI | LI | LI | LI | LI | LI | LI | SC | SC | SA | CP | AQ |
| 1936 | PI | PI | AR | TA | GE | GE | CA | LE | LE | VI | LI | LI |
| 1937 | SC | SC | SA | SA | SC | SC | SC | SA | SA | CP | AQ | AQ |
| 1938 | PI | AR | TA | TA | GE | CA | CA | LE | VI | VI | LI | SC |
| 1939 | SC | SA | SA | CP | CP | AQ | AQ | CP | CP | AQ | AQ | PI |
| 1940 | AR | AR | TA | GE | GE | CA | LE | LE | VI | VI | LI | SC |
| 1941 | SA | SA | CP | AQ | AQ | PI | AR | AR | AR | AR | AR | AR |
| 1942 | TA | TA | GE | GE | CA | LE | LE | VI | VI | LI | SC | SC |
| 1943 | SA | CP | AQ | AQ | PI | AR | TA | TA | GE | GE | GE | GE |
| 1944 | GE | GE | GE | CA | CA | LE | VI | VI | LI | SC | SC | SA |
| 1945 | CP | AQ | AQ | PI | AR | TA | TA | GE | CA | CA | LE | LE |
| 1946 | CA | CA | CA | CA | LE | LE | VI | LI | LI | SC | SA | SA |
| 1947 | CP | AQ | PI | AR | AR | TA | GE | CA | CA | LE | LE | VI |

## MARS SIGN 1910–1975

| | Jan. | Feb. | Mar. | Apr. | May | June | July | Aug. | Sept. | Oct. | Nov. | Dec. |
| --- | --- | --- | --- | --- | --- | --- | --- | --- | --- | --- | --- | --- |
| 1948 | VI | LE | LE | LE | LE | VI | VI | LI | SC | SC | SA | CP |
| 1949 | AQ | PI | PI | AR | TA | GE | GE | CA | LE | LE | VI | VI |
| 1950 | LI | LI | LI | VI | VI | LI | LI | SC | SC. | SA | CP | CP |
| 1951 | AQ | PI | AR | TA | TA | GE | CA | CA | LE | VI | VI | LI |
| 1952 | LI | SC | SC | SC | SC | SC | SC | SC | SA | CP | CP | AQ |
| 1953 | AR | AR | AR | TA | GE | GE | CA | LE | VI | VI | LI | LI |
| 1954 | SC | SA | SA | CP | CP | CP | SA | SA | CP | CP | AQ | PI |
| 1955 | PI | AR | TA | GE | GE | CA | LE | LE | VI | LI | LI | SC |
| 1956 | SA | SA | CP | AQ | AQ | PI | PI | PI | PI | PI | PI | AR |
| 1957 | AR | TA | TA | GE | CA | CA | LE | VI | VI | LI | SC | SC |
| 1958 | SA | CP | CP | AQ | PI | AR | AR | TA | TA | GE | TA | TA |
| 1959 | TA | GE | GE | CA | CA | LE | LE | VI | LI | LI | SC | SA |
| 1960 | CP | CP | AQ | PI | AR | AR | TA | GE | GE | CA | CA | CA |
| 1961 | CA | CA | CA | CA | LE | LE | VI | VI | LI | SC | SA | SA |
| 1962 | CP | AQ | PI | PI | AR | TA | GE | GE | CA | LE | LE | LE |
| 1963 | LE | LE | LE | LE | LE | VI | VI | LI | SC | SC | SA | CP |
| 1964 | AQ | AQ | PI | AR | TA | TA | GE | CA | LE | LE | VI | VI |
| 1965 | VI | VI | VI | VI | VI | VI | LI | LI | SC | SA | CP | CP |
| 1966 | AQ | PI | AR | AR | TA | GE | CA | CA | LE | VI | VI | LI |

## MARS SIGN 1910–1975

|      | Jan. | Feb. | Mar. | Apr. | May | June | July | Aug. | Sept. | Oct. | Nov. | Dec. |
|------|------|------|------|------|-----|------|------|------|-------|------|------|------|
| 1967 | LI | SC | SC | LI | LI | LI | LI | SC | SA | SA | CP | AQ |
| 1968 | PI | PI | AR | TA | GE | GE | CA | LE | LE | VI | LI | LI |
| 1969 | SC | SC | SA | SA | SA | SA | SA | SA | SA | CP | AQ | PI |
| 1970 | PI | AR | TA | TA | GE | CA | CA | LE | VI | VI | LI | SC |
| 1971 | SC | SA | CP | CP | AQ | AQ | AQ | AQ | AQ | AQ | PI | PI |
| 1972 | AR | TA | TA | GE | CA | CA | LE | LE | VI | LI | SC | SC |
| 1973 | SA | CP | CP | AQ | PI | PI | AR | TA | TA | TA | AR | AR |
| 1974 | TA | TA | GE | GE | CA | LE | LE | VI | LI | LI | SC | SA |
| 1975 | SA | CP | AQ | PI | PI | AR | TA | GE | GE | GE | CA | GE |

AR—Aries    LE—Leo    SA—Sagittarius
TA—Taurus    VI—Virgo    CP—Capricorn
GE—Gemini    LI—Libra    AQ—Aquarius
CA—Cancer    SC—Scorpio    PI—Pisces

# 9

# The Planets As "Stars"

## The Astrological Cast of Characters in Order of Their Appearance

As you learned in the chapter "Defining Terms," the planets are the *sine qua non* of astrology—the factor without which there would be no such study. It is the placement of the planets in the signs of the zodiac that give those signs meaning in human terms, and the placement of the planets in an individual horoscope that "spell out" that individual's character/personality. As for forecasting, it is the movement (transits) of the planets throughout our lifetime that activate one part of our chart or another and bring out certain life conditions.

Those planets are moving bodies and not "stars" in the astrological sense, though they are sometimes referred to with that word. In Shakespeare's play, *Julius Caesar*, Cassius, one of the conspirators, states, "The fault, dear Brutus, is not in our stars but in ourselves that we are underlings." Shakespeare (Cassius) actually knew what he was talking about because astrology was part and parcel of daily life in Elizabethan times when the play was written, as well as in Caesar's ancient Rome. However, Shakespeare seems to have preferred "stars" as a more poetic word than "planets." He also was right about another thing: The "stars" (planets) don't push people around unless you let them. The key is to understand the role each planet plays in your basic astrological makeup through your natal chart and to get to know yourself via this ancient and pragmatic science. Then you will better understand how the transits of the different planets are most likely to affect you.

Though the planets are not stars by astronomical definition (except for the sun), they do play the starring roles in the great cosmic drama that is acted out every day of our lives, and has been since the beginning of life on earth. There are other heavenly bodies—like the asteroids—that play supporting roles, but most astrologers take the Big Ten into consideration when they do a chart or a personal forecast: the sun, the moon, Mercury, Venus, Mars, Jupiter, Saturn, Uranus, Neptune, and Pluto. (Some of these planets, like the Moon, Venus, and Mars, are touched on in other parts of this book, and you may want to read those sections to get a better understanding of their characteristics.)

Each planet rules one or more signs of the zodiac—i.e., is very closely associated with that sign or signs. The one that rules your sun sign is your own personal planet, so to speak, and its description will fill in more of the background of your sign.

The following is a rundown of the planetary cast of characters, presented in their order of appearance, their actual position in our solar system As you know, the sun is the center of our solar system, and the orbits of the planets form rings around it. Looking at the planets this way underscores the fact that the *closer* planets influence us much more strongly as individuals. Planets farther out in the solar system are not only farther away, they also move much more slowly. While a transit of the moon lasts two days, for instance, a transit of Uranus (which takes eighty-four years to circle the zodiac) may influence your life for many months. However, even with these distant planets, their position in a specific *house* of your own horoscope will greatly influence your astrological makeup.

## The Sun

*Vital Statistics*: 864,000 miles in diameter; average distance from earth, 93 million miles; gaseous nature. Appears to circle the zodiac in 365 days.

*Rules*:   The sign of Leo
           Fourth period of life: ages 23 to 41
*Role*:    The true "star" . . . the male lead . . . the
           doer . . . the activator.

*Facts and Foibles*:   The position of the sun in anyone's horoscope is the central fact about that person, astrologically speaking. Your sun sign is your core—your individuality. It is your ego in the best sense of the word, the part of you that moves you in a certain life direction. No matter what your sun sign is, true self-development means developing the highest potential of that sign. People really grow into their sun signs as they mature, and the sun symbolically governs that stage of life (23 to 41) at which we are (or should be) mature individuals who are concerned with creating something in our own right. The sun is considered a masculine planet, because it is the fiery, animating force of life. We are meant to *express* our sun sign; those who do not can literally have a lifeless quality about them.

Those born under the sign of Leo have been said to be favored because of their rulership by the most important "planet" of them all. In ancient times, the sun was often the chief deity and was worshipped for its extraordinary power. It was recognized that without the sun, life on earth could not exist, and the dimming of its light via an eclipse was a terrifying experience for early civilizations that recognized their dependence upon its warmth and vitalizing nature. Whether or not Leo is a special sign is debatable, but there is no doubt that there is a tendency in some Leo sun sign people to become overly self-centered. Perhaps even unconsciously, they sense that it is a heady destiny to be ruled by the sun, but they are unable to handle its tremendous energies properly.

## The Moon

*Vital Statistics*:   238,857 miles from the earth; 2,160 miles in diameter (one-fourth earth's size). Revolves around the earth (circles the zodiac) in about 27 ½ days
*Rules*:   The sign of cancer
           The first four years of human life

*Role*:     The leading lady . . . the "feeler" . . . the mother
            . . . the reactor.
*Facts and Foibles*:   The moon is not exactly a planet, either;
it is a satellite of our own planet, earth. However, it is the
largest satellite with respect to its parent planet anywhere
in the solar system that we know of. It has a tremendous
gravitational pull, which is demonstrated on earth by the
changing of the tides and other natural phenomena.

The moon has no light of its own, and we can see it
shining only because it reflects the sun. Therefore, the
moon is considered a *receptive* or "feminine" planet,
rather than an active one like the sun. The moon in
mythology has always been a woman—often the "Great
Mother" to ancient peoples who saw the sun as the
"Great Father." Accordingly, the moon rules the first
four years of human life, when we are totally dependent on our mothers, and the motherly sign of Cancer,
which is closely associated with nurturing and growth.
In an individual horoscope, the position of the moon
indicates our ability to feel and to respond emotionally.
It is our impressionability and sensitivity, i.e., our sub-
jective rather than our objective sign. The moon reacts
to experience and remembers it. All our memories are
stored in our subconscious, which is the part of the
human psyche the moon signifies. In a sense, as the
moon rules the night, it rules our dark or hidden side.
As it takes some time for us to develop or grow into
our sun sign, the moon sign manifests itself much more
strongly in young children than the sun sign does. The
moon represents the instinctual nature connected with
infantile responses; our moon sign acts from habit,
often without thinking.


## Mercury

---

*Vital Statistics*:   36 million miles away from the sun;
2,900 miles in diameter; orbits sun at 108,000 miles per
hour; goes through zodiac in 88 days.
*Rules*:    The signs of Gemini and Virgo
            Age of curiosity: 4 through 14
*Role*:     The young male lead . . . the observer . . . the
            messenger . . . the communicator.

*Facts and Foibles*: Mercury is the hottest, quickest, and smallest of the planets, and is closest to the sun. It is so closely associated with the sun in an astronomical sense, that Mercury is very often in the same sign as the sun in a natal chart. In any horoscope, it is never more than two signs away from your sun sign.

In ancient times Mercury was regarded as the sun's messenger, and the gods with whom it was associated always had some kind of communicating function. In Egypt, Mercury was Thoth—scribe to the gods, keeper of the divine books. The Greeks called him Hermes, the messenger; the Romans renamed him Mercury, but assigned similar functions. Hermes/Mercury always had a golden tongue, and was regarded as the great persuader. Quickness and deftness also associate Mercury with all kinds of human skills requiring manual and mental dexterity.

Mercury has a double role to play as ruler of the signs of Gemini and Virgo. In a sense, Mercury is two-faced; the communicative side in Gemini, his precise specialist side in Virgo. No matter what your sun sign is, in your horoscope Mercury symbolizes your style of thinking and communicating—not so much how intelligent you are as how you tend to put things together mentally.

Mercury is a very human planet, and has a very human foible; occasionally he gets things all mixed up and causes a lot of trouble. About three times a year, for about three weeks at a time, Mercury seems to be going *backwards*. (That appearance is caused by the varying rates of speed of various planets—like two trains traveling in the same direction that can seem as if they are traveling in two different directions.) During these periods Mercury is said to be *retrograde*, it is known to cause problems in all kinds of human interactions. People get the wrong message, or don't get it at all. People who are supposed to meet on a street corner never find each other. Trains and planes are missed, luggage is lost, orders simply never get transmitted or seem to vanish in thin air. There has been quite a bit of research on Mercury retrograde, and it all proves out. Even if people don't know *why* retrograde Mercury

makes things go wrong, they sure know it does. In 1986 Mercury will be retrograde during these periods:
  March 7 through March 30.
  July 9 through August 3.
  November 2 through November 22.

## Venus

*Vital Statistics*:  67.2 million miles from the sun; 26 million to 160 million miles from earth; approximately the same size and volume as earth. Goes through all twelve signs of the zodiac in about 225 days.
*Rules*:  The signs of Taurus and Libra
        Period of developing sexuality: ages 14 to 21
*Role*:  The young, nubile female lead . . . the love interest . . . the artist.
*Facts and Foibles*:  Like Mercury, Venus follows the sun very closely, so in anyone's horoscope it is never very far away from your sun sign. Symbolically, Venus represents your capacity to love and relate, and the capacity to appreciate beauty. In ancient myth, Venus was seen as the daughter of the moon, a feminine planet associated with many of the earthly things traditionally associated with women: the providing of food and shelter, the beautifying of the home, the harmonizing of opposites and settler of strife. Venus is a peaceful planet in every sense of the word. Aphrodite to the Greeks, Venus to the Romans, this goddess/planet was seen as the bounteous giver of life's gifts and pleasures—the personification of beauty. She is supposed to inspire us with the desire for both material and spiritual growth.

Like Mercury, Venus has two faces, but, strangely, one rules a feminine sign, Taurus, and one rules a masculine sign, Libra. In Taurus, Venus shows her earthier side, more concerned with creature comforts, sex, and material prosperity. In Libra, a more refined Venus shines forth as the graceful "hostess," the one who beautifies things and relates to others.

Though most Libra males are quite virile, their rulership by the planet Venus often manifests itself in extremely good looks and a great appreciation of beauty. The virile male hairdresser or interior decorator is the personification of this side of Venus. Because Venus seeks peace rather than war, harmony rather than discord, she rules lawyers, mediators, and arbitrators.

Since Venus rules one feminine earth sign and one masculine air sign, she is sometimes seen as a symbol for the fact that all things in the universe can be made to work in harmony—even the incompatible elements of air (Libra) and earth (Taurus) and the often antagonistic principles of male and female—in real life as in astrology. Divorce courts come under the rulership of Venus.

## Mars

*Vital Statistics:*   14 million miles from the sun; 35 million miles from earth; 10 percent of earth's size; circles the zodiac in about 687 days.
*Rules:*   The sign of Aries
          Ages 42 to 56
*Role:*   The virile male antagonist . . . the lover . . . the warrior.
*Facts and foibles:*   Mars is a rather small planet and has sometimes been called "Earth's little brother." However, since ancient times Mars has been attributed with great powers—possibly because of its fiery red color. Even the earliest peoples associated Mars with strife and sex and a warriorlike attitude. In fact, Mars has had a rather bad reputation in astrology and was sometimes known as the "lesser malefic." But some groups assigned Mars another role and gave him a different dimension. The Egyptians called Mars Artes, and connected him with personal creative expression; to the Hebrews he played a similar role. When you think about it, sex, strife, and creative expression are only a few steps away from each other. Certainly, the act of procreation is a creative one, as it gives new life. War and strife are divisive, but often a new order comes out of them as well.

Mars is pure masculine energy—sometimes a bit rough, but always determined. In a personal horoscope, the sign position of Mars tells how you tend to assert yourself, how aggressive you are likely to be when going after what you want, even how much you will want it. Mars is our desire nature. (See the chapter on Venus and Mars to find out more about Mars in your own horoscope.) As the god of war, Mars is associated with courage and bravery, traits that are available to the Aries sun sign person if he/she cares to develop them. Mars is moral courage too, and the Mars-ruled Aries sun sign person at his/her best will never desert a cause or a person—no matter how rough the going gets.

About once every two years Mars returns to the same place it occupied on the day of your birth; to astrologers this is known as the "Mars return." It is a period of time during which one can make great strides, because Mars is stimulating that area of the natal chart connected with taking on the world. People often feel a great surge of energy during their Mars return, but if that energy is not directed in a productive channel, it can cause a lot of problems in relationships. You are far better taking out your Mars return aggressiveness on another job or another creative project rather than another person.

## Jupiter

*Vital Statistics*:   Largest planet in the solar system, 318 times larger than earth; 365 million to 600 million miles from earth; gaseous nature; circles the zodiac in about 12 years.

*Rules*:   The sign of Sagittarius
            Ages 57 to 68

*Role*:   The hero ... the "father confessor" ... the one who saves the day.

*Facts and Foibles:*   From earliest times, Jupiter was assigned a role in the "cosmic drama" almost as important as that of the sun. Huge and luminous, Jupiter was easily visible to the naked eye eons before the age of the telescope. The sun may have been god in the all-encompassing sense, but Jupiter was *the* god who could make things happen, even interfere in human affairs if he was needed. And he has always been a "good guy." The Hindus, whose roots lie in antiquity, call him Vishnu, the preserver. To the Greeks, he was Zeus, the god who reigned supreme on Mount Olympus; he became Jupiter under the Romans. The important thing about this masculine god-planet is that it has always been very godly but very human at the same time. Zeus frequently came down from Mount Olympus to bestow his favors on people—particularly women who caught his fancy (causing his wife Hera to become jealous). Jupiter-Zeus is the god who keeps one foot in heaven and one foot firmly planted on the earth. Since the planet itself is large and impressive-looking, it has always been associated with benevolence and expansiveness. Our English word "jovial" has its roots in the name Jove, by which name Jupiter was sometimes called.

Joviality is one of the characteristics that is available to people born under the sign of Sagittarius, which Jupiter rules. Some Sagittarians are jovial, they spend all their money and all their energy on making life one long party.

But Jupiter has a serious side, too. Jupiter is associated with the divine law, and the ability to make that law known to men on earth. The higher Sagittarian, ruled by Jupiter, has a sense of this mission, and often takes the real-life role of priest-missionary or teacher of higher studies. While Venus and Libra, the sign Venus rules, are associated with the *practice* of law, Jupiter and Sagittarius are connected with the *making* and *interpretation* of laws.

## Saturn

---

*Vital Statistics*:   75,000 miles in diameter, 95 times as big as earth; 886 million miles from the sun; takes 29 years to circle the zodiac.

*Rules*:   The sign of Capricorn
          Ages 68 on

*Role*:   The "older man" . . . the taskmaster . . . the disciplining father.

*Facts and Foibles*:   Like Jupiter, Saturn is so large it can be seen with the naked eye from earth and was watched carefully by early peoples. It was quickly observed that certain transits of Saturn brought trials and troubles on earth and so the planet earned itself the name of the "greater malefic" by the time astrologers had begun to record their findings. Is Saturn really a "bad guy" as so many astrology books will tell you? There is no question that Saturn represents the principle of limitation; when you go too far out on a limb or get over expansive, Saturn is always there to teach you that there are rules and restrictions. However, as Saturn also represents the principle of contraction, this planet can and does bring periods of time in which we can consolidate our forces and make a secure place for ourselves in this world.

Saturn is also sometimes called the "lord of Karma." Translated into human terms, that means that Saturn represents our inevitable responsibilities, our "fated" duties in this world. Once again, there is a positive side. When Saturn is strongly placed in an individual's chart, that individual is exceptionally able to handle responsibility and achieve worldly success. As ruler of the sign of Capricorn, Saturn brings to that sign an extraordinary talent for working long and hard as well as reaping the material rewards that come with dedication to a task.

Kronos (or Chronos) was the ancient Greek god who is generally regarded as the prototype for Saturn's particular personality or role, and his story sheds a lot of light on the perceptions of this planet. Kronos was born to the very highest ancient god, Ouranos, and to the original earth mother, Ge. Kronos got a little carried away with this position and overthrew his father (castrating him) to take over the throne. When Kronos was told one of his own children would do the same to him, he swallowed them all—except Zeus, who was miraculously saved and became the "avenger." Later on, Zeus banished Kronos into exile. We know Kronos as Father Time—that shadowy old man who reminds us that it's later than we think. Kronos/Saturn also cautions against runaway ambitions, which is often punished by a downfall like his.

One of the most fascinating aspects of Saturn is that it is an uncannily accurate cosmic clock. Taking about 29 years to make a full circle of the zodiac, Saturn returns to the same place it occupied in your horoscope at your birth when you are about 29 years old. The "Saturn return" is regarded by astrologers as the true end of childhood (astrology is kind to us weak mortals by giving us more time to "grow up" than conventional earthly wisdom does). When Saturn begins to creep up on us in our late twenties, we generally begin to feel that it's time to settle down and do something big in the way of taking on earthly responsibility. Many people go through a "life crisis" at this time, because they feel the push that Saturn is giving them, but have trouble knowing what to do about it. Many, many people resolve the dilemma by getting married, buying a home, having a child, or getting divorced. The point is that it is time to *do something decisive* and to take responsibility for our own lives and actions. There are an incredible number of "Saturn return babies" because having a child is probably the most joyful as well as the biggest responsibility a person can assume.

On its second return—at about the human age of 58—people are generally ready to start relaxing their responsibilities and enjoying the fruits of their labors. It is a wise precaution to make ready for the second Saturn return, because just as Saturn tells us we have to *work*, he also tells us when it is time to *stop* working. But remain a productive human being, with real interests and the wherewithal to pursue them.

## Uranus

---

*Vital Statistics*:   1.7 billion miles from earth; 29,300 miles in diameter, 15 times larger than earth; takes 84 years to circle the zodiac; has an erratic orbit.
*Rules*:   The sign of Aquarius
          Teenagers
*Role*:   The rebel . . . the home-wrecker . . . the
          visionary.
*Facts and Foibles*:   Uranus is the first of the "modern" planets, i.e., those unknown to the ancients, and only discovered via the telescope. Uranus, the first planet to be discovered in this manner, was thus a shock to both astronomers and astrologers. Both groups believed the orbit of Saturn defined the limits of our solar system,

and both had to revise their thinking at this discovery. Astrologers took things in their stride by calling Uranus a "planet of the higher octave" and interpreting it as a breakthrough from the realm of purely earthly influences (with Saturn as the dividing line) to the "cosmic" or "higher" order of things. They decided that Uranus— an unconventional planet in many respects—must be the ruler of the quirky sign of Aquarius (which had been formerly ruled by Saturn). In a way it is uncanny that the sudden discovery of Uranus in 1781 heralded all the breakthrough discoveries of the 19th and 20th centuries. In a sense, Uranus ushered in the modern world; it also rules our current Age of Aquarius. As that age (approximately 2000 years long) will continue to shock us with discovery after discovery, it hopefully will also bring us the sense of brotherhood of humanity that is the hallmark of the sign of Aquarius.

As Uranus takes 84 years to circle the zodiac, it stays in each sign about seven years. (It is currently about two-thirds of the way through the sign of Sagittarius.) Whatever Uranus touches as it transits a person's natal chart gets a real jolt. Sometimes very suddenly. Uranus hates the status quo and almost always shakes it up. That means that a lot of changes take place when Uranus comes along, but for most people those changes are eventually positive ones. Uranus gets you out of whatever rut you happen to be in and does it quite forcefully. However, those who resist the changes Uranus "suggests" can cause themselves a lot of trouble. If you aren't willing to bend, Uranus can really "break you up."

Uranus is appropriately associated with the teen years, during which young people are often in a state of rebellion. However, here too, it is a *necessary* fact of life that people must eventually rebel against the strictures of childhood in order to become separate individual human beings. Uranus is associated not only with teenagers, but also with many of the things that represent their rebellion, like rock music, blaring radios, and all that goes with them. In essence, Uranus is the symbol of the electronic modern world.

---

*Vital Statistics*:   2.6 billion miles from earth; 2.7 billion miles from the sun; takes about 165 years to circle the zodiac.

*Rules*:   The sign of Pisces
No specific age.

*Role*:   The fascinating stranger . . . the poet . . . the one who confuses the issue. . . the dreamer of great dreams.

*Facts and Foibles*:   As it is difficult to get a handle on people heavily influenced by Neptune (like Pisceans), it took astronomers a while to figure out what Neptune really was. At first they observed nothing but some rather weird abberations in the orbit of Uranus as they began to plot that planet's orbit. In the early 1840s, some of them proved mathematically that there *must* be another planet out there, although it couldn't be seen. Finally, using all the data at hand, a German astronomer spotted Neptune in 1846.

There is a rather "sneaky" character to Neptune, but what this nebulous planet really symbolizes is the love that passes all understanding, the all-encompassing universal love that is virtually impossible for mortals to feel and give. Venus represents two-way love, the sharing kind. Neptune's love goes only in one direction. Neptune gives in a sense of self-sacrifice, and takes nothing in return.

There is evidence that even though no one really *saw* Neptune until 1846, the ancients knew all about its principles, and embodied them in the mythical figure of Poseidon (later called Neptune), the lord of the seas, master of the deep. When you think that more than three-quarters of the earth's surface is covered by water, you realize that Neptune was pretty important in the overall scheme of things. In fact, according to the Greeks, when the universe was created, it was divided among Zeus-Jupiter, who took the heavens, Hades-Pluto who took the underworld, and Poseidon-Neptune who took the oceans.

Just as water is difficult to contain, it is difficult for many people to get in touch with Neptune's higher qualities in their own charts. Water is soul and spirit, metaphysically speaking, so Neptune should make us aspire to much higher things. Not only universal love, but poetry, music and art in its purest forms. However, what Neptune touches in most people's natal charts often turns into an area of confusion rather than creativity. Neptune rules liquid in all its forms and, unfortunately, some people react to Neptune's confusing vibes by turning to alcohol or drugs. For many drug and alcohol abusers, however, the real goal of their vice is to attain a kind of "cosmic consciousness" which is the real realm of Neptune.

Since Neptune takes 165 years to circle the zodiac, it stays in one sign for 13 years or more. Therefore, it is the zodiacal *sign* Neptune makes to the "personal planets" in your chart that really count. People positively influenced by Neptune make the true artists and poets of this world—as well as the visionaries who interpret its meaning in more philosophical and metaphysical terms.

## Pluto

*Vital Statistics:*   3,666 billion miles from the sun; takes about 242 years to circle the zodiac.
*Rules:*   The sign of Scorpio
           Prenatal
*Role:*   The "heavy" . . . the transformer . . . the tragic
          hero.
*Facts and Foibles:* As you will note, Pluto is a little light on vital statistics. That's because this immensely distant planet, only discovered in 1930, has yet to reveal some of its secrets to astronomers. Like Neptune, it was discovered only because of the erratic nature of the orbit of Uranus. But, even when Pluto was conclusively sighted in 1930, its small size relative to its extremely strong gravitational pull didn't make sense to astronomers. Either Pluto is much larger than we now think or it is so dense that it exerts a force much greater than its size should account for.

Either way, there's no doubt that Pluto represents *power*. In fact, many astrologers connect the discovery of Pluto with the discovery by man of the extraordinary power in matter itself—the power of the atom. As with Neptune, Pluto's "realm" had been staked out in myth and astrology long before its actual discovery. Pluto is Hades, lord of the underworld—the place of darkness that all men fear. However, since most older religions regard life and death as a cycle, Pluto represents rebirth as well. We die only to be reborn. One of the symbols for Pluto is the Phoenix that rises triumphantly from its own ashes. Pluto—and the sign of Scorpio that it rules—hold onto their secrets, but have an incredible power to endure and triumph over life's circumstances. The extremes of life and death that Pluto/Scorpio is associated with connect neatly with the extremism of this astrological sign. "Plutonic" Scorpios often regard the world as totally black and white, with very few grays in between. They can also be the "best" of people, like reformers and religious leaders, or the "worst" of people, like criminals and those who manipulate others for their own purposes.

# 10

## Astrotrivia

### How Do You Rate in the Best Game in Town?

The ancient art of astrology is loaded with bits and pieces of miscellaneous information—all of it fascinating, and some of it more useful than you may think. For instance, did you know that every zodiac sign has a special day of the week and certain colors assigned to it? And, how good are you at guessing sun signs of celebrities—those larger-than-life models of sun signs in the flesh? The Astrotrivia that follows is partly in quiz form, partly in short-take astrological facts. In the first part, you can test your own astrological perceptivity; in the second, you can add a lot to your fund of astrological information—and maybe even learn a few things you can use in your daily life.

### Astrotrivia Part I
### Sun Signs of the Rich and Famous

Try to answer the following questions yourself; if you're stumped you'll find the answers on page 103–104.

1. What famous stripper and the famous actress who played her mother in a Broadway show have the sign of Capricorn in common?

2. What two show biz buddies—who run in the same pack—are both Sagittarians?

3. What do these people have in common: Joseph Stalin, Richard Nixon, Herman Goering, Al Capone, and Mao Tse Tung?

4. What two handsome male movie stars, both known for their progressive ideas, have the same sun sign? And, what is it?

5. What highly Scorpionic actor had an on-again, off-again lifetime romance with a glamourous Pisces actress?

6. What two female tennis pros are both athletic Sagittarians?

7. What U.S. president had a "show-me-I'm-from-Missouri" personality, and what was his sun sign?

8. What two famous "lonely hearts" columnists get their soft Cancerian shoulders cried on all the time?

9. What two "greats" of American popular music were both thoroughly American, and both born on the Fourth of July?

10. Under what sign were these warrior peacemakers all born: Dwight D. Eisenhower, David Ben Gurion, Jimmy Carter, Mohandus Ghandi, and Eleanor Roosevelt?

11. What anti-American villainess of World War II was born on the Fourth of July?

12. What sun sign do these people have in common: Oscar Wilde, Truman Capote, and Gore Vidal?

13. What two famous rock stars—one early, one late—were born not only under the same sign, but on the same day?

14. Which of the following is/was not a Scorpio?

| | |
|---|---|
| Charles Manson | Robert Kennedy |
| Bo Derek | Pablo Picasso |
| Katherine Hepburn | Indira Ghandi |
| Princess Grace | Johnny Carson |
| Henry Kissinger | Billy Graham |

15. All of the following were born under the two most musical signs of the zodiac. What are they?

| Judy Collins | Michael Jackson |
| Barbra Steisand | George Gershwin |
| Stevie Wonder | Luciano Pavarotti |
| Fred Astaire | Paul Simon |
| Irving Berlin | Julie Andrews |
| Bing Crosby | Anthony Newly |
| Beverly Sills | John Lennon |
| Bobby Darin | Guiseppe Verdi |

16. All the following ladies of the stage and screen are masters of their craft. Which craftsman-like sun sign were they all born under?

| Lauren Bacall | Celeste Holm |
| Anne Bancroft | Greer Garson |
| Ingrid Bergman | Twiggy |
| Greta Garbo | Jo Ann Worley |
| Sophia Loren | Claudette Colbert |
| Lilly Tomlin | Raquel Welch |

17. What sun sign do the following famous rebels and rule-breakers have in common: Marlon Brando, Warren Beatty, Eddie Murphy, Charlie Chaplin, Hugh Hefner?

18. What sun sign do these medical and research geniuses have in common: Madame Curie, Jonas Salk, Christian Bernard?

19. What present-day famous Leo "princess" lived in Camelot with her Gemini "prince"?

20. What two great ballet stars were both born in the same country, and share the graceful sun sign, Pisces?

Answers on p. 103–104

## Astrotrivia Part II
## More Celebrity Sun Sign Lore

Just a handful of the many, many stage/screen-struck Leos:

Robert DeNiro            Julia Child
Mike Jagger              Arlene Dahl
Lucille Ball             Alfred Hitchcock
Dustin Hoffman           Mae West
Cecil B. Demille         George Bernard Shaw
John Derek               Dino D. Laurentis
Mike Douglas             Robert Mitchum
Robert Redford           Peter O'Toole
Jason Robards Jr.        Roman Polanski
Esther Williams          Jill St. John
Stanley Kubrick          Robert Taylor
Shelly Winters           Keenan Wynn

And here are some Leos who make/made the international scene their stage:

Fidel Castro             Henry Ford
Jackie Onassis           Alex Haley
Coco Chanel              Lawrence of Arabia
Benito Mussolini         Mata Hari
Rasputin                 Napoleon
Neil Armstrong           Andy Warhol
Mike Conners

Librans are often lovely, like Catherine Deneuve and Brigitte Bardot. Barbara Walters is the ultimate "cool" Libra.

Cancer is the second fame sign, because Cancer rules the public. Cancers who have made it somehow or other are:

Bill Cosby               Ringo Starr
Jimmy Cagney             John Glenn
Ernest Hemingway         Arthur Ashe
Gerald Ford              The Mayo brothers
                            (of the Mayo clinic)

Some outspoken, inventive Aquarians whose opinions have not always been popular, but were always ahead of their time:

Norman Mailer       Ralph Nader
Charles Darwin      Thomas Edison
Jules Verne         Betty Friedan
Ayn Rand            Vanessa Redgrave
Galileo             Franklin D. Roosevelt

## Astrotrivia Part III
## Fascinating Facts About the Signs

Here are the colors that, by tradition, match each of the signs of the zodiac:

1. Aries: bright red, scarlet, magenta

2. Taurus: pastels in most shades, especially pink and turquoise

3. Gemini: beiges and light gray

4. Cancer: shimmery and irridescent shades of gray and silver; anything luminous

5. Leo: bright golds and yellows

6. Virgo: dark navy, brown, gray

7. Libra: cloudy pales, especially blue-green

8. Scorpio: murky colors, especially blood red and black

9. Sagittarius: rich blues, purples, greens

10. Capricorn: black, "no-color" colors

11. Aquarius: checks, stripes, patterns, electric blue

12. Pisces: deep lilac, mauve, sea green

Each Sign/Planet owns a day of the week:

Sunday = Sun/Leo

Monday = Moon/Cancer

Tuesday = Mars/Aries, Mars/Scorpio

Wednesday = Mercury/Gemini, Mercury/Virgo

Thursday = Jupiter/Sagittarius, Neptune/Pisces

Friday = Venus/Taurus, Venus/Libra

Saturday = Saturn/Capricorn, Saturn/Aquarius

(Since there are only seven days and twelve signs, some of the signs double up. Also, since the ancients only knew seven planets, there are only enough days to match seven of the ten planets we now recognize.)

## Astrotrivia Part IV
## Where Do You Belong?

Each sign is said to have certain places where it belongs. Long ago, the world was divided up according to astrological tradition, so there are certain countries, cities, and areas that have the vibrations of certain signs. Tradition divides up other kinds of spaces, too, as you will see.

- *Aries places:* In the world: Birmingham, Oldman, Leicester, and Blackburn, *England* . . . Florence, Naples, Verona and Padua *Italy* . . . Marseilles and Burgundy *France* . . . *Denmark, Germany, Palestine, Syria, Japan.*

  Anywhere: sheepfolds, forges, tool houses, fireplaces, on sandy soil, kilns, ceilings, fire houses, emergency rooms.

- *Taurus places:* In the world: Dublin, *Ireland* . . . Mantua, Parma, Palermo, *Italy* . . . St. Louis, *U.S.A.* . . . *The Greek Islands, Asia Minor,* the *Caucasus.*

  Anywhere: banks, dairies, pastures, shady places, corn fields, middle rooms of houses, altars, maypoles.

- *Gemini places:* In the world: San Francisco, *U.S.A.* . . . London and Plymouth, *England* . . . Bruges, *Belgium* . . . Versailles and Louvaine, *France* . . . Nurenburg, *Germany* . . . *Lower Egypt, Armenia, Wales.*

  Anywhere: buildings with pillars, bookcases, hills and mountains, upper back rooms, graineries.

- *Cancer places:* In the world; St. Andrews, *Scotland* . . . Amsterdam, *Holland* . . . New York City, *U.S.A.* . . . Stockholm, *Sweden* . . . Genoa, Venice, Milan, *Italy* . . . *Paraguay, North and West Africa.*

Anywhere: lakes and brooks, salt marshes, pubs, kitchens, cellars, corner houses facing north.

- *Sagittarius places:* In the world: Avignon, *France* . . . Stuttgart, Cologne, *Germany* . . . Nottingham, Sheffield, Bradford, *England* . . . Provence, *France* . . . *Hungary, Arabia, Tuscany.*

    Anywhere: highest place around, topmost room in house, stables for racing horses, obelisks, places near fire, where incense is burned.

- *Capricorn places:* In the world: Brussels, *Belgium* . . . Port Said, *Egypt* . . . *India, Afghanistan, Mexico, Lithuania, Orkney Islands, Macedonia.*

    Anywhere: vaults, convents, thick forests, gates and hinges, old trees, jails, cattle barns, door knockers, game preserves.

- *Aquarius places:* In the world: Brighton and Trent, *England* . . . Salszburg, *Austria* . . . Hamburg, *Germany* . . . the Piedmont, *Italy* . . . *Prussia, Red Russia, Westphalia.*

    Anywhere: buses, bridges, ladders, garages, airplanes, power transmitters, fountains, springs and streams, sleds, ice caps.

- *Pisces places:* In the world; Alexandria, *Egypt* . . . Seville, *Spain* . . . Southport, Lancaster, Bournemouth, Tiverton, *England* . . . *Portugal, Calabria, Normandy, Sahara.*

    Anywhere: fish ponds, oceans, oil fields, submarines, séances, flooded areas, bars, aquariums, boat yards, swimming pools, hospitals.

- *Leo Places:* In the world: Rome, Ravenna, *Italy* . . . Bath, Bristol, Portsmouth, Blackpool, *England* . . . Philadelphia, Chicago, *U.S.A.* . . . *Bohemia, Sicily, the Alps, Damascus.*

    Anywhere: wild animal preserves, deserts and forests, castles, furnaces, gold mines, porches, forts.

- *Virgo places:* In the world: Paris, Lyons, Toulouse, *France* . . . Boston, Los Angeles, *U.S.A.* . . . Heidelberg, *Germany* . . . *Turkey, West Indies, Brazil, Silesia, Switzerland.*

    Anywhere: pantries, restaurants, refrigerators, medicine cabinets, desks, malt houses.

- *Libra places:* In the world: Dover, Liverpool, New-castle, *England* . . . Messina, *Italy* . . . Halifax, *Nova Scotia* . . . *China, Norway, The Transvaal, the Barbary coast.*

  Anywhere: windmills, wood sheds, harbors, tops of mountains, garrets and lofts, guest rooms, tops of dressers, domed buildings.
- *Scorpio places:* In the world: Copenhagen, *Denmark* . . . Leeds, Nottingham, *England* . . . Johannesburg, *South Africa* . . . Burma, *India* . . . *Tibet, North China, Argentina.*

  Anywhere: junk yards, meat markets, laboratories, low gardens and streams, vineyards, deepest part of ocean.

## Astrotrivia Part V
## Which Animal Best Suits You?

Each sign is said to have an affinity with certain kinds of pets. Here's the rundown.

*Aries:* No animal that needs a lot of taking care of; but if Aries has one pet, he/she will usually have two, so the animals can take care of each other.

*Taurus:* Almost any kind of soft, warm creature. Taurus is a great nature lover, so even a skunk would be welcome.

*Gemini:* Anything with fascinating habits, like bees or ants, or anything that talks, like a parrot or a minah bird.

*Cancer:* Anything in need of a mother is welcome in Cancer's house, no matter how sloppy or in need of care.

*Leo:* Cats, of course, preferably with good breeding. Peacocks or anything with bright colors or plumage are fine too.

*Virgo:* Cats are preferable, because they are clean animals, but any animal in distress brings out Virgo's warmth.

*Libra:* This sign would just as soon do without, but if a pet is preferred, it's the perfectly groomed poodle or other refined breed of dog or cat.

*Scorpio:* This sign goes for rather dangerous pets, such as snakes, or anything with a sting. Basically, animals are creatures to be observed, not coddled.

*Sagittarius:* Horses—at home or at the race track. Any very large dog in the city, almost anything of immense size in the country.

*Capricorn:* Capricorns *need* pets to help pull them out of their frequent depressions. The friendliest kind of animals are the best bet, like sheepdogs.

*Aquarius:* This sign needs a very smart animal, so is picky about the breed of dog or cat. Actually, birds are preferable to this cool sign.

*Pisces:* Many people born under this sign will take in any stray that strays into their path, no matter how scraggly or ugly. They often put animals before humans in their scheme of things.

### Astrotrivia Part I answers

1. Gypsy Rose Lee and Ethel Merman (who played Gypsy's mother in *Gypsy*).
2. Frank Sinatra and Sammie Davis, Jr.
3. They were all born under the calculating sign of Capricorn.
4. Paul Newman and Alan Alda were both born under the sign of Aquarius.
5. Richard Burton was the Scorpio; Liz Taylor the Pisces.
6. Billie Jean King and Chris Evert.
7. Harry S. Truman, a Taurus.
8. Abigail Van Buren ("Dear Abby") and Ann Landers.

 9. George M. Cohan ("Yankee Doodle Dandy") and Louis "Satchmo" Armstrong.
10. Libra.
11. Tokyo Rose.
12. Libra.
13. Elvis Presley and David Bowie (January 5—Capricorn).
14. Henry Kissinger. He's a wily Gemini, but he could easily fool you, because his moon sign is Scorpio.
15. The column on the left are Taureans; those on the right are Librans.
16. Virgo.
17. Aries.
18. Scorpio.
19. Jackie Kennedy Onassis is a Leo; John F. Kennedy was a Gemini.
20. Rudolph Nureyev and Vaslav Nijinsky.

# 11

# Sun Sign Changes. 1920–1975

If you were born "on the cusp" (very near the end or the beginning of a sign) you can find out what your sign really is by using the chart that follows. Many people do not realize that the sun does not "change signs" on the same day every year—or, for that matter, at the same time. For this reason the chart of sun sign changes is calculated to the minute.

## How to Use the Chart

Locate your year of birth, then the month in which you were born. Let's say you were born in April of 1942. In the box for that month and year you will see

20–Tau<br>
12:30 P.M.

That means if you are born *after* 12:30 p.m. on April 20 in 1942, you are a Taurus. If you were born before that date and time, your sun sign is the preceding one, Aries.

In this chart (as well as in the rising-sign chart) the signs are abbreviated as follows:

Ar = Aries<br>
Tau = Taurus<br>
Gem = Gemini<br>
Can = Cancer<br>
Leo = Leo<br>
Vir = Virgo<br>
Lib = Libra<br>
Sc = Scorpio

Sag = Sagittarius
Cap = Capricorn
Aq = Aquarius
Pis = Pisces

**NOTE:** All times given in the sun sign changes chart are Eastern Standard. You must correct for daylight savings time (subtract one hour) and for time zone. For Central Standard Time subtract one hour; for Mountain Standard Time subtract two hours; for Pacific Standard Time subtract three hours.

|      | 1920 | 1921 | 1922 | 1923 | 1924 | 1925 | 1926 | 1927 | 1928 | 1929 |
|------|------|------|------|------|------|------|------|------|------|------|
| Jan  | 21–Aq | 20–Aq | 20–Aq | 20–Aq | 21–Aq | 20–Aq | 20–Aq | 20–Aq | 21–Aq | 20–Aq |
|      | 4:05 am | 8:55 am | 2:48 pm | 8:35 pm | 2:29 am | 8:20 am | 2:13 pm | 8:12 pm | 1:57 am | 7:42 am |
| Feb  | 19–Pis | 18–Pis | 19–Pis | 19–Pis | 19–Pis | 18–Pis | 18–Pis | 19–Pis | 19–Pis | 18–Pis |
|      | 5:29 pm | 11:21 pm | 5:16 am | 11:00 am | 4:51 pm | 11:43 pm | 4:35 am | 10:35 am | 4:20 pm | 10:07 pm |
| Mar  | 20–Ar | 20–Ar | 21–Ar | 21–Ar | 20–Ar | 20–Ar | 21–Ar | 21–Ar | 20–Ar | 20–Ar |
|      | 5:00 pm | 10:51 pm | 4:49 am | 10:29 am | 4:20 pm | 11:13 pm | 4:01 am | 11:59 am | 3:44 pm | 9:35 pm |
| Apr  | 20–Tau | 20–Tau | 20–Tau | 20–Tau | 20–Tau | 20–Tau | 20–Tau | 20–Tau | 20–Tau | 20–Tau |
|      | 4:39 am | 10:32 am | 4:29 am | 10:06 pm | 3:59 am | 10:51 pm | 3:36 pm | 9:32 pm | 3:17 am | 9:11 am |
| May  | 21–Gem | 21–Gem | 21–Gem | 22–Gem | 21–Gem | 21–Gem | 21–Gem | 21–Gem | 21–Gem | 21–Gem |
|      | 4:22 am | 10:17 am | 9:11 pm | 9:45 pm | 3:41 am | 10:33 pm | 3:15 pm | 9:08 pm | 2:53 am | 8:48 am |
| June | 21–Can | 21–Can | 22–Can | 22–Can | 21–Can | 21–Can | 21–Can | 22–Can | 21–Can | 21–Can |
|      | 12:40pm | 6:36 pm | 12:27 am | 6:03 am | 12:noon | 5:50 pm | 5:21 am | 11:30 pm | 11:07 am | 5:01 pm |
| July | 22–Leo | 23–Leo | 23–Leo | 23–Leo | 22–Leo | 23–Leo | 23–Leo | 23–Leo | 22–Leo | 23–Leo |
|      | 11:40 pm | 5:31 am | 11:20 am | 5:01 pm | 11:58 pm | 4:45 am | 10:25 am | 4:17 am | 11:02 pm | 3:54 am |
| Aug  | 23–Vir | 23–Vir | 23–Vir | 23–Vir | 23–Vir | 23–Vir | 23–Vir | 23–Vir | 23–Vir | 23–Vir |
|      | 6:22 am | 12:15 pm | 6:04 pm | 11:52 pm | 5:48 am | 11:33 am | 5:14 pm | 11:06 pm | 4:53 am | 10:41 am |
| Sept | 23–Lib | 23–Lib | 23–Lib | 23–Lib | 23–Lib | 23–Lib | 23–Lib | 23–Lib | 23–Lib | 23–Lib |
|      | 3:25 am | 11:20 am | 5:10 am | 9:04 pm | 2:58 am | 8:43 am | 2:25 pm | 8:17 pm | 2:36 am | 7:52 am |
| Oct  | 23–Sc | 23–Sc | 23–Sc | 24–Sc | 23–Sc | 23–Sc | 23–Sc | 24–Sc | 23–Sc | 23–Sc |
|      | 12:31 pm | 6:03 pm | 11:53 pm | 5:51 am | 11:44 am | 5:31 pm | 11:18 pm | 5:07 am | 10:55 am | 4:41 pm |
| Nov  | 22–Sag | 22–Sag | 22–Sag | 23–Sag | 22–Sag | 22–Sag | 22–Sag | 23–Sag | 22–Sag | 22–Sag |
|      | 9:15 am | 3:21 pm | 8:55 pm | 2:54 am | 8:46 am | 2:36 pm | 8:28 pm | 2:14 am | 8:00 am | 1:48 pm |
| Dec  | 21–Cap | 22–Cap | 22–Cap | 22–Cap | 21–Cap | 22–Cap | 22–Cap | 22–cap | 21–Cap | 22–Cap |
|      | 10:17 pm | 4:08 am | 9:57 pm | 3:53 pm | 10:45 pm | 3:37 am | 9:34 am | 3:18 pm | 9:04 pm | 2:53 am |

| | 1930 | 1931 | 1932 | 1933 | 1934 | 1935 | 1936 | 1937 | 1938 | 1939 |
|---|---|---|---|---|---|---|---|---|---|---|
| Jan | 20–Aq | 21–Aq | 20–Aq | 20–Aq | 20–Aq | 20–Aq | 21–Aq | 20–Aq | 20–Aq | 20–Aq |
| | 1:33 pm | 7:18 pm | 1:07 am | 6:53 am | 10:37 am | 6:29 pm | 12:12am | 6:01 am | 11:59 am | 5:51 pm |
| Feb | 19–Pis | 19–Pis | 19–Pis | 19–Pis | 19–Pis | 19–Pis | 19–Pis | 18–Pis | 19–Pis | 19–Pis |
| | 4:00 am | 9:06 am | 3:29 pm | 9:16 pm | 3:02 am | 8:52 am | 2:33 pm | 3:21 pm | 2:20 am | 8:10 pm |
| Mar | 21–Ar | 21–Ar | 20–Ar | 21–Ar | 21–Ar | 21–Ar | 20–Ar | 20–Ar | 21–Ar | 21–Ar |
| | 3:30 am | 9:40 am | 2:54 pm | 8:43 pm | 2:28 am | 8:19 am | 1:58 pm | 7:45 pm | 1:43 am | 7:29 am |
| Apr | 20–Tau | 20–Tau | 20–Tau | 20–Tau | 20–Tau | 20–Tau | 20–Tau | 20–Tau | 20–Tau | 20–Tau |
| | 3:06 pm | 8:40 pm | 2:28 am | 8:19 am | 2:00 pm | 7:50 pm | 1:31 am | 7:20 pm | 1:15 pm | 6:55 pm |
| May | 21–Gem | 21–Gem | 21–Gem | 21–Gem | 21–Gem | 21–Gem | 21–Gem | 21–Gem | 21–Gem | 21–Gem |
| | 2:42 pm | 8:15 pm | 2:07 am | 7:57 am | 1:35 pm | 7:25 pm | 1:08 am | 6:57 am | 12:51 pm | 6:27 pm |
| June | 21–Can | 23–Can | 21–Can | 21–Can | 21–Can | 22–Can | 21–Can | 21–Can | 21–Can | 22–Can |
| | 11:53 pm | 4:28 am | 10:23 am | 4: 12 pm | 9:48 pm | 3:32 am | 9:22 am | 3:12 pm | 9:04 pm | 2:40 am |
| July | 23–Leo | 23–Leo | 22–Leo | 23–Leo | 23–Leo | 23–Leo | 22–Leo | 23–Leo | 23–Leo | 23–Leo |
| | 10:42 am | 3:21 pm | 9:18 pm | 3:06 am | 8:42 am | 2:33 pm | 8:18 am | 2:07 am | 7:57 am | 1:37 pm |
| Aug | 23–Vir | 23–Vir | 23–Vir | 23–Vir | 23–Vir | 23–Vir | 23–Vir | 23–Vir | 23–Vir | 23–Vir |
| | 4:27 pm | 10:10 pm | 4:06 am | 9:53 am | 3:32 pm | 9:24 pm | 3:11 am | 8:58 am | 2:46 pm | 8:31 pm |
| Sept | 23–Lib | 23–Lib | 23–Lib | 23–Lib | 23–Lib | 23–Lib | 23–Lib | 23–Lib | 23–Lib | 23–Lib |
| | 1:35 pm | 7:23 pm | 1:16 am | 7:01 am | 10:45 am | 6:38 pm | 12:26 am | 6:13 am | 12:noon | 5:50 pm |
| Oct | 23–Sc | 24–Sc | 23–Sc | 23–Sc | 23–Sc | 24–Sc | 23–Sc | 23–Sc | 23–Sc | 24–Sc |
| | 11:25 pm | 4:15 am | 10:04 am | 3:48 pm | 9:35 pm | 3:29 am | 10:18 am | 3:06 pm | 8:54 pm | 2:46 am |
| Nov | 22–Sag | 23–Sag | 22–Sag | 22–Sag | 22–Sag | 23–Sag | 22–Sag | 22–Sag | 22–Sag | 22–Sag |
| | 7:34 pm | 1:25 am | 7:10 am | 10:53 am | 6:44 pm | 12:35 am | 6:25 pm | 12:17 pm | 6:06 pm | 11:59 pm |
| Dec | 22–Cap | 22–Cap | 21–Cap | 22–Cap | 22–Cap | 22–Cap | 21–Cap | 22–Cap | 22–Cap | 22–Cap |
| | 8:40 am | 2:30 pm | 8:14 pm | 1:58 am | 5:49 pm | 1:37 pm | 7:27 pm | 1:22 am | 7:13 am | 1:05 pm |

|       | 1940 | 1941 | 1942 | 1943 | 1944 | 1945 | 1946 | 1947 | 1948 |
|-------|------|------|------|------|------|------|------|------|------|
| Jan   | 20–Aq | 20–Aq | 20–Aq | 20–Aq | 20–Aq | 20–Aq | 20–Aq | 20–Aq | 20–Aq |
|       | 11:44 pm | 5:34 am | 11:16 am | 5:20 pm | 11:09 pm | 4:55 am | 10:44 am | 4:23 pm | 10:18 pm |
| Feb   | 19–Pis | 18–Pis | 19–Pis | 19–Pis | 19–Pis | 18–Pis | 19–Pis | 19–Pis | 19–Pis |
|       | 2:04 pm | 7:59 pm | 1:39 am | 7:41 am | 1:28 pm | 7:15 pm | 1:10 am | 6:53 am | 12:37 pm |
| Mar   | 20–Ar | 20–Ar | 21–Ar | 21–Ar | 21–Ar | 20–Ar | 21–Ar | 21—Ar | 20–Ar |
|       | 1:24 pm | 7:21 pm | 1:03 am | 7:03 am | 12:49 pm | 6:38 pm | 12:34 pm | 6:13 pm | 11:57 am |
| Apr   | 20–Tau | 20–Tau | 20–Tau | 20–Tau | 20–Tau | 20–Tau | 20–Tau | 20–Tau | 19–Tau |
|       | 12:51 am | 6:51 am | 12:30 pm | 6:32 pm | 12:18 am | 6:08 am | 12:03 pm | 5:40 pm | 11:25 pm |
| May   | 21–Gem | 21–Gem | 21–Gem | 21–Gem | 20–Gem | 22–Gem | 21–Gem | 21–Gem | 20–Gem |
|       | 12:23 am | 6:23 am | 12:01 pm | 6:03 pm | 11:51 pm | 5:41 am | 1:34 am | 5:04 pm | 10:58 pm |
| June  | 21–Can | 21–Can | 21–Can | 22–Can | 21–Can | 21–Can | 21–Can | 22–Can | 21–Can |
|       | 8:37 am | 2:33 am | 8:08 pm | 2:13 am | 9:03 am | 1:52 pm | 7:45 pm | 1:19 am | 7:11 am |
| July  | 22–Leo | 23–Leo | 23–Leo | 23–Leo | 22–Leo | 23–Leo | 23–Leo | 23–Leo | 22–Leo |
|       | 7:34 pm | 1:26 am | 6:59 am | 1:05 pm | 6:55 pm | 12:48 am | 6:37 am | 12:12 pm | 6:06 pm |
| Aug   | 23–Vir | 23–Vir | 23–Vir | 23–Vir | 23–Vir | 23–Vir | 23–Vir | 23–Vir | 23–Vir |
|       | 2:21 am | 8:30 am | 1:50 pm | 7:55 pm | 1:47 am | 7:36 am | 1:23 pm | 7:09 pm | 1:03 am |
| Sept  | 22–Lib | 23–Lib | 23–Lib | 23–Lib | 22–Lib | 23–Lib | 23–Lib | 23–Lib | 22–Lib |
|       | 11:46 pm | 5:33 am | 11:10 am | 5:12 pm | 11:02 pm | 4:50 am | 10:41 am | 4:29 pm | 10:22 pm |
| Oct   | 23–Sc | 23–Sc | 22–Sc | 24–Sc | 23–Sc | 20–Sc | 23–Sc | 24–Sc | 23–Sc |
|       | 8:39 am | 2:22 pm | 8:01 pm | 2:09 am | 7:57 am | 1:45 pm | 7:37 pm | 1:27 am | 7:19 am |
| Nov   | 22–Sag | 22–Sag | 22–Sag | 22–Sag | 22–Sag | 22–Sag | 22–Sag | 22–Sag | 22–Sag |
|       | 5:49 am | 11:38 am | 5:23 pm | 11:22 pm | 5:09 am | 10:56 am | 4:47 pm | 10:38 pm | 4:29 am |
| Dec   | 21–Cap | 22–Cap | 22–Cap | 22–Cap | 21–Cap | 22–Cap | 22–Cap | 22–Cap | 21–Cap |
|       | 6:55 pm | 12:44 am | 6:31 am | 12:30 pm | 6:15 pm | 12:04 am | 5:54 pm | 11:44 am | 5:23 pm |

| | 1949 | 1950 | 1951 | 1952 | 1953 | 1954 | 1955 | 1956 | 1957 |
|---|---|---|---|---|---|---|---|---|---|
| Jan | 20–Aq | 20–Aq | 20–Aq | 20–Aq | 20–Aq | 20–Aq | 20–Aq | 20–Aq | 20–Aq |
| | 4:11 am | 10:00 am | 3:53 pm | 9:38 pm | 3:22 am | 9:14 am | 3:03 pm | 8:49 pm | 2:43 am |
| Feb | 18–Pis | 19–Pis | 19–Pis | 19–Pis | 18–Pis | 19–Pis | 19–Pis | 19–Pis | 18–Pis |
| | 6:27 pm | 12:16 am | 6:10 am | 11:57 am | 5:41 pm | 11:33 pm | 5:19 am | 11:05 am | 5:01 pm |
| Mar | 20–Ar | 20–Ar | 21–Ar | 20–Ar | 20–Ar | 20–Ar | 21–Ar | 20–Ar | 20–Ar |
| | 5:49 pm | 11:30 pm | 5:26 am | 11:14 am | 5:01 pm | 10:54 pm | 4:36 am | 10:21 am | 4:17 pm |
| Apr | 20–Tau | 20–Tau | 20–Tau | 20–Tau | 19–Tau | 20–Tau | 20–Tau | 19–Tau | 20–Tau |
| | 5:18 am | 11:00 am | 4:49 pm | 10:37 pm | 4:26 am | 10:20 am | 3:58 pm | 9:44 pm | 3:45 am |
| May | 21–Gem | 21–Gem | 21–Gem | 20–Gem | 21–Gem | 21–Gem | 21–Gem | 20–Gem | 21–Gem |
| | 4:51 am | 10:27 am | 4:15 pm | 10:04 pm | 3:53 am | 9:48 am | 3:25 pm | 9:13 pm | 3:09 am |
| June | 21–Can | 21–Can | 22–Can | 21–Can | 21–Can | 21–Can | 21–Can | 21–Can | 21–Can |
| | 1:03 pm | 6:37 pm | 12:25 am | 6:13 am | 12:noon | 5:55 pm | 11:32 pm | 5:24 am | 11:21 am |
| July | 22–Leo | 23–Leo | 23–Leo | 22–Leo | 22–Leo | 23–Leo | 23–Leo | 22–Leo | 22–Leo |
| | 1:58 pm | 5:30 am | 11:29 am | 5:05 pm | 10:53 pm | 4:45 am | 10:25 am | 4:20 pm | 10:13 pm |
| Aug | 23–Vir | 23–Vir | 23–Vir | 23–Vir | 23–Vir | 23–Vir | 23–Vir | 22–Vir | 23–Vir |
| | 6:49 pm | 12:24 pm | 6:22 pm | 12:03 am | 5:46 am | 11:37 am | 5:19 pm | 11:15 pm | 5:07 pm |
| Sept | 23–Lib | 23–Lib | 23–Lib | 22–Lib | 23–Lib | 23–Lib | 23–Lib | 22–Lib | 23–Lib |
| | 4:05 am | 9:44 am | 3:38 pm | 9:24 pm | 3:07 am | 8:56 am | 2:42 pm | 8:30 pm | 2:27 am |
| Oct | 23–Sc | 23–Sc | 23–Sc | 23–Sc | 23–Sc | 23–Sc | 22–Sc | 23–Sc | 23–Sc |
| | 1:04 pm | 6:48 pm | 12:37 am | 6:22 am | 12:07 pm | 5:58 pm | 11:44 pm | 5:35 am | 11:33 am |
| Nov | 22–Sag | 22–Sag | 22–Sag | 22–Sag | 22–Sag | 22–Sag | 22–Sag | 22–Sag | 22–Sag |
| | 10:17 am | 4:03 pm | 9:52 pm | 3:36 am | 9:23 am | 3:14 pm | 9:02 pm | 2:51 am | 8:45 am |
| Dec | 21–Cap | 22–Cap | 22–Cap | 21–Cap | 21–Cap | 22–Cap | 22–Cap | 21–Cap | 21–Cap |
| | 11:24 am | 5:14 am | 11:01 am | 4:44 pm | 10:22 pm | 4:25 am | 10:12 am | 4:00 pm | 9:49 pm |

|       | 1958      | 1959      | 1960      | 1961      | 1962      | 1963      | 1964      | 1965      | 1966      |
|-------|-----------|-----------|-----------|-----------|-----------|-----------|-----------|-----------|-----------|
| Jan   | 20–Aq 2:20 pm | 20–Aq 2:20 pm | 20–Aq 8:11 pm | 20–Aq 2:02 am | 20–Aq 7:49 am | 20–Aq 1:55 pm | 19–Aq 7:43 pm | 20–Aq 1:30 am | 20–Aq 8:21 am |
| Feb   | 18–Pis 10:49 pm | 19–Pis 4:38 pm | 19–Pis 10:26 am | 18–Pis 6:27 pm | 18–Pis 10:16 pm | 19–Pis 4:09 am | 19–Pis 10:25 am | 18–Pis 3:49 pm | 18–Pis 9:39 pm |
| Mar   | 20–Ar 10:06 pm | 21–Ar 3:55 am | 20–Ar 9:43 am | 20–Ar 5:27 am | 20–Ar 9:30 pm | 21–Ar 3:20 am | 20–Ar 9:43 am | 20–Ar 3:05 pm | 20–Ar 8:53 pm |
| Apr   | 20–Tau 9:28 am | 20–Tau 3:17 pm | 20–Tau 10:06 pm | 20–Tau 2:33 am | 20–Tau 8:51 am | 20–Tau 2:37 pm | 19–Tau 9:00 pm | 20–Tau 2:27 am | 20–Tau 8:12 am |
| May   | 21–Gem 8:52 am | 21–Gem 2:38 pm | 20–Gem 8:33 pm | 21–Gem 1:51 am | 21–Gem 8:17 am | 21–Gem 1:59 pm | 20–Gem 8:33 pm | 21–Gem 1:27 am | 21–Gem 7:33 am |
| June  | 21–Can 4:57 pm | 21–Can 10:50 pm | 21–Can 4:43 am | 21–Can 10:12 am | 21–Can 4:24 pm | 21–Can 11:04 pm | 21–Can 4:43 am | 21–Can 9:56 am | 21–Can 3:33 pm |
| July  | 23–Leo 3:51 am | 23–Leo 9:45 am | 22–Leo 5:38 pm | 22–Leo 9:12 pm | 23–Leo 3:19 am | 23–Leo 9:00 am | 22–Leo 3:38 pm | 22–Leo 8:49 pm | 23–Leo 2:24 am |
| Aug   | 23–Vir 10:47 am | 23–Vir 4:44 pm | 22–Vir 10:35 pm | 23–Vir 3:46 am | 23–Vir 10:13 am | 23–Vir 3:58 pm | 22–Vir 10:35 pm | 23–Vir 3:43 am | 23–Vir 9:18 am |
| Sept  | 23–Lib 5:10 am | 23–Lib 2:09 pm | 22–Lib 8:00 pm | 23–Lib 1:26 am | 23–Lib 7:35 am | 23–Lib 1:24 pm | 22–Lib 8:00 pm | 23–Lib 1:06 am | 23–Lib 6:43 am |
| Oct   | 23–Sc 5:12 am | 23–Sc 11:12 pm | 23–Sc 5:03 am | 23–Sc 10:46 am | 23–Sc 4:41 pm | 23–Sc 11:30 pm | 23–Sc 5:03 am | 23–Sc 10:11 am | 23–Sc 3:52 pm |
| Nov   | 22–Sag 2:30 pm | 22–Sag 8:23 pm | 22–Sag 2:19 am | 22–Sag 8:10 am | 22–Sag 2:02 pm | 22–Sag 7:50 pm | 22–Sag 2:19 am | 22–Sag 7:30 am | 22–Sag 1:15 pm |
| Dec   | 22–Cap 3:40 am | 22–Cap 9:35 am | 21–Cap 5:27 pm | 21–Cap 9:25 pm | 22–Cap 3:15 am | 22–Cap 9:02 am | 21–Cap 3:27 pm | 21–Cap 8:41 pm | 22–Cap 2:29 pm |

| | 1967 | 1968 | 1969 | 1970 | 1971 | 1972 | 1973 | 1974 | 1975 |
|---|---|---|---|---|---|---|---|---|---|
| Jan | 20–Aq | 20–Aq | 20–Aq | 20–Aq | 20–Aq | 20–Aq | 19–Aq | 20–Aq | 20–Aq |
| | 1:05 pm | 6:54 pm | 12:30 am | 6:25 am | 12:14 pm | 6:00 pm | 11:49 pm | 5:47 am | 11:37 am |
| Feb | 19–Pis | 19–Pis | 18–Pis | 18–Pis | 19–Pis | 19–Pis | 18–Pis | 18–Pis | 19–Pis |
| | 3:25 am | 9:11 am | 2:47 pm | 8:43 pm | 2:28 am | 8:12am | 2:02 pm | 8:00 pm | 1:51 am |
| Mar | 21–Ar | 20–Ar | 20–Ar | 20–Ar | 21–Ar | 20–Ar | 20–Ar | 20–Ar | 21–Ar |
| | 2:37 am | 8:22 am | 2:08 pm | 7:59 pm | 1:28 am | 7:22 am | 1:13 pm | 7:08 pm | 12:58 am |
| Apr | 20–Tau | 19–Tau | 20–Tau | 20–Tau | 20–Tau | 19–Tau | 20–Tau | 20–Tau | 20–Tau |
| | 1:56 am | 7:42 pm | 1:18 am | 5:16 am | 12:54 pm | 6:38 pm | 12:31 am | 5:19 am | 12:08 pm |
| May | 21–Gem | 20–Gem | 21–Gem | 21–Gem | 21–Gem | 20–Gem | 20–Gem | 21–Gem | 21–Gem |
| | 1:19 pm | 7:07 pm | 12:41 am | 6:32 am | 12:16 pm | 6:00 pm | 11:54 pm | 5:37 am | 1:25 pm |
| June | 21–Can | 21–Can | 21–Can | 21–Can | 21–Can | 21–Can | 21–Can | 21–Can | 21–Can |
| | 4:23 pm | 1:13 am | 6:55 am | 2:43 pm | 8:21 pm | 2:07 am | 8:01 am | 1:38 pm | 7:27 pm |
| July | 23–Leo | 22–Leo | 22–Leo | 23–Leo | 23–Leo | 22–Leo | 22–Leo | 23–Leo | 23–Leo |
| | 8:16 am | 2:13 pm | 8:05 pm | 1:38 am | 7:15 am | 1:03 pm | 6:56 pm | 12:30 am | 7:23 am |
| Aug | 23–Vir | 22–Vir | 23–Vir | 23–Vir | 23–Vir | 22–Vir | 23–Vir | 23–Vir | 23–Vir |
| | 3:13 pm | 9:52 pm | 2:35 am | 6:35 am | 2:16 pm | 8:04 pm | 1:55 am | 7:29 am | 1:24 pm |
| Sept | 23–Lib | 22–Lib | 23–Lib | 23–Lib | 23–Lib | 22–Lib | 22–Lib | 23–Lib | 23–Lib |
| | 12:38 pm | 6:26 pm | 12:07 am | 5:59 am | 11:47 am | 5:34 pm | 11:22 pm | 4:59 am | 10:56 am |
| Oct | 23–Sc | 23–Sc | 23–Sc | 23–Sc | 22–Sc | 23–Sc | 23–Sc | 23–Sc | 23–Sc |
| | 9:44 pm | 1:30 am | 9:03 am | 3:05 pm | 8:53 pm | 2:42 am | 8:31 am | 2:12 pm | 8:07 pm |
| Nov | 22–Sag | 22–Sag | 22–Sag | 22–Sag | 22–Sag | 22–Sag | 22–Sag | 22–Sag | 22–Sag |
| | 7:05 pm | 12:59 am | 6:23 am | 12:25 pm | 6:15 pm | 12:04 am | 5:55 am | 11:39 am | 5:32 pm |
| Dec | 22–Cap | 21–Cap | 21–Cap | 22–Cap | 22–Cap | 21–Cap | 21–Cap | 22–Cap | 22–Cap |
| | 8:17 am | 2:00 pm | 7:44 pm | 1:36 am | 5:26 am | 1:14 pm | 7:09 pm | 12:57 am | 7:47 am |

# 12

# Gemini: The Big Picture

Because the twelve signs of the zodiac represent twelve ways of being in the world, you will know more about yourself and why you tend toward certain types of behavior and attitudes by knowing more about Gemini. If you read about the elements and qualities in "Defining Terms," for instance, you'll find out that you are one of the active, restless *air signs*, and, as one of the *mutable signs*, you adapt easily to people and situations. You can meet yourself in the Gemini prototype described in "Twelve Places at the Table," and your quick-moving, lively planetary ruler, Mercury, provides some excellent clues about the Gemini style.

However, even with these broad brush strokes, your Gemini portrait is still a bit abstract: to see yourself in totality, you need more of the background filled in. That means going back to some very important basics: your third place position in the zodiac, your picture/symbol, the twins, and the "shorthand figure," or glyph, that astrologers use to indicate Gemini when they draw up a horoscope. In Gemini, as in every astrological sign, these three factors link together, forming a strong "chain of meaning" that holds together everything that is Gemini.

When the sun reaches the first degree of the sign of Gemini, about May 22, the earth is in a state of transition, moving from the exuberance of spring to the more placid season of summer. Gemini, at the tail end

of spring, symbolizes the restlessness of nature as it
completes its growth cycle and looks forward to a steadier and more stable period. It is also the time of year
young animals take their first steps away from the
mothers and begin to explore the world at large. Gemini's position in the zodiac is associated with the adolescent period of human life, when we are virtually
complete physically, but have yet to attain our psychological maturity. It has been said many times that the
typical person born under the sign of Gemini is a
perpetual adolescent, possessing both the refreshing
zestfullness of that age as well as the immature judgment that often accompanies it. As the first mutable
sign of the zodiac, Gemini brings to it the principle of
flexibility, which is vital if things are not to remain in a
static state, as symbolized by the preceding fixed sign of
Taurus. One of the functions of the Gemini person is
to serve as a catalyst to new ways of thinking and doing
things. Gemini sees the infinite variety of possibilities
that exists in any given situation and can quickly switch
gears to adapt.

Gemini's picture symbol, the Twins, turns up many
times in myth and symbol. Perhaps the most famous
pair of twins associated with Gemini is Castor and Pollux,
the twin stars that practically sit on each other in the
constellation Gemini. From earliest times observers of
the heavens could see that the two stars were intimately
involved with each other, a fact confirmed by modern
astronomers. Legend has it that Leda, a human woman,
was seduced by the god Zeus in the form of a swan.
One of the eggs Leda bore contained both Castor and
Pollux. However, one was human and one was divine
(reflecting their mixed parentage). Mortal Castor was
killed in battle, and his twin, immortal Pollux, begged
father Zeus to let him die too so he could join his
brother. Zeus granted his wish, and placed the two of
them in the heavens as twin stars, where they appear to
have their arms around each other to this very day.

In many twin legends, one brother is of a godly
nature and one is purely mortal; the ultimate task the

Gemini person has is to transform his lower nature and blend it with his higher nature to become a whole person. An east Indian epic tells of royal twins who were so close that neither could be killed until one of them slayed the other. The Romans venerated Romulus and Remus, who founded their fair city—but one could not have done it without the other. This concept of two people who are virtually one is at the heart of everything that characterizes the Gemini astrological personality.

One of the obvious readings for the Gemini glyph, or shorthand symbol, used by astrologers (see illustration) is the Roman numeral for the number two, which ties in perfectly with the duality connected with the sign. Some people see in the symbol two pillars—as in the pillars of Hercules. Throughout ancient times, twin gods were the pillars that guarded sacred doorways and entrances, from Solomon's temple to the gates of hell and other underworlds. Gemini, like every other astrological sign, is said to rule or be associated with certain parts of the human body. In the case of Gemini the glyph is interpreted as the hands, arms and lungs. It is uncanny how often a person born under this sign has a special flair for things that require manual dexterity and the jobs and professions that require the breath of the lungs in the form of speech.

# 13

# Gemini: Objectives and Obstacles

## A Game Plan for Being the Most Successful Gemini Under the Sun

Every astrological sign is a set of possibilities; being born under a particular sign does not guarantee you *are* or *will be* all those things that sign is capable of being. Nor would you want to. There are positive characteristics to be cultivated, as well as negative ones you can avoid or overcome. Living "à la carte"—selecting what you want from all the options available—is open to you, within the overall context of your sign.

You can, of course, order the "prix fixe" dinner by living your life as it comes without attempting to direct it. The choice is yours, which is one good reason it is incorrect to regard your astrological destiny as preordained. You are responsible for how you embody your sign, and what results from that embodiment.

Astrologically speaking, your life as a sign is a journey with a starting point, the raw or "primitive" end of the side, and a destination, the evolved or "ideal" realization of that sign. Once again, you don't have to take the full trip; there are plenty of exits if you choose to use them, and few people are ever totally "finished." But if you at least know where you are going, and what potential booby traps lie along the way, you will be way ahead of the game.

Regard the following as a map and use it in charting your course. The most successful way to be the best of your astrological sign is to work with it, in full knowledge of its up side and its down side. The happiest people of any astrological sign are those who aim high and are not afraid to stretch their understanding of themselves in order to reach their goal.

### Where Gemini Starts

In contrast to Taurus, who stands firm, the typical Gemini is all over the place, often accomplishing nothing or causing confusion, both for him-/herself and others. Many Geminis ask astrologers, "Am I really schizoprenic?" For most, the legendary split personality of Gemini does not literally mean abnormality. What the phrase embodies is Gemini's tendency to talk to him-/herself. One part of Gemini says, "Let's go this way"; the other says, "No, it looks a lot more interesting that way." What generally happens is that the unevolved Gemini attempts to go in both directions at the same time. By responding to every stimuli—both mental and physical—Gemini can string him-/herself out so far that there's danger of snapping in two, almost quite literally. The sign is also such an avid observer of the scene that few details go unnoticed. The problem comes when Gemini tries to sort things out; it's all too easy to put the parts back together in a way that forms quite another picture. Are some Geminis actually liars? Perhaps, but for the vast majority of primitives of the sign the tendency to play things back inaccurately is not at all malicious. Gemini simply can't get it straight. This trait in Gemini is simply the shallowness that comes from taking everything at face value.

Here are some buzz words by which you can recognize the primitive Gemini type:

| | |
|---|---|
| Changeable | Insensitive |
| Nervous | Argumentative |
| Superficial | Irritable |
| Double-dealing | Self-centered |
| Gossipy | Can't concentrate |

### Where Gemini Can Go

Ideally, Gemini is the sign of the great communicator, but not the bad reporter who either gets the facts garbled or puts so much in the story that it becomes meaningless. With the sign's extraordinary mental equipment and its capacity to absorb experience and information, Gemini can re-present things so that they are not only clear, but also add to the experience of others. The evolved Gemini has put this sign's greatest strength to work: the power of selectivity. A true Gemini can sort out the wheat from the chaff, weigh all the evidence, and arrive at a well-balanced, totally reasonable assessment of any situation. At Gemini's best, this sign has no equal when it comes to being objective. A mature Gemini can also use the sign's extraordinary adaptability in a positive way. The "chameleon" can change color not just for the sake of change, but for making others feel comfortable and welcome as well. Even though they may not be highly emotional, evolved Geminis are extremely sensitive to the signals they pick up from others, and know how to use that information wisely and well. Instead of merely public relations, the sign can be excellent at human relations.

Some buzz words to recognize the evolved Gemini type:

| | |
|---|---|
| Open-minded | Optimistic |
| Communicative | Attentive to detail |
| Reasonable | Willing to please |
| Understanding | Adaptable |
| Perceptive | Stimulating |

### How Gemini Can Get There

Gemini generally likes things easy, in a lot of ways. Applying the good mind that being a Gemini conveys does not come naturally to many born under the sign. One reason is that when you concentrate hard on one thing you might possibly miss out on another. One vital life-success strategy for Gemini is to become master of one talent before he/she goes on to another. The harder something gets, the more overjoyed Gemini should be that he/she is finally beginning to *learn* something.

On the other hand, success-bent Geminis must also learn to live with confusion. If something doesn't make sense right away, Geminis tend to dismiss it too quickly. Confusion is often the forerunner of understanding, and the Gemini should not run away from it—or any other uncomfortable emotion. Sometimes those of you born under this highly sociable sign should literally *force* seclusion upon themselves, at least for short periods. Quiet meditation and self-study are essential to Gemini's progress. One of the sign's best traits is the ability to see both sides of a story. Unfortunately, many Geminis do so just so they will please everyone, instead of only one faction. Do not fall into that trap, Gemini. Instead, play the great mediator you can be, pointing out the errors in judgment on both sides. You know the world doesn't come in just black and white, and one of your missions in life is to bring that important perception to others, thereby helping to stamp out bigotry and prejudice wherever you find it.

### Potential Pitfalls

One of Gemini's greatest assets, his/her inquiring mind, is also one of their most powerful potential enemies. It is not uncommon for Gemini to immediately pass on every bit of fascinating information he/she comes by, even if Gemini hurts someone else in the process. It is not intentional, perhaps, but it is avoidable. The technique is simple: *Think before you speak.* Another yawning pit the hapless Gemini can fall into is doing too much speaking, and too little listening. Observe an over eager Gemini and you will see someone who asks questions so fast, that he/she doesn't listen to the answers; Gemini is often too busy thinking about how to sound immensely clever the next time he/she speaks. A cardinal rule for any success-bent Gemini is to pay attention. More than that, listen to what the other person is *really* saying.

119

Your infinitely creative mind can all too easily twist a story before you've even heard it out.

Gemini so desires that life be breezy and tension-free that he/she is often tempted to bend the truth in order to avoid unpleasantness. Gemini, no matter what the consequences, face up to the truth, and the *whole* truth. Even if you get away with a certain amount of storytelling in your early years, it's bound to catch up with you sooner or later with unpleasant consequences. And isn't that just what you *don't* want?

# 14

# Pairing Off with Gemini

## Your Compatibility with Other Signs of the Zodiac

Since there are only twelve signs of the zodiac, it would be unusual to go through life without having to interact with each of them at one time or another. Obviously, your astrological makeup is more complex than your Gemini sun sign, but there are some basic truths about how you tend to react when face to face with someone of another sun sign. If you have read about "The Geometry of Relationships," you already know that being an air sign means Gemini relates more easily to certain elements than to others. Now, getting more specific, you will see what the odds are on your matchups with each of the other signs, including your own.

When people talk about "realtionships," they are usually referring to the romantic kind, and there is no doubt that since time immemorial love has been observed to have a great deal to do with keeping the earth revolving in its orbit. However, we also have a lot of other interpersonal interactions, from important ones, like boss-employee and parent-child to more casual ones, like waitress-patron, cabdriver-rider, and buddy-buddy. The general rules that follow apply in all cases; just change the language a little and do a bit of interpretation. You will find that there is more truth than poetry in the matter of astrological compatibility.

***Gemini with Aries***    Chances are you two will hit it off splendidly upon first meeting. You, the "air" element, definitely will "fan" Aries' fire. However, the whole thing could heat up into one big argument if you decide to disagree with Aries. A positive point about this relationship is that neither of you will bore the other; the real danger here is that you two could burn each other out. This is a great combo for business—particularly of the entrepreneurial type. Together you could sell almost anything.

***Gemini with Taurus***    Sometimes-shy Taurus could be a bit put off by your enthusiastic come-on, so if you are really interested, take a slightly quieter approach. You may not find the typical Taurus wildly interesting at first, but it would be good for you to cultivate the relationship. Taurus could teach you a lot about patience and fortitude. Even if you don't find Taurus the most compatible romantic partner, having this sign somewhere in your general scheme of things could truly enhance your life.

***Gemini with Gemini***    Two pairs of twins could be a mutual disaster. The "four of you" might be so busy talking to each other that nothing makes any sense. It is unlikely you will connect romantically, because you are both a bit leery of intense emotion. As friends, however, you could have a great time and certainly would instinctively understand each other. Don't even think about a business relationship—that is, unless you've got a stable Taurus or Capricorn on the staff to keep you two on the right track.

***Gemini with Cancer***    You could be devastating to this sign, so don't get romantically involved unless you are really serious about at least exploring the relationship to its depths. Cancer will pour out his/her troubles, and you had better be ready to give back something more than easy answers. Cancer could offer you the genuine warmth and depth of feeling you so sorely need; you could make Cancer's life a lot more interesting. It can be good, but you'll have to work at it.

***Gemini with Leo***     In spite of the fact that Leo is a fire sign, this person could have a remarkably calming effect on you. Leo's fire burns with a steady heat and would constantly keep you warm. However, Leo is a genuine and sincere sign that has a real problem with anything that smacks of deviousness. One strike and you'll be out. This is one of the best matches in the zodiac for you, Gemini, so if you want it, don't blow it.

***Gemini with Virgo***     You two could make each other awfully nervous. Virgo can't handle as much constant activity as you can; you most likely will not react well to Virgo's tendency to criticize and carp. Though you are both ruled by Mercury, and therefore are both mental types, you are coming from very different places. Romantically, it is better for you both to stay right there. On the other hand, in your professional life you could not find a better backup than Virgo. He/she will gladly pick up all the pieces you drop, and put them back together again. Perfectly.

***Gemini with Libra***     Because Libra is a cardinal sign, there is generally more inner strength there than you possess. Since you both enjoy the same kind of easy, breezy life, there is a high possibility that you could find it together. However, do not depend on Libra to hold you up when the going gets really rough. He/she is going to need a lot of support, and you may not be willing to give enough of it. Still, you two could have a positively dazzling affair!

***Gemini with Scorpio***     You are an emotional lightweight, and Scorpio is an emotional heavyweight. There's really no fair contest here. The question is which of you will back off more quickly. Probably you, because you move faster. Scorprio is likely to stir up things in you that you would rather not think about, and unless you are an unusually sexual Gemini, Scorpio's intense sexuality and possessiveness will feel like prison. However, you could give Scorpio some excellent ideas which he/she has the power to carry out.

**_Gemini with Sagittarius_**     In astrological terms, Sagittarius is your polar opposite in the zodiac, and therefore your true complement or other half. However, it will not be easy going all the way. First off, you both like to move around a lot, and would have to come to some compromises about how much you will be together and how much you will be apart. You sense that Sagittarius has more intellectual depth than you, but you will be inspired by it. On the whole, it is a good thing all around.

**_Gemini with Capricorn_**     Capricorn's "earthiness" may be a bit heavy for you to deal with, but a relationship with this sign would not be all bad for you. Capricorn is not one to cramp your style, especially if he/she sees it as a social asset. You would be loved, adored, and probably pampered as well. What's more, you are both realists. Capricorn could easily be your "steady," in every sense of the word. This works as well in business as in love.

**_Gemini with Aquarius_**     Aquarius will probably be a bit too chilly—even for you. To get romantically involved on a permanent basis, you need more emotional depth than Aquarius can provide. On the other hand, you will see things from a similar point of view and could be great mental companions. Aquarius could teach you a lot about how to back up your ideas with affirmative action. Good marriages have been built on a lot less than there is here, but for best results, keep this one on the professional level.

**_Gemini with Pisces_**     Pisces will confuse you, and vice versa; the two of you simply aren't talking on the same level. Even when Pisces is at his/her most worldly, there is a touch of the poet there which doesn't connect with anything you know or really care about. On the other hand, Pisces could teach you a lot about how to feel—but you probably would find it a bit too much. You may connect across a crowded room, but it is unlikely you will leave together.

# 15

# The Gemini Sex Role Dilemma

One of the most important ways in which the twelve signs of the zodiac are divided is into "masculine" signs and "feminine" signs, and there are six of each. The reason is simple: As one sign follows the other in the zodiac, they alternate energies, much like the Yin/Yang principle of eastern philosophy. The universe is made up of opposites that complement each other; light and dark, hot and cold, black and white, hard and soft. One is not better than the other; rather, each is essential to the existence of its opposite. In other words, you can't have one without the other.

The six fire and air signs are "masculine," since fire and air are connected with *active, assertive, outgoing* energy.

| | |
|---|---|
| Aries | Gemini |
| Leo | Libra |
| Sagittarius | Aquarius |

The six water and earth signs are "feminine," because water and earth represent *reactive, inner-directed, receptive* energy.

| | |
|---|---|
| Taurus | Cancer |
| Virgo | Scorpio |
| Capricorn | Pisces |

To put it rather simplistically, *the masculine fire and air signs are positive, while the earth and water signs are negative.*

To remain neutral and avoid placing a higher value on one or the other kind of energy (or sign) it is useful to think of a battery with positive and negative poles. Without both, it simply doesn't work.

Though the masculine/feminine division of the signs has nothing whatever to do with human physical sexuality or sexual preference, it has very important implications for human behavior. Bluntly put, women born into male signs can be more "masculine"/achieving/competitive than men born in female signs. On the other hand, men born in female signs can be more "feminine"nurturing/cooperative than women born into male signs. Both men and women born into signs that match their own sex may overemphasize the behavior and attitudes connected with that gender. The ideal person, psychologically and metaphysically speaking, has a healthy mix of both masculine and feminine attitudes. Without at least some of both, we cannot be whole people, able to encompass and understand the total range of human emotions, desires, drives, and goals. Since none of us is perfect, just about everyone could stand a bit more gender blending. Your astrological sign offers some excellent clues about how you can accomplish that.

Since Gemini is both a masculine sign and one of the relatively unemotional air signs, Gemini men are more comfortable with their role in the world of business and social life than they are with their personal life. By the same token, Gemini women have a double trip laid on them: Not only must they break through the rational air sign barrier to get in touch with their soft side, they must also deal with the fact that because they are born under a masculine sign, it is that much more difficult for them to express (and even accept) their femininity. To deal with the life problems their respective gender dilemmas are liable to bring, here's a possible prescription. Gemini men: Don't walk away from difficult situations or emotions, especially those involving a member of the opposite sex. When you begin to feel uneasy is the time you should probe deeper and find out what is really going on inside you. Gemini women: Take lessons from some of your feminine-sign sisters in the zodiac, like earthy Taurus and passionate Scoprio. Physical sex may not be a problem for you, but the depth of feeling that accompanies such basic human instincts may be harder for you to grab hold of.

# 16

## The Gemini Female

### Butterfly with a Brain

One of the great astrological myths—most likely perpetuated by those who envy them—are that Gemini women are nothing but flirtatious and flighty butterflies. Quite the contrary; for a great many women born under this quick-witted sign, all that seemingly meaningless activity has a definite purpose, and there is a positive goal in sight. Because they are bright enough to know they've got to live with the attributes they were born with, Gemini women often exhibit many of the characteristics all "good girls" are supposed to have. But underneath, the Gemini woman really wants to match wits and achievements with the opposite sex. Many do so successfully, as far as wordly matters go, at any rate. What's harder for the Gemini woman to achieve is a deep, lasting relationship, possibly because they don't really know what they are looking for. The Gemini female has often grown up observing a parental realtionship that was long on words, but rather short in the expression of true emotions. It's a snap for her to zap a guy with a verbal zinger, but she's virtually defenseless when her emotions threaten to get involved. And threatening is the adjective she most often applies to anything that smacks of the rough-and-tumble of the world where people love and hate—and really live.

*As a child*, the Gemini girl probably identified with Daddy and saw him and his accomplishments as rather special. However, Daddy may have disappointed her by not giving her as much attention as she wanted. Ergo, the Gemini girl often starts out life with some built-in resentment toward men and a lack of respect for the position of women. Gemini girls are usually head-of-the-class types in school, excelling particularly in reading and writing. One of the ways the Gemini girl tries to prove to herself that she's really normal (and lovable) is to outthink all the rest—both girls *and* boys. And it's the boys she most often prefers to run with, since, in her young years at least, she's accepted simply as one of the gang. Gemini girls aren't usually tomboys in the full sense of the word, however. They've got it figured out early on that looking pretty and having the manners to match is an excellent way of getting people to notice them. Mommy may be a bit confused by her, though, because the Gemini girl, for all her surface feminity, can have such a mind of her own that she's even tougher to deal with than Daddy.

*As a young woman,* the Gemini female usually rushes headlong into the job world, eager both to make money and to make her mark. But you won't find many Geminis among the ranks of those women who've opted for tough and traditionally male jobs, like police work or truck driving. Because she's got an enormous fund of nervous energy, she can throw herself into her work and into an active social life as well. When the Gemini woman first begins to date, she's in seventh heaven. There's a big, wide world of fascinating men out there, so there's no way she's ever going to get bored. Later on, when she's gone through quite a few, the Gemini female may begin to wonder why the phone doesn't ring as much as it used to. No matter how well her work life may be going, most Gemini women will eventually have to face up to the fact that most men eventually get attached, and disappear from the singles scene. A lot of Gemini women cope with the situation by preferring (at least on the surface) the company of women. Sooner or later, however, the Gemini female who really *wants* permanent attachment (and most do) will truly meet her match—a man who stimulates and satisfies her mentally and who is able to actively engage her emotions as well. It is liable to be a crisis point in her young life, however, because though she's a quick study in other things, it takes her longer to get the hang of what this somewhat "unpleasant" situation is all about. When she finds out that the reason she's hurting is that she's really in love (often for the first time), her life suddenly becomes complete.

*As a mate,* the Gemini woman is a superb household organizer, though she may shy away from the more mundane aspects of housewifery. In fact, many Gemini women prefer to continue working after marriage for a number of reasons, and one of them is to be able to afford someone else to do the work that requires more elbow grease than brain power. If she marries someone with a real stake in his professional life, she will back him up to the hilt by keeping things running smoothly, and—her real delight—by being the perfect hostess.

Life will not be a total bed of roses, however; throughout her married life, she will have to constantly remind herself that she can't be all talk and no action in order to keep a serious relationship afloat. Her "I'm sorry's" and pat explanations may soon wear out her husband's patience, and he will demand a true show of affection, one that goes beyond the marriage bed to the more difficult area of true communication of feelings. Because the sign of Gemini dislikes real confrontation, she may fake it for a while, but she will eventually be found out. It is of course possible for the Gemini female to reach her golden anniversary with the same mate; but she will have to work harder at it than most.

*As a mother,* the Gemini woman may again experience the problem of painful attachment. She may hesitate longer than some other signs to take the plunge into motherhood, because she's bright enough to see that it's a long and demanding commitment. It would not be unlike her to carefully arrange her pregnancy to fit in with other plans or parts of her life. However, this calculating quality comes in handy when she faces her role as mother; Gemini women can keep a lot of balls in the air without dropping them, because they've got it all figured out in advance. The Gemini mother may have difficulty understanding very young children; in her mind, they should be born at the age of reason. But she learns to love them all the same. Motherhood is the best thing that could possibly happen to the Gemini woman, because through it she will eventually learn the kind of instinctive love and communication of feeling that comes less easily to her than to others.

# 17

## The Gemini Male

### Perpetual Peter Pan

As the first of the air signs of the zodiac, Gemini tends to be the lightest and brightest. Gemini men are often incredible conversationists and superb game players. However, they unfortunately all too often carry over their "weightlessness" into their emotional lives. The Gemini male is a lot more comfortable with women than he is with men, but throughout his lifetime he will make more than one member of the opposite sex quite unhappy. Gemini men are explorers by nature, being irresistibly attracted to anything new and different. Their attention span also leaves a lot to be desired. In their professional lives, Gemini men tend to gravitate toward the communications fields where something is news today and gone tomorrow. You will find Gemini men involved in careers such as law, but you will also find that they have tailored those careers to their own interests and brand of expertise, for instance, entertainment law. Like his Gemini sister, the Gemini man didn't get a lot of attention from his father and he is consequently suspicious of other men. Also, like his female sibling, the Gemini man has no clear idea of what passion and attachment are all about. One of the ways in which Gemini men avoid the heavier emotional responsibilities of life is by refusing to grow up. As a sign,

Gemini represents the adolescent period of human existence; unfortunately too many of the men born under this sign almost literally remain adolescents all their lives.

*As a child*, the Gemini boy is a barrel of laughs. Highly verbal at a very early age, he is likely to astound his parents with his perceptive observations. Later on, his teachers will delight in his brightness, but despair at the way he disrupts the class. Gemini boys are often class clowns, partly because they are bored with the slow pace of their fellow students. More serious, the Gemini boy child is all too often the kind who starts stretching the truth to avoid the consequences. If his parents pick up on it and take steps to put their child on the right path, the Gemini boy is very lucky. When evasive behavior continues into adult life, it can cause Gemini a great deal of serious toil and trouble—both of which he wants to avoid. One of the refuges the Gemini boy seeks is the safe area behind his mother's skirts; she frightens him a lot less than his father, and will always go to bat for him when the chips are down. By handling things this way, the Gemini male often sets up an unfortunate pattern for his later life.

*As a young man*, the Gemini male—like his female counterpart—generally runs headlong into life, eagerly snatching up all kinds of new experiences. Job-hopping is a sport many bright young Gemini males engage in, and their résumés often show it. Their social calendars may be equally crowded, and have few repeats—especially of female partners. Even more than the Gemini female, the Gemini male actively avoids serious emotional attachment. The term "heartbreaker" may have been coined for the Gemini male who talks the sweetest game in the world, but doesn't seriously want to play it. Gemini males can be infuriatingly elusive, causing women to sit alone by the telephone when they neglect to call. Gemini men are rarely deliberately devastating, however; most are simply terrified of involvement and don't even know why. If you're out to trap a Gemini man, don't rely on your sexual prowess alone; he's got to have a mental companion as well. In fact, a lot of Gemini men solve their emotional problem by keeping a lineup of female friends on call.

*As a mate*, the Gemini man generally continues his active interest in other people of both sexes, but is not necessarily unfaithful in the sexual sense. The real problem for his mate is that he may try to lean on her more than she wants him to. One of the classic patterns for the Gemini male is to marry a strong woman and try to pick up where his childhood relationship with his mother left off. It is particularly unfortunate when an attractive Gemini man chooses a stable and solid partner who is not as attractive as he, in several senses of the word. His "grateful" partner may be ecstatic for a while, but later on will realize that she is more valued for her help and support than for her love and romantic companionship. The Gemini mate is a trial to his wife in other ways as well. He often doesn't know what she really wants of him; no matter how many times he says, "But I *do* love you", it doesn't seem to help. What the Gemini man's mate really wants is a demonstration of his caring by meaningful actions rather than words. However, if the partner of a Gemini knows what she's getting into, she can look forward to a long and happy relationship with the most amusing, stimulating of men.

*As a father*, the Gemini man may finally find out what it means to love someone from the very bottom of his heart—and he *does* have one. It is not unlike the Gemini father to want to be a constant companion to his children. As they grow and begin to transfer their interests from their parents to their friends, he may become hurt and resentful. Because he is often still an adolescent himself, he really wants to be part of their crowd. One major pitfall the "intellectual" Gemini father should attempt to avoid is going overboard in teaching his children. He may try to force so many interests on his children that he turns them off com-

pletely from any kind of mental pursuit. However, the
children of a Gemini father will have an actively involved parent whose interest in them will never flag as
long as he lives.

# 18

# Gemini Help Wanted

## Selecting a Career/Your On-the-Job Style

A vitally important aspect of a successful Gemini game plan is making sure you land in the "right" job or career—i.e., the one that best suits your native talents and tendencies. It is more than a truism that people perform better doing what comes naturally. There are some "natural" careers for Gemini, and they have several common denominators. It is not possible to list *all* the specific jobs a Gemini should do well at, but there are some "Gemini images" that provide useful guidelines. Though you may not literally end up *doing* any of these things, try to conjure up an idea of what it takes to do the following jobs, and you'll have a better handle on what kind of inner resources Gemini people have available to them for career success.

Language teacher

Graphic designer

Computer programmer

Reporter/editor

Travel agent

Public relations

Film/book critic

Radio announcer

Lung specialist

Air traffic controller

Singer/lyricist

One-on-one salesman

Equally important to finding the best job slot for you is understanding how your Gemini sun sign affects your modus operandi on the job and your potential for moving up. Every sun sign has certain success skills that can smooth and widen the career path, as well as blind spots that can cause roadblocks. The more you know about both, the better off you will be.

When Gemini hops about from job to job, it isn't always just because the way to move up is to move around. Gemini's *real* motivation is not necessarily ambition, but rather the hyperactivity that arises from restlessness. As a success skill, restlessness can work two ways. When you move fast, some employers think you really want to get somewhere. The down side is that Gemini tends to get bored very easily and when boredom sets in the learning process stops.

All too often Gemini's real problem in the job world is that he/she has a superficial knowledge of a lot of things, but no real grasp on anything. Obviously, you can't force change on yourself overnight, but you can try to stick to one thing longer. The key is making it the right thing—a job where conditions change almost daily in one way or another. Many Geminis are superb commodities traders for instance, because there is no such thing as a dull moment. If you aren't able to dictate your job choice to any great extent, the trick for you is to *bring* freshness to the job every day. No matter how "boring" or tedious the routine, there is always a better/faster way to do it. By figuring out that way, you will not only keep yourself interested, but attract the attention of people who count as well.

A good education is a joy for Gemini, but not all are fortunate enough to get the best. Therefore, your wise course is to continue taking courses, or at least engaging in some kind of activity that brings in new information and new perceptions all the time. If you get absolutely stifled with boredom, take in a movie on your lunch hour, if necessary. Never, never stagnate; if you do, you'll literally never get anywhere.

# 19

# How "Pure" a Gemini Are You?

## Your Moon Sign ... Your Rising Sign

No one is a "pure Gemini"—or pure anything for that matter—when it comes to astrological signs. As you will learn when you read "Defining Terms," there are many other factors in a horoscope that add up to the total person that is "you." Yes, there are twelve basic personality types according to the zodiac, but within those broad groups there are almost infinite variations.

Though you are a Gemini at the core, and can count on the portrait of your sun sign to define you in essence, the two other horoscope factors that count most are in your personality profile: are your moon sign and your rising sign. Many people know their moon sign; anyone can quickly determine it via an ephemeris. If you know your birthtime at least within one hour, you can use the table in this book to find out what your rising sign is.

### The Moon—Your "Dark Side"

Almost more than your sun sign, your moon sign indicates what makes you run. Most of the time, you do not know it yourself, because the moon is your subconscious, your "dark side" not because it is bad, but because it is hidden. When the meaning of your moon sign is added to your Gemini sun sign, it is a fuller picture and a better indicator of your probable personality. Here's how a Gemini sun sign mixes with each of the moon signs.

***Gemini sun sign/Aries moon sign***     Self-control may be a lifetime goal and a perpetual problem for you. On top of being erratic, you are overly impulsive, and possibly a bit insensitive. Make a conscious attempt to get in touch with other people's feelings—before you hurt them. Your wits are sharp and you have the tongue to match. Slow down and try to smell the roses once in a while.

***Gemini sun sign/Taurus moon sign***     It is almost inevitable that you will be a softer Gemini than most, with a more sympathetic ear and instinct to help others in practical ways. Your natural skills tend toward appreciation and performance in a number of artistic areas, especially music and art. Don't waste yourself on "unprofitable" people or circumstances; find out where you are comfortable, and stay there.

***Gemini sun sign/Gemini moon sign***     It would be all too easy for you to live in your head rather than in your emotions, and therefore end up a bit lonely. Even though you *know* you are smarter than everyone else, there are people who can come up to your standards. It is also essential for you to practice self-control and to force yourself to be calm once in a while. If you are not careful, your own nerves can bite you back.

***Gemini sun sign/Cancer moon sign***     You are a most fortunate Gemini, because your moon sign gives you more of the capability of understanding the feelings of others. You are also a bit steadier in the mental department, and more inclined to stick with things. However, you are a bit of a sensationalist and could get carried away by the desire for the unusual. Cool it.

***Gemini sun sign/Leo moon sign***     You probably know by now that you often don't have the determination to carry out some of your ambitious ideas; however, you can develop it. Your Leo moon gives you a wonderfully warm heart, but you may be a bit taken in by your own romantic impulses. Don't be *too* sympathetic. When your self-confidence deserts you—as it often does—retire from the fray to get it back.

***Gemini sun sign/Virgo moon sign***    In spite of your tendency to be rather peevish, this is a great combination. Your Virgo moon gives a lot of direction to your Gemini sun, and should make you a superb analyzer—and an excellent student. However, it is easy for you to get down on yourself, and to lapse into melancholy moods. Give yourself more credit for what you've got and what you can do.

***Gemini sun sign/Libra moon sign***    This is a sun/moon combination that can cause trouble if you do not discipline yourself. It is all too easy for you to take the easy way out, no matter what methods you use. Your heart is in the right place, however, and you always do your best to make people feel loved and accepted. Don't neglect your considerable powers, especially in artistic areas.

***Gemini sun sign/Scorpio moon sign***    All your emotions may be exaggerated—especially your desire for control of every situation. In many cases, you will be a real argumentative type who loses friends easily. Sarcasm comes naturally to you, and you should curb your desire to prove how smart you can be. You are one Gemini who should actually lighten up a little.

***Gemini sun sign/Sagittarius moon sign***    There could be a real lack of continuity in your life. You may bring it on yourself by wanderlust that you overindulge in. Even if you can't always travel far, you all too easily move away mentally from many situations before you let them develop. Don't waste your very good mental energies, and don't deny the real force of character that lies under your surface.

***Gemini sun sign/Capricorn moon sign***    This is a great combination for worldly success, because your Capricorn moon slows you down and makes you capable of steady effort, while your Gemini sun has all the ideas. Your memory should be excellent, but you may tend to reject some of your own best efforts because they don't satisfy you. Congratulate yourself for having more patience than the typical Gemini.

*Gemini sun sign/Aquarius moon sign*    You may be truly distant—even from yourself. While this combination gives exceptional mental ability (sometimes genius), it could make you a loner in spite of all your social activity. For greatest life happiness, you may have to force yourself to get involved with a person or a cause. Use your excellent powers of discrimination to analyze your own problem of detachment.

*Gemini sun sign/Pisces moon sign*    You could be as restless as a willow in a windstorm and have particular difficulty in settling down to a life direction. You are exceptionally open to the problems of others, and inclined to help. However, you may totally lack perspective when it comes to your own life. Depression is possible with this combination, so you should make a special effort to head it off when you see it coming.

**Your Rising Sign—Know Your Cover**
The third of the "big three" astrological factors is your rising sign, which you can think of as an *overlay* to your sun sign. Although it does not carry the psychological weight your moon sign does, your rising sign is also "unconscious" because it is a mode of external behavior that comes so naturally to you you may not be aware of it. In a sense, your rising sign is your cover. It can never totally obscure the real you of your sun sign, but it can temporarily mask that sign, especially when people first meet you. Here's what happens to Gemini when you lay a rising sign over typical Gemini behavior:

*Gemini with Aries rising*    Your childlike charm can be irresistable and refreshing—or extremely annoying. Don't carry it too far if you want to really impress.

*Gemini with Taurus rising*    Many with this combination are real life-of-the-party types that others gravitate towards. Don't hog the limelight.

***Gemini with Gemini rising*** People with this combination sometimes move with the speed of lightning and talk the same way. Slow down, if you want to be truly understood.

***Gemini with Cancer rising*** Glamorous is the word for you—even if you aren't conventionally beautiful. There's a sexiness to your speech and movement.

***Gemini with Leo rising*** Some people may regard you as just too self-involved for words; try to get to know the other person before you blow your own horn.

***Gemini with Virgo rising*** There is an edgy quality to the way you speak and move, although you choose your words with care. Try to loosen up a bit more.

***Gemini with Libra rising*** You've got class written all over you, regardless of your actual physical features. When you speak, people are even more impressed with you. Enjoy!

***Gemini with Scorpio rising*** You express your opinions with such vehemence you may intimidate some people; take a more casual approach for greatest social success.

***Gemini with Sagittarius rising*** Your clowning around sometimes makes people take you less seriously than you would like. Make them realize you're more mature than you may appear.

***Gemini with Capricorn rising*** It's easy for you to command attention and respect. Just make sure you really know what you're talking about if people are going to take you so seriously.

***Gemini with Aquarius rising*** You could easily be labeled that "queer duck" who says the *strangest* things. Know your audience before you go into your act.

***Gemini with Pisces rising*** Females with this combination run the risk of simpering; males can be just too charming. Let your sincerity shine through.

# 20

# Find Your Rising Sign

It is easier than many people think to find out your rising sign. One reason is that it is based on "universal" or "sidereal" time—the measure used in space travel. To ascertain your rising sign, look through the following chart and locate the birthdate nearest your birth date; look across and locate the time nearest your birth time. Remember that if daylight saving time was in effect at your birth, you must subtract one hour from the time stated on your birth certificate. In the section for your date and time, you will find an abbreviation for the sign that was rising when you were born. For instance, if your birthdate is June 12 at 9:30 a.m., your rising sign is Leo; if you were born on the same date at 9:30 p.m., your rising sign is Capricorn.

You will notice that the *year* you were born does not affect your rising sign. However, the geographical latitude does. These tables are calculated for the middle latitudes of the United States. If you were born far to the south, it is wise to look at the sign that *follows* your rising sign as well. If you were born far to the north, check out the *previous* sign.

# Rising Signs—A.M. Births

| | 1 AM | 2 AM | 3 AM | 4 AM | 5 AM | 6 AM | 7 AM | 8 AM | 9 AM | 10 AM | 11 AM | 12 NOON |
|---|---|---|---|---|---|---|---|---|---|---|---|---|
| Jan 1 | Lib | Sc | Sc | Sc | Sag | Sag | Cap | Cap | Aq | Aq | Pis | Ar |
| Jan 9 | Lib | Sc | Sc | Sag | Sag | Sag | Cap | Cap | Aq | Pis | Ar | Tau |
| Jan 17 | Sc | Sc | Sc | Sag | Sag | Cap | Cap | Aq | Aq | Pis | Ar | Tau |
| Jan 25 | Sc | Sc | Sag | Sag | Sag | Cap | Cap | Aq | Pis | Ar | Tau | Tau |
| Feb 2 | Sc | Sc | Sag | Sag | Cap | Cap | Aq | Pis | Pis | Ar | Tau | Gem |
| Feb 10 | Sc | Sag | Sag | Sag | Cap | Cap | Aq | Pis | Ar | Tau | Tau | Gem |
| Feb 18 | Sc | Sag | Sag | Cap | Cap | Aq | Pis | Pis | Ar | Tau | Gem | Gem |
| Feb 26 | Sag | Sag | Sag | Cap | Aq | Aq | Pis | Ar | Tau | Tau | Gem | Gem |
| Mar 6 | Sag | Sag | Cap | Cap | Aq | Pis | Pis | Ar | Tau | Gem | Gem | Cap |
| Mar 14 | Sag | Cap | Cap | Aq | Aq | Pis | Ar | Tau | Tau | Gem | Gem | Can |
| Mar 22 | Sag | Cap | Cap | Aq | Pis | Ar | Ar | Tau | Gem | Gem | Can | Can |
| Mar 30 | Cap | Cap | Aq | Pis | Pis | Ar | Tau | Tau | Gem | Can | Can | Can |
| Apr 7 | Cap | Cap | Aq | Pis | Ar | Ar | Tau | Gem | Gem | Can | Can | Leo |
| Apr 14 | Cap | Aq | Aq | Pis | Ar | Tau | Tau | Gem | Gem | Can | Can | Leo |
| Apr 22 | Cap | Aq | Pis | Ar | Ar | Tau | Gem | Gem | Gem | Can | Leo | Leo |
| Apr 30 | Aq | Aq | Pis | Ar | Tau | Tau | Gem | Can | Can | Can | Leo | Leo |
| May 8 | Aq | Pis | Ar | Ar | Tau | Gem | Gem | Can | Can | Leo | Leo | Leo |
| May 16 | Aq | Pis | Ar | Tau | Gem | Gem | Can | Can | Can | Leo | Leo | Vir |
| May 24 | Pis | Ar | Ar | Tau | Gem | Gem | Can | Can | Leo | Leo | Leo | Vir |
| June 1 | Pis | Ar | Tau | Gem | Gem | Can | Can | Can | Leo | Leo | Vir | Vir |
| June 9 | Ar | Ar | Tau | Gem | Gem | Can | Can | Leo | Leo | Leo | Vir | Vir |
| June 17 | Ar | Tau | Gem | Gem | Can | Can | Can | Leo | Leo | Vir | Vir | Vir |
| June 25 | Tau | Tau | Gem | Gem | Can | Can | Leo | Leo | Leo | Vir | Vir | Lib |
| July 3 | Tau | Gem | Gem | Can | Can | Can | Leo | Leo | Vir | Vir | Vir | Lib |
| July 11 | Tau | Gem | Gem | Can | Can | Leo | Leo | Leo | Vir | Vir | Lib | Lib |
| July 18 | Gem | Gem | Can | Can | Can | Leo | Leo | Vir | Vir | Vir | Lib | Lib |
| July 26 | Gem | Gem | Can | Can | Leo | Leo | Vir | Vir | Vir | Lib | Lib | Lib |
| Aug 3 | Gem | Can | Can | Can | Leo | Leo | Vir | Vir | Vir | Lib | Lib | Sc |
| Aug 11 | Gem | Can | Can | Leo | Leo | Leo | Vir | Vir | Lib | Lib | Lib | Sc |
| Aug 18 | Can | Can | Can | Leo | Leo | Vir | Vir | Vir | Lib | Lib | Sc | Sc |
| Aug 27 | Can | Can | Leo | Leo | Leo | Vir | Vir | Lib | Lib | Lib | Sc | Sc |
| Sept 4 | Can | Can | Leo | Leo | Leo | Vir | Vir | Vir | Lib | Lib | Sc | Sc |
| Sept 12 | Can | Leo | Leo | Leo | Vir | Vir | Lib | Lib | Lib | Sc | Sc | Sag |
| Sept 30 | Leo | Leo | Leo | Vir | Vir | Vir | Lib | Lib | Sc | Sc | Sc | Sag |
| Sept 28 | Leo | Leo | Leo | Vir | Vir | Lib | Lib | Lib | Sc | Sc | Sag | Sag |
| Oct 6 | Leo | Leo | Vir | Vir | Vir | Lib | Lib | Sc | Sc | Sc | Sag | Sag |
| Oct 14 | Leo | Vir | Vir | Vir | Lib | Lib | Lib | Sc | Sc | Sag | Sag | Cap |
| Oct 22 | Leo | Vir | Vir | Lib | Lib | Lib | Sc | Sc | Sc | Sag | Sag | Cap |
| Oct 30 | Vir | Vir | Vir | Lib | Lib | Sc | Sc | Sc | Sag | Sag | Cap | Cap |
| Nov 7 | Vir | Vir | Lib | Lib | Lib | Sc | Sc | Sc | Sag | Sag | Cap | Cap |
| Nov 15 | Vir | Vir | Lib | Lib | Sc | Sc | Sc | Sag | Sag | Cap | Cap | Aq |
| Nov 23 | Vir | Lib | Lib | Lib | Sc | Sc | Sag | Sag | Sag | Cap | Cap | Aq |
| Dec 1 | Vir | Lib | Lib | Sc | Sc | Sc | Sag | Sag | Cap | Cap | Aq | Aq |
| Dec 9 | Lib | Lib | Lib | Sc | Sc | Sag | Sag | Sag | Cap | Cap | Aq | Pis |
| Dec 18 | Lib | Lib | Sc | Sc | Sc | Sag | Sag | Cap | Cap | Aq | Aq | Pis |
| Dec 28 | Lib | Lib | Sc | Sc | Sag | Sag | Sag | Cap | Aq | Aq | Pis | Ar |

# Rising Signs—P.M. Births

| | 1 PM | 2 PM | 3 PM | 4 PM | 5 PM | 6 PM | 7 PM | 8 PM | 9 PM | 10 PM | 11 PM | 12 MIDNIGHT |
|---|---|---|---|---|---|---|---|---|---|---|---|---|
| Jan 1 | Tau | Gem | Gem | Can | Can | Can | Leo | Leo | Vir | Vir | Vir | Lib |
| Jan 9 | Tau | Gem | Gem | Can | Can | Leo | Leo | Leo | Vir | Vir | Vir | Lib |
| Jan 17 | Gem | Gem | Can | Can | Can | Leo | Leo | Vir | Vir | Vir | Lib | Lib |
| Jan 25 | Gem | Gem | Can | Can | Leo | Leo | Leo | Vir | Vir | Lib | Lib | Lib |
| Feb 2 | Gem | Can | Can | Can | Leo | Leo | Vir | Vir | Vir | Lib | Lib | Sc |
| Feb 10 | Gem | Can | Can | Leo | Leo | Leo | Vir | Vir | Lib | Lib | Lib | Sc |
| Feb 18 | Can | Can | Can | Leo | Leo | Vir | Vir | Vir | Lib | Lib | Sc | Sc |
| Feb 26 | Can | Can | Leo | Leo | Leo | Vir | Vir | Lib | Lib | Lib | Sc | Sc |
| Mar 6 | Can | Leo | Leo | Leo | Vir | Vir | Vir | Lib | Lib | Sc | Sc | Sc |
| Mar 14 | Can | Leo | Leo | Vir | Vir | Vir | Lib | Lib | Lib | Sc | Sc | Sag |
| Mar 22 | Leo | Leo | Leo | Vir | Vir | Lib | Lib | Lib | Sc | Sc | Sc | Sag |
| Mar 30 | Leo | Leo | Vir | Vir | Vir | Lib | Lib | Sc | Sc | Sc | Sag | Sag |
| Apr 7 | Leo | Leo | Vir | Vir | Lib | Lib | Lib | Sc | Sc | Sc | Sag | Sag |
| Apr 14 | Leo | Vir | Vir | Vir | Lib | Lib | Sc | Sc | Sc | Sag | Sag | Cap |
| Apr 22 | Leo | Vir | Vir | Lib | Lib | Lib | Sc | Sc | Sc | Sag | Sag | Cap |
| Apr 30 | Vir | Vir | Vir | Lib | Lib | Sc | Sc | Sc | Sag | Sag | Cap | Cap |
| May 8 | Vir | Vir | Lib | Lib | Lib | Sc | Sc | Sag | Sag | Sag | Cap | Cap |
| May 16 | Vir | Vir | Lib | Lib | Sc | Sc | Sc | Sag | Sag | Cap | Cap | Aq |
| May 24 | Vir | Lib | Lib | Lib | Sc | Sc | Sag | Sag | Sag | Cap | Cap | Aq |
| June 1 | Vir | Lib | Lib | Sc | Sc | Sc | Sag | Sag | Cap | Cap | Aq | Aq |
| June 9 | Lib | Lib | Lib | Sc | Sc | Sag | Sag | Sag | Cap | Cap | Aq | Pis |
| June 17 | Lib | Lib | Sc | Sc | Sc | Sag | Sag | Cap | Cap | Aq | Aq | Pis |
| June 25 | Lib | Lib | Sc | Sc | Sag | Sag | Sag | Cap | Cap | Aq | Pis | Ar |
| July 3 | Lib | Sc | Sc | Sc | Sag | Sag | Cap | Cap | Aq | Aq | Pis | Ar |
| July 11 | Lib | Sc | Sc | Sag | Sag | Sag | Cap | Cap | Aq | Pis | Ar | Tau |
| July 18 | Sc | Sc | Sc | Sag | Sag | Cap | Cap | Aq | Aq | Pis | Ar | Tau |
| July 26 | Sc | Sc | Sag | Sag | Sag | Cap | Cap | Aq | Pis | Ar | Tau | Tau |
| Aug 3 | Sc | Sc | Sag | Sag | Cap | Cap | Aq | Aq | Pis | Ar | Tau | Gem |
| Aug 11 | Sc | Sag | Sag | Sag | Cap | Cap | Aq | Pis | Ar | Tau | Tau | Gem |
| Aug 18 | Sc | Sag | Sag | Cap | Cap | Aq | Pis | Pis | Ar | Tau | Gem | Gem |
| Aug 27 | Sag | Sag | Sag | Cap | Cap | Aq | Pis | Ar | Tau | Tau | Gem | Gem |
| Sept 4 | Sag | Sag | Cap | Cap | Aq | Pis | Pis | Ar | Tau | Gem | Gem | Can |
| Sept 12 | Sag | Sag | Cap | Aq | Aq | Pis | Ar | Tau | Tau | Gem | Gem | Can |
| Sept 20 | Sag | Cap | Cap | Aq | Pis | Pis | Ar | Tau | Gem | Gem | Can | Can |
| Sept 28 | Cap | Cap | Aq | Aq | Pis | Ar | Tau | Tau | Gem | Gem | Can | Can |
| Oct 6 | Cap | Cap | Aq | Pis | Ar | Ar | Tau | Gem | Gem | Can | Can | Leo |
| Oct 14 | Cap | Aq | Aq | Pis | Ar | Tau | Tau | Gem | Gem | Can | Can | Leo |
| Oct 22 | Cap | Aq | Pis | Ar | Ar | Tau | Gem | Gem | Can | Can | Leo | Leo |
| Oct 30 | Aq | Aq | Pis | Ar | Tau | Tau | Gem | Can | Can | Can | Leo | Leo |
| Nov 7 | Aq | Aq | Pis | Ar | Tau | Tau | Gem | Can | Can | Can | Leo | Leo |
| Nov 15 | Aq | Pis | Ar | Tau | Gem | Gem | Can | Can | Can | Leo | Leo | Vir |
| Nov 23 | Pis | Ar | Ar | Tau | Gem | Gem | Can | Can | Leo | Leo | Leo | Vir |
| Dec 1 | Pis | Ar | Tau | Gem | Gem | Can | Can | Can | Leo | Leo | Vir | Vir |
| Dec 9 | Ar | Tau | Tau | Gem | Gem | Can | Can | Leo | Leo | Leo | Vir | Vir |
| Dec 18 | Ar | Tau | Gem | Gem | Can | Can | Can | Leo | Leo | Vir | Vir | Vir |
| Dec 28 | Tau | Tau | Gem | Gem | Can | Can | Leo | Leo | Vir | Vir | Vir | Lib |

# 21

# Gemini Astro-Outlook for 1986

Among the more significant things 1986 brings to the sign of Gemini is a heightened awareness and understanding of life. As you go beyond the superficialities to the deeper meaning of existence, you may very well begin to reevaluate your goals as well as your relationships and all your current situations.

People will be drawn to you by your enhanced magnetism and willingness to give as you have never given before. More than one friend and/or associate will come to you seeking to tap into your new vein of sensitivity to help solve their problems.

1986 is a year of exploration in every sense of the word, and you will want to experience all kinds of new ideas and activities—perhaps to travel. In the course of "stretching" yourself, you may find a certain relationship has become too restricting. Your solution may be to terminate it or reestablish it on an entirely new basis.

In your career life you will be focusing on long-range objectives; some Geminis may decide a new job is in order, or even a total career switch. Anything that does not allow for advancement will not fit into your game plan. In some cases, a sparky new associate—possibly an Aries—will be the one to help you focus on future opportunities.

The months of January and October are excellent for getting new things off the ground, while March and

May look light and romantic, and June is a distinct
possibility for a change of residence. For more details
on what 1986 holds for Gemini, see the day-to-day
forecasts on the pages that follow.

# 22

# Fifteen Months of Day-by-Day Predictions

## OCTOBER 1985

*Tuesday, October 1 (Moon in Taurus)*     No matter what the weather, the sun is shining for you today— and shedding some light on an area that's been an uncomfortable one for you of late. Now you know there was no reason to be suspicious or to doubt someone's motives. Keep all your dealing aboveboard today; when someone tried to draw you into a gossip session, politely refuse.

*Wednesday, October 2 (Moon in Taurus)*     Don't worry about following your hunches today; one in particular is right as can be. When someone gives in to you, be nice; there's no point in rubbing it in and continuing the battle. When the sense of harmony is restored, your sense of direction will come back. Someone turns up to help you out of a tight spot.

*Thursday, October 3 (Moon Taurus to Gemini 8:26 a.m.)*     Early today the moon moves into your sign, and you get a shot of ambition and energy. Keep your agenda wide open today because you may have to make some quick changes and show how adaptable you really are. It will be fun, however, so dress up a bit and be prepared to be in the spotlight. The lucky number is 3.

*Friday, October 4 (Moon in Gemini)*     Nobody but nobody can get ahead of you today. In this high cycle it is easy for you to see what you've done that needs to be redone, and you plunge into it with vigor. An Aquarian or a Scorpio may be on the scene today and try to share the spotlight. Be generous; you've got enough going for you today to spread it around.

*Saturday, October 5 (Moon Gemini to Cancer 8:42 p.m.)*    Someone very exciting could waltz onto the scene today—and possible try to waltz you around. It could be very romantic and possibly very promising; romance is definitely on the calendar. If it isn't love that occupies you today, it should be some kind of creative project. No matter what it is, you will do it well now.

*Sunday, October 6 (Moon in Cancer)*    A little dispute that turned into a big one could be resolved today; it looks like the battleground is right on your doorstep. Do your bit to restore harmony. When you do, you find that someone is very supportive of your efforts after all; don't let money matters break the peace again. Your lucky number is 6.

*Monday, October 7 (Moon in Cancer)*    Be sure to protect what belongs to you today; there is a possibility that someone could try to take something away from you. Be aware of the possibility, but don't let it ruin your day, which could otherwise be a good one. In fact, you may be finding your way out of a dilemma that has been quite annoying recently. A solution is at hand.

*Tuesday, October 8 (Moon Cancer to Leo 6:38 a.m.)* This is "pressure cooker" time and the heat may definitely be on. Don't feel swamped; you will get out from under, and the way you handle things now could do a lot for your future in terms of tangible rewards. As you accept more responsibility, you see that more authority goes along with it. Nice going.

*Wednesday, October 9 (Moon in Leo)*    If you keep on dragging something out, you will never finish. Don't be afraid to complete—or toss out—what isn't relevant anymore. You may have to go a bit out of your way for a friend or relative today, and you will feel inclined to grumble about it. Keep the ability to laugh at yourself, and try your luck with number 9.

***Thursday, October 10 (Moon Leo to Virgo 1:24 p.m.)*** Someone comes along and shows you where you are wasting money. As you plug up that hole, your morale rises. Be prepared to show how adventurous you can be when something interesting—and possibly profitable—comes your way. Sometimes it's fun to play pioneer—especially when the stakes are not too high.

***Friday, October 11 (Moon in Virgo)*** You are right about something, and you decide to follow through on a first impression. However, it isn't much fun, and you feel very hemmed in by circumstances. Don't worry; a freer time is coming. Concentrate your mind on matters of law and property in order to get the sense of security you need.

***Saturday, October 12 (Moon Virgo to Libra 2:38 p.m.)*** Look beyond the immediate possibilities; a trip or journey could be looming. Whatever it is, there is an element of the educational in it, and you do love to learn about many things. What's important now is to ask a lot of questions, which is your style anyway. Make sure others are aware of what good work you do.

***Sunday, October 13 (Moon in Libra)*** You are in the mood for fun now, and you should easily be able to find it today. Seek out some other playful types and get them to go along; you won't have any problem convincing people today that what you want to do is the thing to do. Leave time to put something back together that has been falling apart lately.

***Monday, October 14 (Moon Libra to Scorpio 2:50 p.m.)*** It's a good day to tie up some loose ends, catch up on calls and letters, and generally do a clean-up job. You may find it necessary to be very frank and direct with someone who has to be set straight; it could be a member of the opposite sex. The lucky number is 5.

*Tuesday, October 15 (Moon in Scorpio)*     Focus your efforts on your job and your health today; you could have been neglecting both of late. Show your skill to those who rely on you and you will get the kind of appreciation you've been looking for. In fact, you may get a rather abject apology from someone who says he/she has been underestimating you.

*Wednesday, October 16 (Moon Scorpio to Sagittarius 2:25 p.m.)*     You may have to exercise patience today if you are to get your hands on what you want. Some people will be talking all around the subject when all you want is the facts. You will have to be very firm about defining where you are in a situation; you will receive solid support from someone who shares your concerns.

*Thursday, October 17 (Moon in Sagittarius)*     You may have to take on some responsibility you didn't bargain for—and realize a relationship is more serious than you had thought. Put your mind to a partnership and see where ideas that clash can be integrated into each other. It's something you are very good at.

*Friday, October 18 (Moon Sagittarius to Capricorn 3:37 p.m.)*     Love plays a bit part in the day's scenario, and once again you may be called upon to smooth the waters with someone you love. Don't let it distract you from the work at hand where you are able to take some definite steps toward a future goal. The lucky number is 9.

*Saturday, October 19 (Moon in Capricorn)*     Today you will have to have the courage of your convictions when someone attacks your master plan. Be prepared to give all the logical reasons why you are doing what you are doing. It is obvious you want to act independently, but perhaps you should bring others who are equally concerned into the decision-making process.

*Sunday, October 20 (Moon Capricorn to Aquarius 8:04 p.m.)*     Now you are being pulled in two directions and have to resolve your dilemma. There is no doubt that you should go in the direction of loyalty to family and those you love. Your integrity may be at stake, and you know how important it is to you. Fulfill your obligations before you go on to anything else.

**Monday, October 21 (Moon in Aquarius)**  It is a relief to get back to firm ground where you are sure about what has to be done first. Don't get bogged down today, however, because there are some excellent ideas floating around that could be very useful to you in improving yourself. Education has been on your mind, and you should heed what you hear today.

**Tuesday, October 22 (Moon in Aquarius)**  Check into a travel or education scheme that has drifted into your view. It may not be as great as it sounds. However, that obstacle that appears in your path may not be the problem you think it is. If you look into it carefully, you may see where you can take a few steps forward and get nearer your goal.

**Wednesday, October 23 (Moon Aquarius to Pisces 3:35 a.m.)**  Be ready for a new start, some unusual new contacts and the possibility of putting some extra cash in your pocket. You may have to put something down on paper in order to get in the running, however. Don't hesitate. Look into the motives of someone who seems almost too helpful.

**Thursday, October 24 (Moon in Pisces)**  Someone is going around spreading nice stories about you and how you have helped in a certain situation. Take the pat on the back and let it do wonders for your morale. There is a possibility that love could walk in today; keep your eyes wide open. The lucky number is 6.

**Friday, October 25 (Moon in Pisces to Aries 2:09 p.m.)**  Someone who appears to be your friend has really been bitten by the green-eyed monster; play down your good fortune in front of this individual. You are going to have to keep alert in order to protect your rights. No one means any harm, but they could walk in and take over. It causes a minor crisis.

***Saturday, October 26 (Moon in Aries)*** If you've done your homework properly, you can put some lessons of the recent past to good use today. Your practicality impresses someone older, who proves he/she is now on your side. A wish comes true when you get credit for something you thought nobody would ever recognize.

***Sunday, October 27 (Moon in Aries)*** No matter what you are selling, you can sell it to anyone today because your powers of persuasion are excellent. Someone from whom you've been a bit estranged comes back into the picture and you kiss and make up. Don't let small things interfere with this relationship in the future; it is too important to you.

***Monday, October 28 (Full Moon 1:59 p.m., Moon Aries to Taurus 2:11 a.m.)*** An "exclusive" makes you the star reporter today and provides the key to doors that have been locked. As you make this breakthrough, insist on getting a new deal, and don't be intimidated by idle threats. Someone is definitely a paper tiger, and you are holding all the cards.

***Tuesday, October 29 (Moon in Taurus)*** You may feel like hiding during this full moon; you may feel as if there are secrets you don't want anyone else to know. It's okay to hole up, but don't be a total recluse. There are things that need doing. What's more you may have been letting some idle threats intimidate you. See them for what they are.

***Wednesday, October 30 (Moon Taurus to Gemini 2:35 p.m.)*** You now come out of your shell with a vengeance, and literally burst onto the scene. Now you can see the whole picture and feel a little foolish for having been so fearful. Another Gemini, or possibly a Sagittarian is very helpful in pulling you out of your "paranoid" state. The lucky number is 3.

***Thursday, October 31 (Moon in Gemini)***    You are at the peak of a high cycle and could enjoy this particular Halloween immensely. Even if you don't celebrate it in the traditional manner, you may decide to treat yourself and someone special to a special evening. You are starting to rebuild and you feel much more secure.

# NOVEMBER 1985

***Friday, November 1 (Moon in Gemini)***    Realize that what appears to be a dead halt is only a temporary delay; things will start moving again fast enough. Since this is your high cycle, you can enjoy the feeling of being just where you should be when you should be there. A number of people will be attracted to you; one may even profess feelings you didn't suspect were there.

***Saturday, November 2 (Moon Gemini to Cancer 3:12 a.m.)***    Diversify your interests today, and be sure not to get stuck in a rut. The more you look around the more likely you are to spot a new opportunity. Accept any invitation that comes your way today, and feel free to ask all the questions you like. No one will be offended because of your friendly, open manner.

***Sunday, November 3 (Moon in Cancer)***    A family gathering is a nice touch that lifts your morale and makes you feel more optimistic about the future; at least you know there are people you can call on if the going gets too rough. However, you should take a good look at the budget and see that you are not overspending where it can be avoided.

***Monday, November 4 (Moon Cancer to Leo 3:12 a.m.)***    Get ready for an opportunity for a change in scene; you need a little variety in your life. A unique idea you have should be protected; don't tell everyone and anyone about it. You are delighted to find out that you have everything you need to finish off a certain project. The lucky number today is 5.

*Tuesday, November 5 (Moon in Leo)*    Someone who is passing through brings good news of people at a distance. It reminds you that you have been very out of touch, and you should vow to keep on top of your long-standing relationships. Someone gives you a delightful surprise that shows how much he/she cares.

*Wednesday, November 6 (Moon Leo to Virgo 9:14 p.m.)*    Romance is definitely in the air, but it may not all be open and aboveboard. Intrigue can be fun, but it shouldn't get carried to the point where you are roped in. Be diplomatic with someone you must question for the "story behind the story." A Pisces or a Virgo could be an annoyance today.

*Thursday, November 7 (Moon in Virgo)*    It's nice to feel on solid ground again, emotionally speaking. Don't forget the lesson you just learned. As you turn your thoughts to stabilizing your environment, an older person shows how much support you have. Feel good about it and say "thanks" in some tangible way. The lucky number is 8.

*Friday, November 8 (Moon in Virgo)*    Don't start anything new today; finish off what needs to be finished and close a transaction. This can't go on forever. There's a lot of goodwill to be gotten from associates who admire your deft way of doing things. You may get a chance to present your platform to a wider audience.

*Saturday, November 9 (Moon Virgo to Libra 1:14 a.m.)*    It would be wise to get the opinion of a professional in a matter of evaluation; your own estimate is probably unrealistic. You will have the chance to show your style in a very unique way and prove to others that you are the creative person you like to think you are. Don't overdo in the area of exercise.

*Sunday, November 10 (Moon in Libra)*    Children could be a great source of pleasure today, as you stay close to your home base. It's much more pleasant now that harmony has been restored there. A search turns up something you thought you had lost, and someone close to you compliments you on your thoroughness. A Cancer or a Capricorn may interrupt the peace.

**Monday, November 11 (Moon Libra to Scorpio 1:53 a.m.)** You didn't even realize it, but you scored a direct hit rather than a near miss. Nice going! Now you have the luxury of considering several options instead of being forced to go with one. Examine things carefully so you will make the best decision. Take a good look in the mirror and decide if a diet is necessary.

**Tuesday, November 12 (Moon in Scorpio)** Things at work get abruptly turned upside down, and you may feel a little disoriented. Don't get rattled, and realize that the new rules work very much in your favor. As you consider how to make the most of the situation, resolve to work out a minor dispute with someone important to the scene. The lucky number is 4.

**Wednesday, November 13 (Moon Scorpio to Sagittarius 1:12 a.m.)** It is difficult for you and someone else to see eye to eye on something; cooperation is possible if one of you backs down. Though it may have to be you, figure that you may have lost a battle, but not the war. What you do is important to your image, and you are really practicing public relations.

**Thursday, November 14 (Moon in Sagittarius)** Your mind may be very much on a domestic situation that desperately needs straightening out. A simple solution should occur to you, and you should be the one to make the adjustment. In other matters, keep a low profile and do some quiet persuading. A Taurus or a Scorpio really knows you count.

**Friday, November 15 (Moon Sagittarius to Capricorn 1:10 a.m.)** You just seem to know what is going to happen before it happens; your ESP powers are running high. Even though some will say it was just a lucky guess, play it up. A glamourous person is rather effusive in what he/she says to you; enjoy the flattery but do not think that it runs very deep. The lucky number is 7.

**Saturday, November 16 (Moon in Capricorn)**     Listen to someone who gives you a tip today; it could lead to financial gain. If it is some form of investment, you are in a good time to take advantage of it. A minor crisis arises which you solve quite handily, and prove your worth to some important people.

**Sunday, November 17 (Moon Capricorn to Aquarius 3:54 a.m.)**     Today again you find yourself around some interesting and informative people; today they inspire you to think in a creative direction. You can break new ground now because you have gotten some kind of burden off your back and have more time to spend on the pursuits you enjoy. Think about travel.

**Monday, November 18 (Moon in Aquarius)**     Today you feel quite certain that you can handle a rather large project, and you indicate your willingness. Your enthusiasm is catching, and soon you find there are a number of others who want to go along with you. Be direct when you tell them that this is serious business and will require steady application. A friendship becomes stronger as a result.

**Tuesday, November 19 (Moon Aquarius to Pisces 10:04 a.m.)**     You are not thrilled by something that happens today; in fact, you are quite disappointed. Though it is difficult, try to realize that it is all for the best this way and that your time will come. Concentrate on matters of security and make sure that you and yours are totally protected.

**Wednesday, November 20 (Moon in Pisces)**     Your career gets a boost today through a contact you make at a social event, keep your eyes open for the main chance. A Virgo or Sagittarian could be very instrumental in furthering some plans of yours; rely on their help. The lucky number is 3.

*Thursday, November 21 (Moon Pisces to Aries 8:00 p.m.)* Don't let yourself be outmaneuvered today by a co-worker or supervisor; make it clear that you want what you should have. It may mean you have to streamline your way of doing things, but indicate that you are willing to do so. And that you have friends who support you in this matter.

*Friday, November 22 (Moon in Aries)* In a roundabout way one of your wishes comes true today; and you are amazed at the person who makes it possible. It just goes to show that you never can be certain how people will act. You get excellent playback from a recent proposal you put forth, and find that higher-ups are willing to have you try a new tack. Don't be afraid to display all your talents.

*Saturday, November 23 (Moon in Aries)* Today you feel "surrounded"—but in the nicest way possible. It is nice to know there are so many friends and that they will support you when the chips are down. A member of the opposite sex is particularly sympathetic and declares you the most important person in his/her life. The lucky number is 6 today.

*Sunday, November 24 (Moon Aries to Taurus 8:37 a.m.)* If you had your way, today you might be someone else. Not that things are bad, but that you are in the mood for adventure and romance. Feed the feeling by dressing up or buying some new clothes or makeup. They will come in handy when you are asked to make an "appearance" at a social gathering.

*Monday, November 25 (Moon in Taurus)* Someone wants you to take on a special responsibility that will benefit a particular group of people. Accept, while realizing that you will be doing something for yourself as well as others. There is a trick to this project which you will learn if you look behind the obvious. Lucky number today is 8.

*Tuesday, November 26 (Moon Taurus to Gemini 9:02 p.m.)* Someone may confide in you today and tell you more than you would like to know; realize that you must keep it under your hat. Though you are a bit annoyed at being put in this position, try to be helpful and sympathetic with the one who has the problem. Don't get caught in the trap of lending more than your hand, however.

**Wednesday, November 27 (Full Moon 7:58 a.m., Moon in Gemini)** This is your best full moon of the year, as it occurs in your own sign. You may be filled with confidence and courage, and you should trust yourself to take a risk that comes your way. Your willingness to help others as well as yourself is sincere, and you may find that you have started in a whole new direction. The lucky number is 1.

**Thursday, November 28 (Moon in Gemini)** You are still on your full moon "high" and people find you especially attractive now. You are very able to gather forces around you and get the information you need to pull off a coup. When you take your bows, you will realize that someone of the opposite sex is applauding particularly enthusiastically.

**Friday, November 29 (Moon Gemini to Cancer 8:59 a.m.)** Your sense of humor is called into play today, as is your colorful personality. When you are asked to expand something in order to include more people, you should respond affirmatively; you can handle it. If you have a gut feeling about something today, it is probably correct.

**Saturday, November 30 (Moon in Cancer)** It's back down to earth today, but not with too loud a crash. You are easily able to turn your thoughts to practical matters of bill-paying and the like. When you go on a search, you find exactly what you are looking for and it is very gratifying. Among the people you run into and must deal with today may be a Scorpio or a Leo. Your lucky number is 4.

# DECEMBER 1985

**Sunday, December 1 (Moon Cancer to Leo 8:04 p.m.)** Your appearance is cause for comment today, and you are aware that people are attracted. As your personality sparkles, use the situation to further your cause with people who count. Don't be surprised if you turn up a clue about something that you thought was lost. A little looking around will reveal it.

**Monday, December 2 (Moon in Leo)** It's nice to know you are not alone; those around you really do understand and are ready to back you up. Let this give you heart as you plunge into the process of rebuilding something on a firmer foundation. In another matter, you get a message that cheers you and gives you the will to proceed.

**Tuesday, December 3 (Moon in Leo)** It is obvious that some changes are necessary, and you must revamp things in a way not everyone is going to like. You can get your point across and convince others this is the only way to do it. You will feel a lot more secure when someone you trust a lot says he/she is with you all the way. The lucky number is 5.

**Wednesday, December 4 (Moon Leo to Virgo 4:38 a.m.)** You are feeling the pinch of some restrictions today; remember they are only temporary. In fact this delay gives you the opportunity to play the waiting game—and win. Make sure you are observing all the rules, and check out the fine print. Someone may talk about a change in martial status.

**Thursday, December 5 (Moon in Virgo)** It may be necessary to demand an accounting from someone, and the results may leave you disillusioned. Remember that you must be realistic about people and not overestimate what they can do. Refine your techniques of assessing people and you will make fewer mistakes. The lucky number is 7; you may find yourself playing with a Pisces or a Virgo.

***Friday, December 6 (Moon Virgo to Libra 9:44 a.m.)***
Keep long-range goals in mind today, and realize
that you must commit yourself to a specific course of
action in order to achieve them. You can be very productive today; particularly when someone with more
experience helps you over the rough spots. It may be a
Cancer or a Capricorn who lends the helping hand.

***Saturday, December 7 (Moon in Libra)*** You are
very glad to be relieved of a project that's been a drag
of late, and you feel in the mood to celebrate your new
freedom. A talk you have with someone makes you
realize how important such values as love and friendship are to you. You may feel adventurous enough to
venture into untried waters.

***Sunday, December 8 (Moon Libra to Scorpio 1:05
p.m.)*** Today you continue your dialogue with others, and find that a young person wants your advice
and counsel. You like the feeling of being depended
upon and are very willing to spend time getting to the
heart of the matter. Your actions today bring a nice
compliment from someone whose opinion you respect.

***Monday, December 9 (Moon in Scorpio)*** You can
smooth over the rough waters of a family dispute if you
listen to both sides, but follow your first impression. It
may be necessary to devote some time to health—your
own, a dependent's, or possibly that of a pet. Don't
delay in getting professional advice if you think it is
needed. The lucky number is 2.

***Tuesday, December 10 (Moon Scorpio to Sagittarius
1:11 p.m.)*** Try to look at the total picture instead of
the little part you can see. If you are going to make any
headway, you are going to have to put more effort into
communicating with someone who is difficult to penetrate. Take a tip from another Gemini who has an
absolutely inspired idea.

***Wednesday, December 11 (Moon in Sagittarius)*** You
may have to wade through miles of red tape today to

get the information you want, but is worth the effort. Make a special note to check out every detail, however, because it is a confusing situation. Listen carefully to someone rather shrewd—possibly a Taurus or a Scorpio—who has the right idea. The lucky number is 4.

***Thursday, December 12 (Moon Sagittarius to Capricorn 1:03 p.m.)*** Toss out the old junk that is no longer of any use; when you clear the decks for action, you will be able to operate much more effectively. Don't spend time in wishful thinking; look at the facts and only the facts. When you see things realistically, you will be much better able to plan ahead.

***Friday, December 13 (Moon in Capricorn)*** A decision comes down in your favor, and you are very much relieved. Now, was that worth all the worrying? Try to keep a better perspective on things that may look bad, but are really going to boomerang in the right direction. A Libra could provide a pleasant diversion.

***Saturday, December 14 (Moon Capricorn to Aquarius 1:34 p.m.)*** There is a mystery in the air today, but an exciting rather than a disturbing one. You feel like a child wild with anticipation as you wait for it to unravel. Part of it could involve a stimulating individual who doesn't exactly see eye to eye with you, but certainly provides an interesting interlude.

***Sunday, December 15 (Moon in Aquarius)*** You might have to think about a different base of operations; a change is in the air and you must be willing to be flexible. Someone tells you about a wonderful trip or course he/she is involved in, and it may spark you to similar activity. A family consultation may be necessary to clear the air.

***Monday, December 16 (Moon Aquarius to Pisces 6:21 p.m.)*** When you finally finish something off, you will begin to look beyond the immediate into your not-too-distant future. It is important to maintain a sense of balance and not go too swiftly forward; this is one time when haste will definitely mean waste. Someone gives you added recognition, and you are gratified.

**Tuesday, December 17 (Moon in Pisces)**    You get the opportunity to prove a major point today, and to show everyone that you were not very far off the mark. When you correct a minor mistake, let others in on the situation so you do not feel so isolated. Later on, consult with a loved one about the situation. And try your luck with number 1.

**Wednesday, December 18 (Moon in Pisces)**    Someone who has been a pal in the past proves that he/she is still behind you. Show your gratitude in some tangible way. Some credit due you for some time finally comes through, and the one who recognizes your talents is in a position to better your position. The lucky number is 2.

**Thursday, December 19 (Moon Pisces to Aries 2:55 a.m.)**    Your sense of humor will come in very handy today and help you shine at a social event. Something you invested a lot of hope in not too long ago is beginning to take shape; your wish may even come true. Another Gemini or a Sagittarian will be key to the day's events.

**Friday, December 20 (Moon in Aries)**    Take the broad view today and you will not get bogged down by petty details and small-minded people. You are aware that certain things are not as solid as they could be and need some revisions, but not everyone is willing to work at it. Use your powers of persuasion to get some needed allies.

**Saturday, December 21 (Moon Aries to Taurus 3:09 p.m.)**    You should be ready for some rather unusual activity today—particularly in the area of relationships. Someone you didn't expect may drop in suddenly and upset your particular apple cart. If you have some explaining to do—especially to someone of the opposite sex—you may be better off putting it on paper. The lucky number is 5.

**Sunday, December 22 (Moon in Taurus)**    Someone is in a concilatory mood today, and you should accept an apology graciously. However, you mainly want to be alone and should let others know that. Don't neglect someone who is alone, but lonely too. Hearing from you would help.

**Monday, December 23 (Moon in Taurus)**    Keep alert today and let yourself be optimistic; there is going to be a change for the better in your present situation. The more confident you appear, the more confidence others will have in you. Get the facts you need from someone who is accurate; a Virgo might be just the person.

**Tuesday, December 24 (Moon Taurus to Gemini 3:46 a.m.)**    With the holiday upon you, you are definitely in the spirit of the season. You can afford to be as others show their love and appreciation of you. You have real faith in the future and are able to instill optimism in those close to you. Keep the faith!

**Wednesday, December 25 (Moon in Gemini)**    This could be one of your most memorable holidays; your cycle is high and points to fulfillment of wishes, pleasure, and a deep understanding of what you really value. Today you are secure in the knowledge that you have a loyal and loving circle of people around you. The lucky number is 9.

**Thursday, December 26 (Moon Gemini to Cancer 3:41 p.m.)**    The warm glow of yesterday flows over into today, and you are ready to face a new situation without nervousness. You are right to feel secure; don't hesitate to assert your views in a very positive manner. The direct approach allows you to get right to the heart of the matter. Leave some time to play—particularly with real children.

**Friday, December 27 (Full Moon 2:46 a.m., Moon in Cancer)**    This full moon falls smack in your sector of income and compensation; yours could actually increase.

On the other hand, feelings may be running high today, so try not to let anyone rub you the wrong way. Some people may have had too much holiday. Trust the fact that your timing is excellent right now.

**Saturday, December 28 (Moon in Cancer)**   Today you get into a very lively discussion that could lead to a most interesting travel plan. You are very much in the spotlight as friends and family enjoy your sense of humor and upbeat approach. Whatever you attempt today, you will derive a lot from your efforts. Another Gemini could be good company.

**Sunday, December 29 (Moon Cancer to Leo 1:51 a.m.)** Today you are totally immersed in a family project and enjoy every minute of it. Well, almost every minute. Someone may throw you off temporarily by disagreeing on a matter of detail. The dispute is quickly resolved, however, and you get the pleasure of knowing you are very much appreciated.

**Monday, December 30 (Moon in Leo)**   The future seems very sharp and clear today, and you are able to keep your goals very much in sight. You know you are on the right track if you keep things in focus. You have some obligations to fulfill, and you might as well take care of them before they weigh too heavily on your conscience. Make the effort, even if it means going a little bit out of the way.

**Tuesday, December 31 (Moon Leo to Virgo 10:06 a.m.)** Don't think you can find any better place to celebrate New Year's Eve than your own home base. This is one time when all you need are those closest to you. However, as you spend a pleasant evening, you will discover there is more excitement than you thought. Especially when someone starts to entertain quite spontaneously.

# J A N U A R Y   1 9 8 6

**Wednesday, January 1 (Moon in Virgo)**   You start off the new year in a mood to take up the slack and pay attention to things that were neglected during the recent holiday days. Someone shares your enthusiasm, and ingenuity. Together you are able to make significant progress during a very active day. Don't get caught short by a quick change of plans—remain flexible and pleasant. Some important news comes in through an older person. The lucky number today is 2.

**Thursday, January 2 (Moon Virgo to Libra 3:45 p.m.)** It is possible you are considering a change of residence—for yourself or for someone else who values your opinions. Be practical in making suggestions. You sometimes go for the facade rather than the foundation. You could get rather charged up by an opportunity to express yourself. It could lead to a whole new activity—possibly a sport or a hobby.

**Friday, January 3 (Moon in Libra)** You heave a sigh of relief as the roadblock is removed from your path. Now you can steer your way clear and go full speed ahead to your destination. An opportunity could present itself today to have a lucky break. Don't get so distracted you miss it. Extreme physical attraction is possible now; keep things in perspective. The lucky number is 4.

**Saturday, January 4 (Moon Libra to Scorpio 7:44 p.m.)** If you aren't already involved, get ready for a new contact with a scintillating individual who compliments you on your charm and humor. It gives your ego a big boost and it could lead to something very interesting. Others are beginning to make constructive changes and learning how to imprint their own style on a situation. Another Gemini or a Sagittarian could be very helpful in this regard.

**Sunday, January 5 (Moon in Scorpio)** It is important to make sure you are very familiar with your rights. No one can fool you if you don't allow yourself to be fooled. The more attention you pay to money matters now, the more work and worry you'll save yourself in the future. Realize that someone very reliable is there and willing to help; he/she will prove a sincere and valuable ally.

**_Monday, January 6 (Moon Scorpio to Sagittarius 9:47 p.m.)_** No matter how you are tempted, do not take a shortcut that appears to be the easy way. It can only cause endless problems. The best way to handle things is to streamline your techniques and get rid of unproductive methods. In other words, stick to the familiar—but spruce it up a bit. Some may be wavering about recent resolutions concerning diet and nutrition; get serious about it again. Someone drops a hint, and you should pick it up for future use.

**_Tuesday, January 7 (Moon in Sagittarius)_** Today you come out of the tunnel and into the light. In fact, you should prepare yourself to be a "public figure" today. This could be a very productive period and you might even be able to hurdle a challenge that's been put between you and some thing or some one you want. Partnerships of all kinds are emphasized, including marriage. Be willing to look at things fairly and squarely.

**_Wednesday, January 8 (Moon Sagittarius to Capricorn 10:42 p.m.)_** Your reputation as a good and helpful friend is getting around. Someone may want to consult you and actually seems to believe you have healing powers. Be helpful, but set this person straight. You should be feeling a lot more emotionally secure and satisfied that you have completed a big task or project. Start thinking about things farther down the road.

**_Thursday, January 9 (Moon in Capricorn)_** Start off the day on a new footing, and take pleasure in your sense of well being. Some have not been feeling great lately, but today that is all changed. It is important to take the lead now—particularly in a romantic situation. However, if you are not willing to give up any independence, make that clear upfront. No point in not getting right to the heart of things. The lucky number is 1.

*Friday, January 10 (Moon in Capricorn)* Something goes well and you get the credit. Good going! Realize what you did in this situation, but don't overestimate your importance. The best thing that happens out of it is that your sense of purpose is restored. A family situation improves, and you could be on the road to a much more constructive arrangement.

*Saturday, January 11 (Moon Capricorn to Aquarius 12:01 a.m.)* You experience an almost spiritual feeling as things that mean the most to you come into sharp clear focus. Suddenly you know exactly the Right thing to do. And that's Right with a capital R. You find yourself far from cloistered, however, and the social pace could be quite a quick one now. Pick up all the information you can; it will come in handy later on.

*Sunday, January 12 (Moon in Aquarius)* Some confusion and resentment you may have been feeling lately is totally put to rest when you get a message that someone really does care. It's nice to feel emotionally satisfied rather than drained. An intellectual challenge may come your way today, and you should accept it. Refuse to be discouraged by people who are envious of you and therefore quite bitter. They can't hurt you.

*Monday, January 13 (Moon Aquarius to Pisces 3:39 a.m.)* No matter how hard you try, you will not be able to hide today. Somehow or other, you find yourself right out there on the firing line—but you come off the winner. You should be feeling more ambitious than usual, and you should take advantage of it. You love to win, and there are more ways to do it than you have been practicing. The lucky number today is 5.

*Tuesday, January 14 (Moon in Pisces)* Something doesn't sound quite right to you, and it shouldn't. You've got to do some checking out and checking up. Be discreet, however, because you don't want to tip your hand. In another matter, someone makes a conciliatory gesture to you and you should be willing to respond in kind. Something that appears to be a bargain really is; go ahead and buy it, it is an intelligent purchase.

**Wednesday, January 15 (Moon Pisces to Aries 11:03 p.m.)** Some have had a falling out recently and are not happy about it. Today you have the opportunity to patch things up when someone extends a hand to you. Realize how much this individual wants your approval, and how much you want the relationship on good footing. Some will have the opportunity to show off their unique way of doing things. When asked what you want, speak up and be frank. No point in not defining your terms.

**Thursday, January 16 (Moon in Aries)** Everybody has self-doubts, and you are no exception. That's why you should let a small victory of the day give you the lift you deserve. No matter that you do not regard it as a significant incident; others do. You should be quite popular during this period and have no lack of social life. Some will find a wish comes true—even though it is in disguise. The lucky number is 8.

**Friday, January 17 (Moon Aries to Taurus 10:14 p.m.)** You haven't learned your lesson yet; you are still giving up too much for too little in return. It's nice to be openhanded, but sometimes you are absolutely ridiculous. You should know it and clean up your act accordingly. You won't lose any friends thereby. A lucky streak runs through the day, and you should take advantage of it.

**Saturday, January 18 (Moon in Taurus)** Things are begining to work out for you the way they should; you are starting to get back in proportion to what you give out. Others are getting your message and it is becoming increasingly clear. A murky problem turns out to be a lot less complicated than it looks on the surface. It's time for some to get involved in community activity.

**Sunday, January 19 (Moon in Taurus)** Someone may talk about things you would rather not hear; listen anyway. It's possible to remain neutral yet to give a show of support. If you are nervous about it, realize that everybody has moods of the moment. Some of you will feel a bit on edge today and should guard against eating on a queasy stomach.

**Monday, January 20 (Moon Taurus to Gemini 11:12 a.m.)**    When something turns out to be a paper tiger, you may feel a bit silly that you were so afraid of it. No problem, it's intelligent to be self-protective under such circumstances. Many will have a reason to celebrate or a lot of social contact. Let your sense of humor shine in company. Indulge your intellectual curiosity in a fascinating discussion. The lucky number today is 3.

**Tuesday, January 21 (Moon in Gemini)**    With the moon in your sign, your cycle is high. Take advantage of it and refuse to take a backseat to someone who doesn't appreciate you as much as he/she should. Speak openly and frankly and what you want will come to you. You should have personality plus—and receive some heartening news on top of it. Trust your intuition now.

**Wednesday, January 22 (Moon Gemini to Cancer 11:14 p.m.)**    Once again you are bright-eyed and full of energy and ambition. Even if you don't feel that great, realize that this is *your* day—and make the most of it. Dress up and stride out full of confidence and in full knowledge of the fact that you can communicate on an excellent level today. Romance should be on the sunny side too. A Virgo could play a key role today.

**Thursday, January 23 (Moon in Cancer)**    Be sure to stick to the budget today, even though you are tempted to go out and splurge. You can't always get what you want—but you can get what you need. Your cash flow may be very much on your mind now, and you can find ways to improve the situation. On the bright side, you will discover some income potential you have overlooked. The lucky number today is 6.

*Friday, January 24 (Moon in Cancer)*    Your ideas will crystallize now and you should know exactly what to do where money is concerned. Your clarity of mind is helped by the fact that your moon cycle is still high. That also means you should be at the right place at exactly the right time. Take advantage of it. The lucky number today is 7.

*Saturday, January 25 (Moon Cancer to Leo 8:47 a.m.)*    This could be a power play day! That is, if you take full advantage of the full moon. Money and love in abundance could be yours—if you communicate with the right people. It is no time to hang back and be shy; nor is it a time to compromise your principles. All in all a promising but possibly complex day awaits you.

*Sunday, January 26 (Moon in Leo)*    Some may find themselves involved in a serious discussion about a change of residences—possibly involving a major real estate purchase. Even if that is not the scenario, your mind and your energy will be focused on home and security. Whether it is internal or external, a significant transaction is about to be completed. Make sure you are on the right side.

*Monday, January 27 (Moon Leo to Virgo 3:51 p.m.)* If you aren't careful, you could be fooled by someone who appears to be trying to attract your interest but really is just fooling around. It will be necessary to protect your pride and to maintain your dignity. Avoid the whole issue by continuing to concentrate your interest on domestic matters. Some will get an opportunity to make a new start and to become more independent. Investigate it thoroughly before rejecting it out of hand. The lucky number today is 1.

*Tuesday, January 28 (Moon in Virgo)*    For many, news comes in which is extremely helpful in planning future moves and strategies. All should learn exactly where they stand in no uncertain terms. That does not mean you will necessarily like it. Once again it may be necessary to shrug off mild insecurities and stress the positives in your life. Make sure you are on a solid foundation. The lucky number today is 2.

*Wednesday, January 29 (Moon Virgo to Libra 9:10 P.M.)*    Get out and move around and diversify your interests today. Things should be a lot lighter than they have been in the recent past. Take a suggestion from a friend whose loyalty is beyond question, and you will be glad of it. Most will be breathing easier and find they have more working room. If you've got a favorite cause, this is the time to promote it.

*Thursday, January 30 (Moon in Libra)*    Most will wake with a feeling of anticipation, and it is justified. Almost anything can happen today, and you should be aware that the surprise element is very much with you. In fact, some of you could get a rather rude shock to your status quo; however, it is positive in the long run. Those in love with love will find it returned now.

*Friday, January 31 (Moon in Libra)*    Don't give away any of your ideas now—they are too good. Reveal your thoughts only to the right people and get things in writing. Once again, your emotions may be chaotic and some may find themselves in search of new sensations. Not a bad activity, if you keep things in perspective. Get out and get around with another Gemini or Sagittarian.

# FEBRUARY 1986

*Saturday, February 1 (Moon Libra to Scorpio 11:19 a.m.)*    Try to stand back and look at the whole picture now; leave details for another time because they will only confuse you. Realize that an invitation is not inconsequential, and could lead to valuable contacts and necessary new experiences. Cast out fear and plunge on ahead. Some may have new employment opportunities.

*Sunday, February 2 (Moon in Scorpio)*    Keep your thoughts to yourself and your money in your own account when someone talks about a new scheme or a possible new living arrangement. It is possible to be a good listener without getting financially involved. Or involved in any other way. Realize that you have a tendency to be gullible when people pluck at your heartstrings. Focus your attention on your own rebuilding program and realize there is much to be done. The lucky number today is 4.

**Monday, February 3 (Moon Scorpio to Sagittarius 4:31 a.m.)** Let someone else take the initiative today; lie low and do not fret about the fact that your visibility is eclipsed. You should know from experience that you can ruin things for yourself by speaking out of turn. If you must be involved with others, put on your public relation hat and keep it there. Marriage is a subject of discussion now; if that is your state, you may be questioning your status.

**Tuesday, February 4 (Moon in Sagittarius)** Things take a turnaround and there is an adjustment for the better. Duties are outlined and responsibilities assigned. It is very obvious that cooperation is essential for keeping things afloat. In less stressful scenarios, there is still the need to make intelligent concessions or to agree to some repairs or redecorating in the family compound. Your lucky number today is 6.

**Wednesday, February 5 (Moon Sagittarius to Capricorn 7:02 a.m.)** Some should take care not to overstay their welcomes now. That means you should know when to take the last bow and to get offstage. Others could experience a loss but should realize it is not permanent. Things are merely delayed. You should definitely not count yourself out of the game. Take solace with a Pisces or Virgo who can offer moral support. The lucky number today is 7.

**Thursday, February 6 (Moon in Capricorn)** You can get the job done if you put your shoulder into it. You may not be feeling overambitious, but your conscientious streak should be showing. On a positive side, financial help could come from a rather surprising source. Those who make a commitment now may not be totally sure; realize that uncertainty and security can be coexisting emotions.

*Friday, February 7 (Moon Capricorn to Aquarius 7:35 a.m.)* Now is the time to dump a losing proposition and to reach out for the new. You have been unhappy too long. Some will find a rather large audience awaiting them, and they should prepare for an extremely important performance. For some, it could be the performance of a lifetime. There is a haze of mystery over this day, and you should try to penetrate it. The lucky number today is 9.

*Saturday, February 8 (Moon in Aquarius)* This is an excellent phase of the moon for you to state your case—and get positive feedback. Even if you do not hear what you would like, at least you will know exactly where you stand. You can be confident if you form a solid front in your own mind. Sometimes your thoughts get scattered, and that makes you disheartened. It doesn't have to be that way. Try some silent meditation to get to the heart of the matter.

*Sunday, February 9 (Moon Aquarius to Pisces 11:32 a.m.)* Help is there when you need it—and you may need it now. Don't let pride stand in your way of accepting it. Some will experience a rather offbeat day during which they will experiment with something new and possibly exotic. The experience should make you realize there are new worlds to conquer, and you should go after them with determination. Travel anyone? A Cancer or an Aquarian could be a prominent person in your life now.

*Monday, February 10 (Moon in Pisces)* Recent experiences should make you willing to tear down something you've built in a rather flimsy manner. Something tells you—and it's right—that you can make things a lot stronger and more suitable. It is important to keep all your options open now and not to get locked in. There is more than one way you can beef up your bank account—and your ego. The lucky number today is 3.

***Tuesday, February 11 (Moon Pisces to Aries 6:21 p.m.)*** Don't let anyone fault you for not having all the information you need at your fingertips. Someone may be trying to trip you up. However, others may discover that an individual who acts in a surprising manner is merely trying to get your attention. Give it, because you may form a fascinating new relationship. Don't be shy in dealing with superiors or authority figures.

***Wednesday, February 12 (Moon in Aries)*** You should be feeling up rather than down today. In fact, most should experience a renewal of strength and vigor. Along with that goes excellent morale—and consequently excellent performance. Make sure the right people notice. With a lot less effort than you think, you could make a dream come true. Hang out with a Sagittarian or another Gemini.

***Thursday, February 13 (Moon in Aries)*** No matter how low your spirits may be, they will receive a boost today. One possible way is through a token of affection that comes from an unexpected source. Isn't it nice to know that somebody cares? Don't get edgy when someone wants to discuss a rather touchy subject; you can handle it with aplomb. The lucky number today is 6.

***Friday, February 14 (Moon Aries to Taurus 5:38 a.m.)*** Someone tries to strum your heartstrings today, but your logic should prevail. It's easy to get sentimental at a time like this, but if you don't see things the way they are, you will do yourself a disservice. Some will be delighted when a person from the past gets in touch and wants to renew old ties. Someone could confide a secret.

***Saturday, February 15 (Moon in Taurus)*** You probably will be most comfortable today behind the scenes— possibly even in isolation. If at all possible, get some private time and communicate only with yourself. There are certain things you must get clear in your mind if you are to attain your goals. Some should give time and attention to a friend or family member who is confined in some way. If you need help, someone will give it if you only give the signal.

**Sunday, February 16 (Moon Taurus to Gemini 5:17 p.m.)**    Some good news you hear today concerns someone else—but someone you care for. When you compare your situation with him/her, you should feel quite well off. You may not feel like revealing all your thoughts—or all your activities—and you shouldn't feel compelled to. Some things are better left unsaid. For some, a romantic liaison is heating up. The lucky number today is 9.

**Monday, February 17 (Moon in Gemini)**    Your recent tendency to brood vanishes completely as the moon moves into your sign. In fact, you may now have a tendency to be overly optimistic. Realize that, no matter how good things are, nothing is really going to happen unless you make it happen. That means you should plunge right in where a loved one is concerned and discuss a new course for the relationship. You may be surprised at how receptive your partner is. A Leo may play a prominent role today.

**Tuesday, February 18 (Moon in Gemini)**    Most should have a strong sense that they know where they are going now; intuition is an accurate guide. A sticky financial problem gets resolved in a most satisfactory manner. Some may even find they have more assets than they originally thought. Others will be making important plans in connection with where they really live. Both physically and emotionally.

**Wednesday, February 19 (Moon Gemini to Cancer 7:39 a.m.)**    Timing and luck are on your side and you should take full advantage of them. That means, don't turn down any invitations—even if they sound as if they mean work. The demands that are made on you will be returned fourfold. A lot of you will be feeling very popular and your need for social activity should be satisfied.

*Thursday, February 20 (Moon in Cancer)*    It isn't often that you get a second chance to right something that went wrong. Take full advantage of it. Start to get your act together by lining up your facts and getting all your thoughts in order. That way you won't get caught offguard when an excellent opportunity comes your way. Don't neglect some small debts that could prove annoying if you don't take care of them immediately. The lucky number is 4.

*Friday, February 21 (Moon Cancer to Leo 3:25 p.m.)* Here it comes—the chance to make a big change in your life. The area could be love or it could be money, but either way you stand to gain. Realize that you can be very persuasive when you try—and when your arguments carry real authority with them. That means you cannot rely on flimsy facts. Even if nothing so dramatic occurs in a particular Gemini's life today, it is a significant date. Get your ideas on paper for future use.

*Saturday, February 22 (Moon in Leo)*    You should be back to your old Gemini self today, full of humor and a willingness to exchange ideas. Even if you do not feel you are in a critical situation, it is important to speak clearly and to moderate your tone. A diplomatic approach can get you almost anything you want now. You also can find a genuine bargain if you look around a little bit.

*Sunday, February 23 (Moon Leo to Virgo 11:58 p.m.)* You may not be altogether happy with today's turn of events. Ask yourself, "Do I feel left out?" You may discover that you are simply being petulant and a bit childish. Your day will come; others deserve the limelight now. Don't scatter your forces by getting involved a little bit in a lot of things. Give some of them "benign neglect." Let a Pisces show you how to relax.

**Monday, February 24 (Moon in Virgo)**     This month's full moon falls smack in your center of emotional security—the place where you really live. That means you could experience some kind of upheaval in your domestic sphere; you can handle it if you let your good rational mind take over. On the other hand, some will find an opportunity to advance themselves and do some self promoting. All relationships—particularly the personal kind—are under the moon's influences. They could grow stronger, or suffer a few bad moments. Realize that it is only temporary. The lucky number is 8.

**Tuesday, February 25 (Moon in Virgo)**     Know that when something is over it's over. Don't overstay your welcome or linger longer than is necessary. Take away with you a sense of accomplishment. Some will be dealing with an older or more prestigious individual who is impressed by your dedication and sincerity. Don't let him/her down. A special occasion may be coming up and you should remember to remember it in a special way. If you don't, someone may fault you.

**Wednesday, February 26 (Moon Virgo to Libra 4:07 a.m.)**     Now you should feel you are out of the woods and more able to be your freewheeling Gemini self. Have fun, but also spend some serious time on serious questions. Realize you need explicit answers and don't let anyone get away with anything. If you keep on a straight course, all will go well. Relationships could get quite electric now; realize it and do not flirt with danger.

**Thursday, February 27 (Moon in Libra)**     Be aware that you run the risk of thinking with your heart instead of your head now. That means your emotions could dominate your logic, but as long as you know it you should be able to protect yourself. On the positive side, your intuition is strong and you should be able to sense what is exactly the right thing to do. Don't get sentimental; the key is to act in your own best interest. The lucky number today is 2.

*Friday, February 28 (Moon Libra to Scorpio 7:06 a.m.)*    Get set for change, variety, and a lot of creative activity. Some could experience a real stroke of luck—even winning a contest. Realize that you are particularly intriguing to members of the opposite sex now; use your attractiveness intelligently. If you wish, you can have your pick. Make sure that you pick wisely—and do not dabble with anyone's emotions. Have a ball with a Sagittarian or another Gemini. The lucky number is 3.

## MARCH 1986

*Saturday, March 1 (Moon in Scorpio)*    You may suddenly be struck between the eyes by a startling fact that previously escaped your attention. Don't panic; use it to your best advantage. For all, this is a day to locate loopholes and close them. There are ways you can correct past errors and make a whole new beginning. The key is to keep all your senses alert and not to miss a trick.

*Sunday, March 2 (Moon Scorpio to Sagittarius 9:51 a.m.)*    An important relationship could be tested now. Someone may want to discuss practical issues, and you should not try to avoid them. Sometimes you do not love responsibility, but you are intelligent enough to know that without it there can be no meeting of the minds. You can make concessions without abandoning your principles. Some will meet a stimulating new person who is absolutely inspiring in terms of getting you to think about what you really can do. Don't let the moment pass.

*Monday, March 3 (Moon in Sagittarius)*    Once again you may have to give rather than get in a relationship. This is one time patience is truly a virtue; also realize that time is on your side. Some may be considering a new important relationship—a business partnership or marriage. Make sure you know who you are dealing with—that means, investigate your own motives as well as those of your opposite number. Talk it over with a serious type like a Taurus or a Scorpio. The lucky number is 6.

*Tuesday, March 4 (Moon Sagittarius to Capricorn 12:56 p.m.)* Don't let anyone force you into anything you are not ready for. Your worst course now would be premature action. As you refuse to move, take time to see others in a realistic light. It is possible you are being conned. Become thoroughly familiar with your legal rights—and your moral ones. Someone is working in your behalf, though it is in a quiet discreet manner.

*Wednesday, March 5 (Moon in Capricorn)* You've got more information now and should be able to plot out the wisest course. You may also find it necessary to make a commitment; but you should be ready—and armed with a sense of self-protectiveness. Some may find their finances are better than they thought. You see what can be accomplished through cooperation. The lucky number today is 8.

*Thursday, March 6 (Moon Capricorn to Aquarius 4:42 p.m.)* The most important message you get today is that old ways of doing things will not work; you've got to break new ground and get more experimental. You can get beyond this hurdle if you keep your mind open. For many, love is very much in the air and the key to success is to communicate. If you don't let others know how you feel, nothing can happen. Keep your eye on an Aries who might want to edge you out of the way.

*Friday, March 7 (Moon in Aquarius)* Now you are off and running—in an exciting new direction. The moon's position highlights adventure and romance. If you are a little confused by recent events and unable to see a pattern, realize that you are the only one who can create a new status quo. It may be scarey, but it is necessary. And it is more than possible for you. Fight for what you want.

*Saturday, March 8 (Moon Aquarius to Pisces 7:48 p.m.)* Your best course today is to retire from company and commune only with yourself. You may find some of the answers you seek. If that is not possible, seek out someone who has played a "teacher" in the past. While in the real world today you will find yourself dealing with some rather unusual people and grappling with some fascinating new concepts. It is excellent for your self-development. On a more mundane level, you may get what you want by following through on a hunch.

*Sunday, March 9 (Moon in Pisces)* It's a big surprise when someone you thought was totally uninterested in you now comments and wants to get involved in your activities. And your aspirations. He/she could be helpful, but you should also keep your own counsel when it comes to certain matters. Someone may be trying to play you like a violin. It is important to try to come back down to earth today and deal with the familiar; as much as you would like to be visionary, realize that you must also be practical.

*Monday, March 10 (Moon in Pisces)* This month's emphasis on accomplishment and professional activity is no accident; that is where the new moon falls in your chart now. On the positive side, you should be feeling strong enough to try some new things to improve your position. However, you may also not be feeling that much like making the effort. Remember, it is up to you—but you can't complain later on if you do not make your move now. For some, a conversation with someone out of the area or out of touch helps clarify direction. Your best buddy now may be an Aquarian, a Taurean, or a Scorpio—any of whom can give you direction.

*Tuesday, March 11 (Moon Pisces to Aries 5:03 a.m.)* You should be feeling off the hook now, but even more public than you have been in recent days. One of your fondest desires is coming close to fulfillment, and you should take care not to blow your chances. Chance-taking is highly likely for you now, and you may be in the mood for some special excitement. If you must get carried away, do it with another Gemini or a Sagittarian. A Virgo may try to dampen your enthusiasm.

**Wednesday, March 12 (Moon in Aries)**    Some Geminis may be the object of a surprise event that someone puts together in an effort to show how much you are loved and adored. No matter what your mood, express your appreciation and enthusiasm. Others may experience this day as one in which the urge to redecorate or remodel becomes paramount. The subject could be your own home or your own wardrobe or personal image. Enjoy the urge to splurge, but keep things in perspective. Take a Taurus or a Libra along to give you advice on good taste. The lucky number is 6.

**Thursday, March 13 (Moon Aries to Taurus 3:04 p.m.)**    Most will welcome the change of routine when it comes along today; few Geminis can stand the status quo very long. As you get out and about, you should get a sense of how many friends you have and how valued your opinions are. Some will learn a secret about someone and it is one you should keep. It should also make you resolve never to be the one to throw the first stone. In this and any situation that arises today, attempt to be mature.

**Friday, March 14 (Moon in Taurus)**    You may be feeling rather deflated today, and it could be a result of yesterday's excesses. Even if you did not overdrink or overdo, you may have had just a bit too much of the world. Retire within yourself now and try to relieve the emotional pressure. You will emerge much stronger as a result of the experience of confronting the self you may not like that much. Spend some time thinking about or visiting a person who very much needs help and support.

**Saturday, March 15 (Moon in Taurus)**    Today you should be feeling much more in sync with the world and in tune with yourself. In fact, you should be able to accomplish something by completing a job you've been puttering away at for a while. Suddenly fewer people will be on your back, and more will be giving you credit for what you can do. Seriously consider a proposition someone makes today for a joint effort. It could be just the thing you need now. The lucky number is 9.

***Sunday, March 16 (Moon in Gemini)*** With the moon completely in your sign now, you should have a fresh start feeling and the courage of your convictions should be returning. Depending on your situation, love could play a major role. Whether it is a new love or a long-standing relationship, you will be able to cut through a lot of emotional talk and get right to what is bothering both of you. The end of the day is much happier than the beginning.

***Monday, March 17 (Moon in Gemini)*** What a great way to start the week! Put on your brightest and prepare to act accordingly; if you feel anything but optimistic, you are missing the influence of the moon in your sign. Even if there are nagging worries, cast them off and prepare to go directly toward what you really want. Most will be able to discover a loss or at least restore stability to their situation. Trust your judgment—and someone who extends a hand to you. He/she deserves your trust.

***Tuesday, March 18 (Moon Gemini to Cancer 4:04 p.m.)*** Okay, now catch your breath, relax, slow down. Now you can catch up with personal matters and other concerns which seem neglected; however, not everything is completely calm. You could find yourself with two different views and unable to choose a correct path. The important thing is to keep your plans flexible and realize a major opportunity is on the horizon. The lucky number is 3 today.

***Wednesday, March 19 (Moon in Cancer)*** A recently tight cash flow may now be relaxed. Money is definitely the issue today, and the influences are positive. For

many, a frustrating roadblock is removed and it should
be a cause for celebration. Don't avoid a frank discussion which is frankly inevitable; it will clear the air and
restore a sense of balance—both for you and the other
party involved.

**Thursday, March 20 (Moon in Cancer)**    Don't jump
at the first offer someone makes you today; you should
continue to look around. There are a lot of opportunities, and your wisest course is to be selective. Ignore an
urge to be frivolous where you should be practical. A
dramatic scene may be unavoidable but by keeping cool
you can keep it in proportion. Do admit that your
opposite number has cause to be emotional.

**Friday, March 21 (Moon Cancer to Leo 2:38 a.m.)**
Everything you need should be at your fingertips
today; you have no excuse for procrastinating. Be as
thorough as possible, and don't let anything slip between the cracks. You may get some favorable news of
a financial nature. You may also get a chance to display
your excellent sense of humor—and thereby save what
could be a rather tense situation. Don't hesitate to ask
questions and expect the right answers.

**Saturday, March 22 (Moon in Leo)**    You could have
fun experimenting today, but you could overextend
yourself by scattering your efforts. Try to zero in on
the things that would be most fun—and most profitable. Some run the risk of falling prey to a fast-talking
individual. Be curious, but not gulliable. No one should
listen to "sweet nothings" without a bit of skepticism.

**Sunday, March 23 (Moon Leo to Virgo 9:39 a.m.)**
This day should find your feeling stronger and more
confident—or at least surrounded by supportive people. There is no need to be intimidated by anyone.
Those who are feeling financially insecure should make
a careful review of the balance sheet; things may not be
as bad as you suppose. It may be your accounting
procedures need some redoing. For many, a family
reunion is the best way to boost morale.

*Monday, March 24 (Moon in Virgo)*     Don't let anyone attempt to invade your territorial rights; be aware of what is yours and be ready to protect it. For some, the challenge will be not to make a compromise where quality is concerned. If you can't have the best, don't have anything at all. That is not snobbery—it is practicality. Others may find their integrity is at stake, and should act accordingly. This rough period will pass.

*Tuesday, March 25 (Moon Virgo to Libra 1:22 p.m.)* This is "new deal" day. Suddenly you have the upper hand again, and can call the shots. One of the reasons is that you are confident that you have allies. Let others know it. Be very careful not to buy or sell anything without a professional appraisal; you are not always the best judge of that. The lucky number today is 1.

*Wednesday, March 26 (Moon in Libra)*     This full moon could be a positively glorious one for you—full of excitement and a variety of new experiences. However, some Geminis should take care not to be carried away. Let your inner feelings serve as your guide, and you will remain afloat despite confusion. There will be many diversions and you should enjoy them; just be sure you do not lose your sense of direction altogether. Know that you are the winner in the end.

*Thursday, March 27 (Moon Libra to Scorpio 3:05 p.m.)*     Some may be experiencing "full-moon hangover." Others may realize that a change of pace is necessary and buckle down to the here and now. Show that your sense of humor is good enough to laugh at your own little foibles; you will will be amazed at how much stock this buys you with someone you admire. If you have the time, devote some energy to a creative pursuit. It's an excellent way to recover from "the nerves."

*Friday, March 28 (Moon in Scorpio)*     It will probably be a relief today to find that you must deal with practical affairs, details, perhaps even some temporary restriction. Even Gemini sometimes desires quiet. The privacy you seek now has nothing to do with loneliness, and you should know it. Spend some time thinking about how you can improve your general health and vitality. That may mean giving up something, but you should be willing to do it.

***Saturday, March 29 (Moon Scorpio to Sagittarius 4:20 p.m.)*** A message—most likely a written one—comes in today and gives you great encouragement. Even if it is a small thing, you should take heart from it. Some will find that it is an excellent time to speak out frankly to someone you know has your best interests at heart. A compromise can be struck, and you can feel less threatened than you do now. Gemini does not like to think deeply too often, but this is one time you should examine what is really going on in your inner depths. There lies the clue as to how you should proceed. The lucky number today is 5.

***Sunday, March 30 (Moon in Sagittarius)*** Your mood should be mellow today if you followed your heart yesterday. That means you should be willing to give in to someone new and dear who desperately wants something. You lose nothing by saying "Yes," and you have everything to gain. Some will be pleased and surprised when they receive a compliment or more tangible expression of confidence. All should be willing to go along with those around them who suggest some budget revisions. It is possible to tighten up without strapping yourself entirely.

***Monday, March 31 (Moon Sagittarius to Capricorn 6:25 p.m.)*** It isn't always easy to see the other side of the story; but you will make your life a lot easier now by doing so. Even though you are convinced you are right, there is no point in holding out. In fact, the moon position dictates that you should be the one to go more than halfway. Some should take care to steer clear of some sensation gossip and startling accusations. You could find yourself smack in the middle of a rather messy situation. Remain above it, and take your fun with an easygoing Pisces or a practical Virgo. The lucky number today is 7.

# APRIL 1986

**Tuesday, April 1 (Moon in Capricorn)**    This is definitely a day to keep all your options open; don't box yourself in whatever you do. Some may be experiencing a new attitude towards their work in this world; ambition may be stirring where before there was an indifferent attitude. Take advantage of your change of heart and take some positive steps toward putting yourself in a better place than you are now. Others should take great care to unravel a rather garbled message that comes in now. You could easily misinterpret it. The lucky number is 5.

**Wednesday, April 2 (Moon Capricorn to Aquarius 10:11 p.m.)**    Where yesterday your job was the focus, it is very possible that today your thoughts are very much home, in every sense of the world. There may be a surprise in connection with the real feelings of someone who shares that home with you. It doesn't have to be a dull day, but there will be demands on your time for a fair number of routine matters; treat yourself to something nice to alleviate the boredom if you feel it. The lucky number today is 6.

**Thursday, April 3 (Moon in Aquarius)**    Someone may drop a hot potatoe in your lap today; you might want to pass it right on to someone else. There is a scheme in the air that you should count yourself out of. Some could get carried away with their own self-importance today; be realistic about what you can do and where you fit into the picture. Take some time out to explore your own "inner space." If a call comes in that settles a dispute, don't be surprised.

**Friday, April 4 (Moon in Aquarius)**    Both your emotions and your actions should be clear and well directed today; you could be exceptionally productive as a result. Apply some of your reason to a romantic relationship that may be getting off the track. A calm, cool discussion should clarify things and make both parties feel more secure. The lucky number today is 8.

***Saturday, April 5 (Moon Aquarius to Pisces 4:03 a.m.)*** Don't hesitate to take the hard line with someone who is blocking your path; if you are too soft, you will never be able to get over or around this hurdle. Sometimes it's necessary just to end things and say "That's that." Once again you should be able to accomplish brilliant things—if only in your small sphere. Something happens that raises your stock with others. Take advantage of your new prestige.

***Sunday, April 6 (Moon in Pisces)*** Finally, you are being appreciated! Realize this would not have happened if you had not taken that first step. No matter what your situation, you should have a more constructive outlook than in the recent past. Someone near and dear—possibly a romantic partner—flashes the green light and you can go full speed ahead. The lucky number is 1.

***Monday, April 7 (Moon Pisces to Aries 12:12 p.m.)*** You may be particularly "wired" today; that means, steer clear of a possible confrontation. Even if you really do know more than the other person, realize you are not going to get anywhere now. Wait it out and things will improve. Spend some time helping out someone who needs the benefit of your greater knowledge; it's a good feeling to learn by teaching. Trust those vibes you get from a situation; they are most likely right.

***Tuesday, April 8 (Moon in Aries)*** This should be a much lighter day, in every sense of the word. Some slight depression you might have been feeling vanishes with the swing in your moon cycle. You should be bubbling with good spirits—accept an invitation where you can show off your marvelous sense of humor. A stroke of luck is possible now, in money or love—possibly both. A Sagittarian could be an excellent companion today. The lucky number is 3.

*Wednesday, April 9 (Moon Aries to Taurus 10:36 p.m.)*    Don't get overconfident about something you think you know very well; if you don't check your facts, you could get tricked up. And it would be a shame to ruin such a good day. Try talking someone into something today; you may be amazed at how easily you get your way. Some may even have a wish come true. Good companions today would be a Scorpio, a Leo, or an Aquarian. One of them may figure prominently even if you do not seek him/her out. The lucky number today is 4.

*Thursday, April 10 (Moon in Taurus)*    Get set for a puzzling but possibly intriguing day. Something is going on and you get some clues about it; if you are tempted to dig further, do so. You may feel like a snoop, but this is one time you are justified. Some will feel like retiring from the scene and trying to figure out exactly where they stand on important issues. It is a wise idea.

*Friday, April 11 (Moon in Taurus)*    You could be tempted to splurge in some way today—your wisest course is to keep your checkbook closed. Shop, but do not buy. Some may be thinking about moving, and a likely new spot could be found today. For others, the urge to splurge may be in the goodies department; remember that you promised to watch your weight.

*Saturday, April 12 (Moon Taurus to Gemini 10:51 a.m.)*    The day may start out a bit slowly but you can expect the pace to pick up later on. The reason is the moon is really into your sign and it's difficult to live an absolutely quiet life at that time. In fact, a delay you experience is merely temporary and you should use the time to get your second wind; a lot more will be going on. Don't get carried away by your first impression of someone; if you are realistic, you will see that he/she is a talker rather than a doer. You don't need any more deadwood. Watch your weight again!

*Sunday, April 13 (Moon in Gemini)*    This should be a superexcellent day for you, Gemini! Not only is the moon in your sign, but you have the advantage of a "free day" on top of it. Feel free to do all the wheeling and dealing you like today, because you are most likely to be successful. At least you'll be noticed! Enjoy, and keep it all in perspective. Even though it seems like it today, remember that you don't always get what you want.

*Monday, April 14 (Moon Gemini to Cancer 11:42 p.m.)*    Don't be intimidated by someone who wants to trim your wings; realize that you can soar as high as you like now. And realize that others may be envious. Don't be satisfied with your own status quo; show how inventive you can really be and you can count on the fact that you will receive points for it. Get in touch with someone you're feeling a bit sentimental about. He/she would love to hear from you.

*Tuesday, April 15 (Moon in Cancer)*    Money could be very much on your mind today, but it should be bringing you positive thoughts around this time. If that is not the case, realize you can do something about it—and today is an excellent day to start. There are ways that your money—no matter how little you have—can make more money. Some will rejoice when the lost is found. In the personal area, it is essential to be absolutely honest today. That applies particularly to your relationships. No little Gemini tricks!

*Wednesday, April 16 (Moon in Cancer)*    What a relief! Finally the pieces of the puzzle are beginning to fall into place, and you are losing that "all at sea" feeling. However, some may feel they are being pulled in two directions at the same time. This is one of those times you should trust your intuition, and go with the thing or person you have the best gut feeling about. Just make sure you have all the facts.

***Thursday, April 17 (Moon Cancer to Leo 11:10 a.m.)***
You may be feeling the results of too much of a
good thing. The last few days have been rather hectic,
and you may have to make an effort to pull together
your scattered forces. Time is still on your side, however, so make the most of it. Somebody may say, "You
owe me one," and you should take the remark seriously. That means, grant their request. In the midst of
a lot of activities, some may experience a kind of spiritual revelation. It is important to record it.

***Friday, April 18 (Moon in Leo)***    Okay, now it's
time to get organized. That may mean reorganizing
something—but you don't have to do it alone. A quiet
person will be right there at your side and you should
express your gratitude. Some may have to deal with a
detour that seems to throw the day out of whack: don't
worry, you can recover. Others will experience the satisfaction of having their views proven to be correct.

***Saturday, April 19 (Moon Leo to Virgo 7:24 p.m.)***
Easy does it today. That means, steer clear of a hot
topic that could lead to a heated argument. Let things
roll off your back as Gemini is often able to do. A light
touch and sense of humor are desirable; a close scrutiny of someone's motives is essential. Write things down.
Let another Gemini or Sagittarian play witness. The
lucky number is 5.

***Sunday, April 20 (Moon in Virgo)***    Don't take anything for granted today. Something that looks A-OK
on the surface may have a shakey foundation. Some
may be literally dealing with home repairs; others will
deal in less tangible areas. The point is in either case
to follow through on instruction and make sure you are
interpreting them correctly. It's possible that an old
debt will be repaid now.

***Monday, April 21 (Moon Virgo to Libra 11:50 p.m.)***
Once again you may have to plumb the depths of a
situation to make sure there are no flaws. The more
attention you pay now, the more secure you will be in

the future. In another matter, be aware that someone wants something for nothing. If you play the "good guy," you are likely to be shortchanged. Protect your assets and keep your eyes open. Check in with an analytical Virgo.

**Tuesday, April 22 (Moon in Libra)** Someone may throw you the reins today and say, "Take charge." You should be very much up for it. Whatever you do, you will flirt with pleasure today. For some that means actual sexual physical attraction. The romantic mood is everywhere and so is a desire for variety. As long as you know it, you are safe. The lucky number is 8.

**Wednesday, April 23 (Moon in Libra)** Once again love is in the air. That includes all kinds, meaning TLC and affection are also part of the scene. Those who are involved with children should be particularly sensitive to their needs. Many will experience the relief of having a burden removed; you may say to yourself why did't I speak up sooner? Others will receive praise for a "good deed."

**Thursday, April 24 (Moon Libra to Scorpio 1:15 a.m.)** This is a tricky full moon for Gemini. Some of you may experience an upheaval that means all bets are off and all plans are canceled. Some basic premises may be shaken. Whatever you do, do not panic. Realize that others who share your concerns are right there with you and will cooperate. You will come smiling through if you keep your wits about you. Be very careful of some devious activity that may be going on around you.

**Friday, April 25 (Moon in Scorpio)** Today someone steps in and helps you pick up the pieces and reorganize your plans. In fact, some may start a whole new routine—and be grateful for it. Many will experience an inkling about a future event or situation; this is one time you may actually be clairvoyant. Use your foreknowledge. The lucky number today is 2.

**Saturday, April 26 (Moon Scorpio to Sagittarius 1:16 a.m.)** Whatever you do today, make it a twosome.

Relationships and partnerships of all kinds are emphasized and joint efforts should go very smoothly. You will feel very curious about something and tempted to experiment. Go ahead! Some may have a new awareness of their physical image and feel like making some changes. It is an excellent time to do so. Remember a special anniversary.

**Sunday, April 27 (Moon in Sagittarius)**   Don't stir up trouble today; keep a low profile. It is possible there are storm clouds on the horizon. The most productive thing you could do today is reevaluate something you've already done; you may have to go back to square one and start all over again. It's worth the effort. Your legal rights may be in question.

**Monday, April 28 (Moon Sagittarius to Capricorn 1:41 a.m.)**   Some information may come your way today that is a bit unsettling. However, you are much better off knowing the whole truth. It may mean you revise your opinion of someone or decide to take a very different course. A person who talks big may shake your confidence in yourself; don't let him/her intimidate you. Spend some time on your personal financial situation. It could be better.

**Tuesday, April 29 (Moon in Capricorn)**   Finally a disruptive element is eliminated and you feel much more "together." The sweet harmony could extend to the person closest to you. Someone pays you back—either in money or a favor—but immediately makes another request. Realize this will always be the case. Some will have a delightful romantic interlude that boosts morale. The lucky number today is 6.

**Wednesday, April 30 (Moon Capricorn to Aquarius 4:06 a.m.)**   If you are thnking lofty thoughts today, it is no accident—it is the moon position. Let your mind soar and take advantage of what it comes into contact with. It is definitely a day to learn something new. For some, that may mean experiencing a new culture in some way—possibly simply through a gourmet exotic meal. Open up and communicate with someone you've been a bit at odds with recently. The lucky number today is 7.

# MAY 1986

**_Thursday, May 1 (Moon in Aquarius)_**    It is essential to be diplomatic today if you are to avoid conflict with people around you. The battleground is most likely your domestic sphere. You are going to have to make a concession; realize it is the most practical thing to do under the circumstances. At least a final decision will be reached. Some will find themselves involved with a Taurus or a Scorpio who has a lot to say; listen. The lucky number today is 6.

**_Friday, May 2 (Moon Aquarius to Pisces 9:30 a.m.)_** Some may find themselves feeling disillusioned or deserted today. Realize it is a feeling and that your real situation does not reflect it. As a matter of fact, ask yourself if you are merely feeling sorry for yourself. Some may be getting involved in an underground arrangement; Geminis are often excellent illusionists, so you should be able to get away with it.

**_Saturday, May 3 (Moon in Pisces)_**    You're going to have to accept some added responsibility now but you should realize that the end result will be a better situation for you. Remember that you get back what you give out, so try to maintain a positive attitude. Things are definitely improving and you will feel happier and more prosperous soon. You will be!

**_Sunday, May 4 (Moon Pisces to Aries 8:01 p.m.)_** This could be an unusually quiet day—especially for action-oriented Gemini. However, some will finish off a large project and feel greatly relieved. Others may be considering whether or not to end an important association; get some advice from someone who knows this kind of situation. Your resolve to be more ambitious could pay off.

***Monday, May 5 (Moon in Aries)***     Off you go into the workweek full of pioneering spirit. Good for you—it's an excellent time to make a new start or start down a new road. Soften up with someone who expresses affection; it's okay to make yourself vulnerable. Many will be particularly persuasive today and should be able to swing others over to their side. A wish may soon be a reality.

***Tuesday, May 6 (Moon in Aries)***     You've got that "take charge" feeling today, and you should use it to the fullest. Remind yourself that you are in charge of your own destiny and can call the shots your way. That does not mean, however, that you should ride rough-shod over others. Use your energy to penetrate right to the heart of a rather confusing situation, one which you can be the one to straighten out. The lucky number today is 2.

***Wednesday, May 7 (Moon Aries to Taurus 4:59 a.m.)*** The social pace is definitely picking up and you are in a position to make a lot of new contacts now. If you are your curious Gemini self, so much the better, because there is a lot of extra information to be obtained. Don't get so carried away with the party atmosphere that you forget your resolutions about health and diet. You know you can very easily run yourself down.

***Thursday, May 8 (Moon in Taurus)***     Some one may confide his/her feelings today and you must be prepared to deal with them. That means you cannot simply clam up. Some will experience a breakthrough, even if it is only a mental one. In fact, it is possible to have a real revelation now that erases a lot of doubts and fears. You are right to be hopeful about the future. The lucky number is 4.

***Friday, May 9 (Moon Taurus to Gemini 5:26 p.m.)*** Don't hesitate to be frank and open with someone; you may have to "draw pictures" to get this person to understand. It's possible to get a new chance to fix up a situation or a relation where you goofed the first time. Some of you may find yourselves reunited with loved ones. All should realize that more is going on behind the scenes than they are aware of. It is positive for you.

***Saturday, May 10 (Moon in Gemini)***  Here you go off into your excellent Gemini moon. Your timing should be a lot better and your personality should absolutely sparkle. Things at home should go a lot more smoothly than in the recent past; there may even be a whole new arrangement. The tide is definitely going your way. Share your luck with a Taurus or a Libra.

***Sunday, May 11 (Moon in Gemini)***  Now you are beginning to get the answers you've wanted for so long. And you will be able to confront the person who has been avoiding you. Do it with a smile. An opportunity to display your talents may come along; take advantage of it because there is more here than meets the eye. Some may be offered a new deal and should accept it. Just read the fine print. The lucky number is 7.

***Monday, May 12 (Moon Gemini to Cancer 6:18 a.m.)*** Your emotions should be stabilizing now and the result should be a calm secure feeling. Among the good things that happen today is your receiving access to someone who has been hard to see. It could mean an increase in income. Check out your financial situation with a canny Cancer or a Capricorn. The lucky number is 8.

***Tuesday, May 13 (Moon in Cancer)***  Once again you should have that nice warm feeling. For some it will come through being asked to solve a problem—and having someone express absolute faith in your ability to do so. However, if someone shares a confidence, vow to keep it secret. In another area you should be absolutely direct and say "I'll do it." You definitely are the one for the job.

***Wednesday, May 14 (Moon Cancer to Leo 6:15 p.m.)*** Your willingness to try a new approach really pays off now. Trust your judgment when you are asked to make a decision; know that you will be in the right place at the right time. You may be exuding confidence now, but you should take care not to be overbearing. The lucky number is 1 today.

**Thursday, May 15 (Moon in Leo)**    A seemingly unimportant invitation could lead to something big; accept it immediately. You can easily live by your wits today and score a lot of points in the process. Just don't overuse your sense of humor and play the clown. Some may start planning a trip or receive an unexpected visitor. Be cordial.

**Friday, May 16 (Moon in Leo)**    You may experience a sudden urge to toss out everything you own and start all over again. It's possible your closets may need some revamping, but don't go overboard. Realize that spending money is not always the cure for a touch of the blues. Realize you have more options than are apparent at the moment. In all things, this is the time to choose quality over quantity. Take off for some fun with some other Gemini or a Sagittarian. The lucky number is 3.

**Saturday, May 17 (Moon Leo to Virgo 3:45 a.m.)** Your spirits should be better—especially when someone has a change of heart that affects you in a positive way. Many will have pressures relieved and actually feel like celebrating. Rights of possession may be an issue today; don't be greedy! Double-check your facts in a tricky financial matter.

**Sunday, May 18 (Moon in Virgo)**    If you handled things right yesterday, there should be smooth sailing today. However, you must be careful not to let a pleasant change of ideas deteriorate into a messy argument. Don't be so opinionated! Also realize that someone has your best interests at heart when he/she speaks out and gives you advice. Have a frank talk.

**Monday, May 19 (Moon Virgo to Libra 9:41 a.m.)** Okay, so it's necessary to make an adjustment. Don't make a big deal of it. Instead, do your bit to brighten up the atmosphere—possibly even by spending some money on a gift. You may be mingling with a Taurus or a Scorpio—either of whom could teach you some new twists on an old subject. Many will feel like indulging in a gourmet meal.

**Tuesday, May 20 (Moon in Libra)** You are really gullible, but this is one time you must protect yourself. You are usually able to analyze what you hear; this time, really pick it apart. There's an aura of excitement about this day and some may find themselves irresistably attracted to a new sensation. Just remember you never get something for nothing. The lucky number is 7.

**Wednesday, May 21 (Moon Libra to Scorpio 12:02 p.m.)** There may be nothing you desire more than a change of scenery. However, realize that you can never walk away from a problem. It will simply go with you. Some may experience confusion today over meeting times and schedules. Don't let it ruin your day. Some may be encouraged to adopt a whole new policy; be willing to go along. The lucky number is 8.

**Thursday, May 22 (Moon in Scorpio)** Stick to the job at hand; you probably won't have much choice. Some basic things need doing before you can goof off and feel justified in doing so. Some may miss out on an opportunity but should not let it get them down. This is merely a delay—you'll get a second chance later on. Don't overlook someone who could be very helpful to you in your job or career. The lucky number is 9.

**Friday, May 23 (Moon Scorpio to Sagittarius 11:57 a.m.)** This month's full moon falls in an area of relationships and partnerships for Gemini. You may find more people relying on you than usual; don't let them down. Even if you feel you need emotional support as well. You will get it. It is an excellent time to open up and express your feelings and your desires to a member of the opposite sex. One could be a Leo or an Aquarian.

**Saturday, May 24 (Moon in Sagittarius)**   Once again the emphasis is on others—what is theirs versus what is yours. It is also an excellent time to join forces—even to marry. No matter what else happens today let others express their views; be a good listener and do not force issues. The lucky number today is 2.

**Sunday, May 25 (Moon Sagittarius to Capricorn 11:15 a.m.)**   Some kind of confusion is highly possible today, and you should know it in advance. That means don't take anything at face value and don't box yourself in. You may have to suddenly turn on a dime. Some may be feeling a bit run down and in need of R&R. Make sure you get it. A Sagittarian could be very prominent on the scene today.

**Monday, May 26 (Moon in Capricorn)**   Be willing to pay attention to some rather technical terms that someone throws your way. A lot could depend on your understanding of them. It's most important to be aware of all your rights as well as your restrictions. Don't get sentimental when someone asks you for a favor; you could end up giving a lot and getting absolutely nothing. Some may be contemplating signing a lease or some other kind of legal paper; read everything carefully.

**Tuesday, May 27 (Moon Capricorn to Aquarius 12:00 noon)**   Your creative ideas should be coming like crazy now, and you should be able to impress others with your own special style. Never let it be said that you imitated anyone but yourself. Some quick changes may be the order of the day, but they should provide interest and variety. Some should force themselves to put things in writing. It's easy to be misunderstood when you don't. The lucky number today is 5.

**Wednesday, May 28 (Moon in Aquarius)**   Many may find themselves smack in the middle of a discussion about a move—meaning a change of residence. Or possibly an additional home. Even if you think nothing is possible now, take things seriously and give things your undivided attention. There is a lot you can learn now, even if you are not able to put it to good use till later on. Many will find love and romance is definitely in bloom. Don't let it wither.

**Thursday, May 29 (Moon Aquarius to Pisces 3:54 p.m.)**     Even Gemini can be discreet when he/she tries. Someone may tempt you to divulge personal information about someone else, and you should not give in to this test. Show how honorable you can be. Don't get involved in any kind of scheme—especially the get-rich-quick variety. Do everything necessary to clarify some rather fuzzy statements someone has made to you.

**Friday, May 30 (Moon in Pisces)**     This could be an excellent day for advancement on the job. In fact, someone could offer you the opportunity to take on a whole new set of responsibilities. Realize it is an honor, no matter what happens. Isn't it nice to be recognized? All should be rather productive now and have the opportunity to increase their visibility in a positive way. The lucky number is 8.

**Saturday, May 31 (Moon Pisces to Aries 11:43 p.m.)** You may have to forgive and forget now; don't take a hard line. The more generous you are and willing to patch things up, the happier you will be. You certainly do not like apparent dissension. Some will find yourselves in a position to reach more people with your message. Take full advantage of the situation. Don't hang back; this is no time to be shy.

# JUNE 1986

**Sunday, June 1 (Moon in Aries)**     Today you should be able to transform what is apparently a defeat into a rousing victory. Show that you can be a real fighter when the tide is against you. Some of you will have access to privileged information and should keep it to yourselves. Just be content to know a lot is going on behind the scenes. Even though this is not the most spectacular of days, a wish could come true in an unusual manner.

*Monday, June 2 (Moon in Aries)*     Now you get what you want—and that could include money. If it does, resolve to make good use of it. A relationship is getting a lot more serious and deepening in intensity; if it is what you want, rejoice. However, do not play with fire. Your powers of persuasion are good today and you could get some credit that is long overdue.

*Tuesday, June 3 (Moon Aries to Taurus 10:45 a.m.)* Be willing to let go of the past; it is nothing but a burden on you now. You can still maintain ties without having them tie you down. For some of you, an emotional wound is healing and you're beginning to feel whole again. Realize it is possible to fall in love again. Some will receive recognition today and should bask in the glow. The lucky number today is 9.

*Wednesday, June 4 (Moon in Taurus)*     If you think something big is about to happen, you are right. For many, it could be an important discovery or clarification of an area that has been shrouded in doubt and suspicion. This is one time you should not be afraid to express your feelings and go right to the heart of things. You will be out of the woods soon. A Leo could be very important today.

*Thursday, June 5 (Moon Taurus to Gemini 11:26 p.m.)*     If two different people are pulling you in two different directions, stick with the one you know is truly loyal. Don't be too trusting. The important thing is to keep your sense of self-worth intact and to clarify your sense of purpose. Do whatever makes you feel the most secure; don't flirt with intrigue now.

*Friday, June 6 (Moon in Gemini)*     You should sense a renewed vitality and even a burst of energy. With the moon in your sign, you can strut your stuff and take full advantage of whatever comes your way. That means, jump in and take the initiative when you see a gap. You can look like a hero—and be one. A lot of messages will be coming in now; be sure to decode them properly. The lucky number is 3.

**Saturday, June 7 (Moon in Gemini)**    With both the sun and the moon in Gemini, you are experiencing a personal "new moon." That should mean fresh starts, optimism, and renewed vigor. All of which should help you build something really solid now. Do not let this excellent day go by without making some positive step—even if it is a bit scarey. Refuse to be intimidated by others who may tell you you are overstepping your bounds. You are not.

**Sunday, June 8 (Moon Gemini to Cancer 12:15 p.m.)** There are definitely positive vibes around you now. You should be able to take a situation by storm. However, another situation, possibly a family reunion, be a bit more laid back. You don't need to star among those who love you the way they do. Your judgment is excellent now and you should not hesitate to trust it. The lucky number today is 5.

**Monday, June 9 (Moon in Cancer)**    If you followed your heart yesterday, today you will find that a loved one makes a major concession to you. The important thing is to be gracious about being the winner. Your money cycle is quite high now and you should have no difficulty funding your activities. However, remember that tomorrow is another day.

**Tuesday, June 10 (Moon in Cancer)**    Your position is still strong so you should not lose heart; you can renegotiate an agreement. Be sure to realize who is on your side and that you are not without allies. Some may find the focus is on bills and payments of all kinds. Even here, you should realize your position is stronger than you think. The lucky number today is 7.

**Wednesday, June 11 (Moon Cancer to Leo 12:11 a.m.)**    Past experience pays off today when you have to deal with a rather tricky and sticky situation. Keep your cool and learn even more from it. Your mind may be on a lot of different things, and you should attempt to narrow it down to the thing that most needs doing.

Some may be distracted by a new relationship gradually getting more serious.

**Thursday, June 12 (Moon in Leo)**    It's definitely a day to get out and get around; there's a lot of fun to be had, and for the most part Gemini likes nothing better. Your up mood should make you reach beyond your current expectations. Keep this sense of optimism on darker days. Some of you may find out that you have a secret admirer—or at least someone who's working behind the scene on their behalf. Someone might return a favor and it could be someone who's helped you before. Be doubly grateful. The lucky number today is 9.

**Friday, June 13 (Moon Leo to Virgo 10:18 a.m.)** There is a shake-up in the status quo today, but you are the winner. In fact, some who have been feeling trapped recently will have a lot more freedom. Keep the courage of your convictions and do not lose heart; there are even better things down the road. When someone says "You were right all along," take it graciously and do not gloat. A Leo or an Aquarian could figure big in the scenario today.

**Saturday, June 14 (Moon in Virgo)**    If you keep your sense of proportion, you will be able to rise above some petty differences that surface today. The way to handle things is to stick to the facts and put your reason to work. That way, you will be able to overcome the other person's emotionalism. There may be a question of territorial rights and what belongs to whom. You may have to remind someone of a long-standing arrangement. However, be willing to bend.

**Sunday, June 15 (Moon Virgo to Libra 5:38 p.m.)** This is an excellent day for the gathering of the clan. For many, there will be something to celebrate. For some, that might be a major new purchase, such as a home. For others, the scene is a bit different, but equally pleasurable. Gemini should play with Gemini today, or possibly a Sagittarian.

**Monday, June 16 (Moon in Libra)** Open your mouth and speak up for what you want. You can be much more convincing than you think. The key is to be as specific as possible and do not hedge about any of your opinions—even if they are controversial. For many there will be some kind of new experience or refreshing change. Don't hesitate to show how clever you can be.

**Tuesday, June 17 (Moon Libra to Scorpio 9:36 p.m.)** You may be tempted to be a sensationalist today; give in to it, as long as it doesn't spoil anything for you. One of your relationships could be in jeopardy. To avoid trouble, keep the lines of communication open and be willing to try some alternatives. If you overindulge yourself, you will shortchange someone else and kick yourself later. The lucky number is 5.

**Wednesday, June 18 (Moon in Scorpio)** This should be a cooler, calmer day. In fact, it may be a rather quiet one for normally gregarious Gemini. As you play the strong silent type, you find others relying on your judgment and letting them know you are respected. Maintain a close contact that is becoming a bit unglued. You can create harmonious atmosphere.

**Thursday, June 19 (Moon Scorpio to Sagittarius 10:36 p.m.)** You may experience an inner tension today that tempts you to find dangerous ways to relax. Stay away from them! If you do a little internal communication, you can renew your values and your sense of well-being. For some, the scenario could include the temptation to do something slightly underhanded. Stand tall for your principles. A Pisces could play a key role. The lucky number is 7.

**Friday, June 20 (Moon in Sagittarius)** You're going to have to protect your interests today through creative intelligent action. Don't do anything rash! The more responsible you are the better off you will be. Call your logic into play and calmly check out your rights. A

Cancer or a Capricorn could be extremely helpful in this regard.

**Saturday, June 21 (Moon Sagittarius to Capricorn 10:00 p.m.)** Start feeling the effects of tonight's full moon early in the day. For Gemini, this means a heightening of your ability to get your point across in a meaningful dramatic fashion. If you want to sell something, today is an excellent day to do it. Cooperative efforts of all kinds are favored, and that includes marriage. Your sexual urges could be particularly aroused.

**Sunday, June 22 (Moon in Capricorn)** Gemini may experience some particularly turbulent emotions under the current lunar position. They need not be disturbing; in fact, they could be absolutely sensational! However, it is important to be selective—to go for quality rather than quantity. For some, money is the big emotional issue and should be treated rationally. The lucky number is 1.

**Monday, June 23 (Moon Capricorn to Aquarius 9:50 p.m.)** The atmosphere lightens and Gemini feels more "at home." You should be able to rise above some minor obstacles that crop up in your path today; if you have the opportunity to pull a surprise, it will work in your favor. Someone comes through and proves his/her loyalty, and it gives you a nice warm feeling. Be careful to watch your diet and get proper rest. You want to look your best!

**Tuesday, June 24 (Moon in Aquarius)** Some could find themselves reunited with people they love and possibly have not seen in a while. All should feel the benefit of a change in routine and a sparky atmosphere. If you have the urge to get in touch with someone at a distance, give into it. The communication will be very beneficial.

**Wednesday, June 25 (Moon in Aquarius)** Something rather nebulous and hazy now takes solid form, and it is a relief to be able to look at the real thing. You should like it! Your Gemini curiosity will be piqued by something today, and you should investigate it. You may find yourself intrigued with a whole new subject—and in a whole new group of people. It is a day to be creative about everything, including love and romance. Put some zest back in your life. The lucky number is 4.

**_Thursday, June 26 (Moon Aquarius to Pisces 12:12 a.m.)_** If someone makes you a promise today, be sure to get it in writing. That goes double for people who get a vague hint about a possible promotion in the future. It may come out in a meaningful compliment from someone higher up. Don't miss the subtlety. All should be quite productive today and feel like getting in their and participating. Another Gemini, a Virgo, or a Sagittarian could lead to all kinds of good things. And a lot of excitement.

**_Friday, June 27 (Moon in Pisces)_** The way to get what you want is by being your sweet smiling self and exercising every bit of diplomatic talent you have. Do not give in to a fit of temper that threatens to work against you. Some will feel an increase in cash flow and along with it the desire to spend. Remember that a special anniversary is coming up and you should think about a special gift. The lucky number today is 6.

**_Saturday, June 28 (Moon Pisces to Aries 6:35 a.m.)_** If you kept your cool yesterday, things should be smooth and harmonious on the homefront now. Many will find themselves with greater freedom of action and the desire to do something interesting with it. Don't just scatter your interests and your energies; zero in on something potentially fulfilling—both emotionally and financially. Some will have a secret meeting that adds spice to the day—or evening.

**_Sunday, June 29 (Moon in Aries)_** A welcome change of pace wipes out any traces of down feelings you start the day with. It's nice to get a second wind. For some, an important relationship is getting to a critical stage; be confident it will go the way you want it. However, you must do your part—particularly by being absolutely frank and open with your partner. A Cancer or a Capricorn will provide excellent advice and support.

*Monday, June 30 (Moon Aries to Taurus 4:54 p.m.)* The week starts out on a rather low-key note, but you should feel a sense of expectancy—even the possibility that something very exciting is about to happen. At the very least, you will go up a notch in prestige today and experience the pleasure of being recognized in a positive way. It should prove to you that even if you try to hide, you are noticed. Some will complete an important project and want to plunge right into another. Give yourself a break for a while. The lucky number is 9.

# JULY 1986

*Tuesday, July 1 (Moon in Taurus)* Don't get bent out of shape when you have what is really a minor setback today; if you stand your ground this delay will eventually work out in your favor. Use this valuable time to gather your forces, get organized and straighten out your life in general. That goes doubly for a special relationship. Realize you are going to come out of this thing a lot stronger than you were when you went into it. The lucky number is 8.

*Wednesday, July 2 (Moon in Taurus)* You may still be stalled and doing a bit of nervous foot-tapping; don't despair because you are almost out of the woods. Once again the most productive thing you can do today is start getting all your ducks in a row and planning the future. Even though things are rather low-key, you can still make some very necessary contacts. You can come out from under the raps soon now. An Aries would be a good person to buddy with today.

*Thursday, July 3 (Moon Taurus to Gemini 5:32 a.m.)* There could be a spectacular and rather dramatic turn of events today. With things going in your direction, of course. At the very least, you are in for a top-notch time of it and should be able to pull off some cherished plans. Some will experience romantic vibes—and could even get carried away by a new romance. Don't hang back today, take the initiative. The lucky number is 1.

***Friday, July 4 (Moon in Gemini)*** Most should have the best July 4 in years; make the most of it. Some will be smacked in the middle of a display of family pyrotechnic; you are the one who should come to the rescue and cool everyone down. With a light touch you can ensure the fact that everyone comes out unscathed. It's an excellent day to follow your hunch about someone or something—your radar is working extremely well.

***Saturday, July 5 (Moon Gemini to Cancer 6:19 p.m.)*** For you at least, the holiday spirit is still in full swing. In fact, you could still feel so much like partying that you run the risk of burning yourself out. Don't end up like one of yesterday's fireworks. Some of you will get smart and start pulling in the rein where food, drink, and excesses of other kinds are concerned.

***Sunday, July 6 (Moon in Cancer)*** One smart way to work off excessive nervous energy is via a shopping spree. You should be able to grab off some great stuff at good prices. Keep alert when you pick up a piece of conversation; someone drops a hint you could find valuable. Resist an urge to "pig out" on rich foods by working out with some mildly strenuous exercise. You'll feel a lot better.

***Monday, July 7 (Moon in Cancer)*** You generally like to have more of everything than you need; this is one day you may have to make do with what is available. That could mean money. Use your smarts and you will be able to make it stretch and go as far as you need to make it go. Some of you may receive a love letter—it may not be a class one, but it should warm your heart. Catch up on calls and other kinds of interpersonal correspondence. All should try to get their ideas across now. The lucky number is 5.

**Tuesday, July 8 (Moon Cancer to Leo 5:56 a.m.)** The natives are definitely restless today. There is dissatisfaction with things the way they are, and you may be called upon to change them. Your best course is to remain open-minded and be willing to give in—even if it goes counter to your own interests. Some may be actually contemplating a change of residence—or even of live-in status. Don't walk out on a good thing before you think it over carefully.

**Wednesday, July 9 (Moon in Leo)** Now you are going to have to put up or shut up. At the very least, you are going to have to make yourself absolutely clear and define terms. Some fuzzy communication has been the cause of a rift between two people; now is the time to fix it up. On a pleasanter note, some should be taking a short trip with a pleasant destination. Others get much-needed moral support. The lucky number is 7.

**Thursday, July 10 (Moon Leo to Virgo 3:50 p.m.)** Something or someone you had given up on bounces right back into your life now, and it should be a pleasant turn of events. For many, a relationship is growing stronger and the ties are binding more and more. Be honest with yourself about whether or not you are willing to accept this responsibility. For those who have bright ideas, this is an excellent time to submit them where they will be heard or seen. You will get attention.

**Friday, July 11 (Moon in Virgo)** Don't hog the spotlight; do your number and then get offstage. Know when enough is enough and when a transaction is completed. It is a time when many can lead rather than follow, and can do their very own number successfully. Others are going to have to keep an eye open for someone who would trespass on their property; stand up for your rights.

*Saturday, July 12 (Moon to Libra 11:40 p.m.)*     There is a great chance today to smooth out some wrinkles in a job that is not as polished as it should be. Grab it! By now you should know that presentation is everything in life, and that the more attractive the package the more appreciated it is. As you start over, a member of the opposite sex jumps in and gets very involved—helping you immensely. Good going! The lucky number today is 1.

*Sunday, July 13 (Moon in Libra)*     Most can find a lot of pleasure right around home today. Warm vibes and close relationships are emphasized. Some get a special bonus in the form of an offer of help from an old pal or associate; remember how much you learned from this person in the past. If a first impression tells you someone or something is fishy, you are right.

*Monday, July 14 (Moon in Libra)*     You could find yourself mixing with the high and the mighty. For some, the opportunity comes through an invitation you can't refuse. Maintain your balance and your sense of humor and you will come smiling through. Others will enjoy a feeling of sudden popularity and wish that it would continue. It could; it's all up to you. The lucky number today is 3.

*Tuesday, July 15 (Moon Libra to Scorpio 4:58 a.m.)* Don't settle for scanty answers today; you deserve the truth and the whole truth. Someone may not actually be lying, but he/she may not regard something as seriously as you do. You are in a strong position and should insist on having things your way. In this case, you have the greater integrity. Some may find themselves having to deal with a number of responsibilities concerning their job or dependents. Give it your all.

*Wednesday, July 16 (Moon in Scorpio)*     Don't hold back where you should give out today; it is important to relate your feelings to the right people. If you simply refuse to communicate, you can make the situation a lot worse than it is. Some should renew some promises to themselves about health, diet, and nutrition. Talk it over with a careful Virgo.

**_Thursday, July 17 (Moon Scorpio to Sagittarius 7:34 a.m.)_** A "glamorous" individual could be the pivot point of the day's activities. You could very easily be swayed—and not necessarily in the right direction. Watch it! Some will find there is an excellent give and take with others today—particularly those who share your basic interests and concerns. Such as a marriage partner. Do some thinking about how you can make your living surroundings more attractive. The lucky number is 6.

**_Friday, July 18 (Moon in Sagittarius)_** Once again, joint efforts are highlighted and you should take advantage of the harmonious vibes. A potential clash of ideas turns into a brilliant new insight. Some will be plagued by perfectionism today and should not get bogged down in details. Look at the big picture. Don't make a hasty judgment about someone or something that annoys you today.

**_Saturday, July 19 (Moon Sagittarius to Capricorn 8:10 a.m.)_** Once again, you do not have to be hasty. In fact, if you play a waiting game, you are in a much better spot. Don't toss off as unimportant a gesture of friendship that someone makes today; it could be a beginning of an excellent enterprise and a productive partnership. "Biggies" are on your side today too.

**_Sunday, July 20 (Moon in Capricorn)_** You are uncharacteristically occupied with deep thoughts today—that is, for a Gemini. It is possible that some event in your life has made you focus on the mystery of it. Even if that is not the case, most will be digging deep for answers now—and having the effort pay off. You could have a very productive discussion with an Aries or a Libra. The lucky number today is 9.

**_Monday, July 21 (Moon Capricorn to Aquarius 8:17 a.m.)_** This full moon finds you once again thinking deeply about your feelings—and possibly the whole meaning of your life. Even if you do not experience this on a very conscious level, you should use your time now to have a frank discussion of intimate matters with those closest to you. You may find that it gives you a new sense of purpose and a willingness to forge ahead. A Leo, a Virgo, or an Aquarian could be the source of inspiration. The lucky number is 1.

**Tuesday, July 22 (Moon in Aquarius)**    You run the risk of false hero worship now. Someone you think is 10 feet tall really has feet of clay. Don't let it disillusion you; use the lesson wisely. It's an excellent time to get out and get around, reopening an occasion with a variety of people. Someone has an excellent tip for you; do not turn a deaf ear.

**Wednesday, July 23 (Moon Aquarius to Pisces 9:59 a.m.)**    You should be tough with yourself today and force yourself to edit your own ideas and actions. Be sure there is nothing excessive in either of these two areas. You can toss out old things successfully now. This refining process will be very valuable for some—who will have a light go on about exactly where they want to go and how they can get there. The lucky number today is 3.

**Thursday, July 24 (Moon in Pisces)**    Reach as high as you like today, because you have an excellent chance of grabbing off the brass ring. However, you must be willing to accept some changes and the fact that you are not perfect. Be willing to go back and retrace your steps. Some of you will get solid support—possibly from a Scorpion—and should express their gratitude for it.

**Friday, July 25 (Moon Pisces to Aries 3:02 p.m.)** Orders come down from "on high" today and they could prove to be exciting. If it is not travel that is involved in your newest assignment, it will at least be something new and refreshing. Be glad for this change of pace. Some will finally have a decision made for them; don't dispute it if you didn't help make it. The lucky number is 5.

*Saturday, July 26 (Moon in Aries)*     Surprised? Why should you be? After all you do deserve praise for all that hard work you've been doing. More praise will be coming your way, so get ready for it. In some cases, the vote of confidence will be a silent one—but at least harmony will be restored. If you need to convince someone of something today, be aware that you could charm the birds out of the trees.

*Sunday, July 27 (Moon in Aries)*     You are going to have to be aware of the subtleties in a certain situation; it is not going to be crystal-clear now. Once again you are in an excellent cycle to win friends and influence people. Don't hesitate to use the influence of someone who makes it available to you. Do your homework!

*Monday, July 28 (Moon Aries to Taurus 12:11 a.m.)* Your position is getting stronger and you should start to feel it. Realize you are on the verge of a major breakthrough. However, you are going to have to be selective as far as current opportunities go—both for relationships and for reward. Some are involved seriously and are right to feel that this is right. A Capricorn could be influential.

*Tuesday, July 29 (Moon in Taurus)*     Many will find themselves in the mood for beauty and illusion; some can work it off via a good book or film. Others may find themselves involved in a rather dangerous flirtation—not necessarily with a person. It could be with an opportunity for some minor fame. Make sure it is worth it to you. Remember the future is beckoning.

*Wednesday, July 30 (Moon Taurus to Gemini 12:19 p.m.)*     You can prove a point today by sticking to your convictions. It may take some courage, but you can summon it up. The more loyal you are to some one or some cause the more loyalty you will get in return.

Many will have some nagging fears totalling dispelled when light is shed on a murky area. The lucky number is 1.

***Thursday, July 31 (Moon in Gemini)*** With the moon well into your sign now, you can expect a successful day in every sense of the word. However, as usual, if you simply stand back, nothing much is likely to happen. Take a big step, even if it is slightly scary. Some will have a money arrangement settled and will come out looking like a hero.

# AUGUST 1986

***Friday, August 1 (Moon in Gemini)*** There's no doubt about it—you'll be in the right place at a very special moment. Call it luck, if you will. At any rate, you are going to have an opportunity to start off in a whole new direction, or to get on a new footing with an intense emotional involvement. Don't waste a moment! The lucky number today is 9.

***Saturday, August 2 (Moon Gemini to Cancer 1:04 a.m.)*** Money and everything connected with it is the focal point of the day. Some may be counting their financial blessings, and taking an inventory of possessions. It is a necessary activity at this time. Many will find themselves reunited with an old friend or lover; be aware that you have a second chance, and make the most of it.

***Sunday, August 3 (Moon in Cancer)*** Don't get knocked off your feet when you receive a surprise visit—take it in your stride. Once again, matters of personal security could be occupying your mind. Some will find that new information about outgo is helpful in conserving income. Something that was misplaced may suddenly turn up. The lucky number today is 2.

***Monday, August 4 (Moon Cancer to Leo 12:26 p.m.)*** Don't miss a word when somebody starts talking about the thing closest to your heart right now—money. There are some valuable tips being offered and you should accept them gratefully. On the personal side, it is time to diversify your interests; it's possible that gregarious Gemini has been limiting him-/herself to a rather small circle lately. Remember, you bore easily.

***Tuesday, August 5 (Moon in Leo)***    There is a change of pace and a change of scene. Some may literally find themselves in a new setting via a surprise side trip. A surge of energy should make you willing to rethink and redo a part of your life that is not the most solid. Keep your sense of humor at hand, because you should have a chance to display it.

***Wednesday, August 6 (Moon Leo to Virgo 9:44 p.m.)*** Tell yourself to roll with the punches today—they certainly will not be hard blows. However, a willingness to be flexible is necessary as changes are indicated. Some will get excellent news about a pet project or bright new scheme. Travel may well be involved. The lucky number today is 5.

***Thursday, August 7 (Moon in Virgo)***    Get up, get out, and get going. You should be aware by now that you do have the wherewithal to make a success of a project once you apply yourself to it. What you have to keep in mind are two words: Get started. All the building material you need will be virtually handed to you today. Accept help from a Taurus, a Libra or a Scorpio.

***Friday, August 8 (Moon Virgo to Libra 5:05 a.m.)*** You've won the esteem of an admirable person. Here's your chance to enhance your place in his or her life. Let this new relationship develop to its full potential. Some will have to be discreet when a secret is revealed to them—mark it "strictly confidential" in your mind. Do some soul-searching today; it could be productive.

***Saturday, August 9 (Moon in Libra)***    Sensation and stimulation are two things you want very much now; you will have the opportunity to indulge yourself. Remember, however, that your emotional responses are heightened at this time. Some will find themselves very much involved with children—and very pleasurably. Listen to a serious person who wants to offer constructive suggestions; don't laugh them off.

**Sunday, August 10 (Moon in Libra)**   If you separate the fluff from the fact, you can get some invaluable information now. It will help you shove an obstacle out of the way and perhaps even save you money. You may find yourself in some kind of game or contest today; don't show off your smarts to other people's detriment.

**Monday, August 11 (Moon Libra to Scorpio 10:36 a.m.)**   Someone may reveal his/her secret feelings to you today; give back by opening up yourself. Once again, you are in the mood for some rather sensational fun and games; make sure they are safe ones. Many will find they have more independence than in the recent past—isn't it nice to walk alone?

**Tuesday, August 12 (Moon in Scorpio)**   Back to the grindstone today and to the serious work-a-day world. Though there's a lot you must do, you should be able to cut through things easily. Spend some time concentrating on your own health and well-being; you could discover there is good news in one of those areas. A Cancer or a Capricorn may be the one to get you out of your rut.

**Wednesday, August 13 (Moon Capricorn to Sagittarius 2:17 p.m.)**   There are those who rely on your good judgment and your good taste; don't drop the ball for them now. You may run into a curious type who questions you more closely than you like; you can be polite and still refuse to divulge what you do not choose to divulge. Some will receive a rather pleasant invitation to an unusual social event. Enjoy your popularity! The lucky number is 3.

**Thursday, August 14 (Moon in Sagittarius)**   Though patience is not generally a Gemini virtue, you are going to have to summon up some now. If you don't, you will rush in and thereby ruin your own game. If you go slowly, you will be able to put together all the pieces—and know exactly what to do. For some, some revamping of procedures is necessary before anymore progress can be made. Take some advice from an Aquarian or a Scorpio.

***Friday, August 15 (Moon Sagittarius to Capricorn 4:22 p.m.)*** Your mate or partner may make you reconsider some of your plans. It might be a very good idea, because during this period you could make some rash moves. Let's face it, you can sometimes be your own worst enemy. Do the necessaries in terms of catching up with those who are waiting to hear from you. Most will get a generous gesture of affection from the most important person in their life; be sure to respond in kind. The lucky number today is 5.

***Saturday, August 16 (Moon in Capricorn)*** It's possible you may be thrust right into the middle of a mix-up; keep cool throughout the fuss and fury. And be careful not to say anything that might be misunderstood. Your best course is to deliberate rather than participate. This is one time you could be an excellent peacemaker if you don't attempt to force any issues. The lucky number today is 6.

***Sunday, August 17 (Moon Capricorn to Aquarius 5:44 p.m.)*** Even without trying, you will learn the difference between fact and fiction—even fantasy—today. Someone is really off-the-wall, and it's a good thing you know it right now. It's up to you to straighten things out. Some may have to protect themselves when an overly emotional person "attacks"; you can handle it.

***Monday, August 18 (Moon in Aquarius)*** It's time to come to terms with a fact of life: you are involved, and the sooner you know it, the better for all. You can no longer play the role of observer—get in there and participate. Some of you will find yourselves in a position where you can make their views known—quite dramatically. Don't overplay it. You have the power, but you don't have to throw it around.

*Tuesday, August 19 (Moon Aquarius to Pisces 7:52 p.m.)* This full moon puts the focus squarely on fairness and broadmindedness. That means you should be able to rise above pettiness in a minor dispute that erupts. Play it cool and give where you must. A loving atmosphere is on tap for most. Some will be thinking in long-range terms—and should consult with an experienced Aries.

*Wednesday, August 20 (Moon in Pisces)* This is one of those times you can mix business with pleasure quite successfully. For some, a creative hobby is now becoming something more, and could be transformed into profit. All should be a bit daring now, and speak up about their rather offbeat ideas. You are an original—and you should not hide it. The lucky number is 1.

*Thursday, August 21 (Moon in Pisces)* You may not be altogether sure which direction to go in today. Some kind of conflict exists. This is one time you should chose the familiar over the adventurous; if you stick with what you know, you will be in a much better position. Some will find themselves mixing and mingling with people in power; do not hesitate to speak up and express your aspirations.

*Friday, August 22 (Moon Pisces to Aries 12:27 a.m.)* You could go on a "sentimental journey" today—if only in your mind. However, you run the risk of letting your feelings overpower your logic. Realize that you are living in the here and now. Most should be particularly persuasive today and able to get what they want; just don't press your luck. There is no doubt that an element of luck is with you now, but you could overdo it. The lucky number is 3.

*Saturday, August 23 (Moon in Aries)* This could be a profitable day—in several senses of the word. It could simply work out as a period in which you get a lot done and therefore feel self-satisfied. On the other hand, it is a much more tangible reward you could receive. Some will feel on much more secure ground now and should try to store away some of that confidence for a future time.

**Sunday, August 24 (Moon Aries to Taurus 8:36 a.m.)** This could be a particularly pleasurable summer Sunday for fun-loving Gemini. Relaxation and recreation are the key words for the day. Some will make progress in a special relationship; others will find that a chancy venture has paid off. All should flow with the holiday spirit.

**Monday, August 25 (Moon in Taurus)** There is a more sober note today, and someone could confide a rather disturbing secret to you. Try to be understanding, and realize that you are no angel. It never helped anyone to cast the first stone. Some will be moved to help those less fortunate—it could be as simple as a visit to a sick friend. Some kind of change in living arrangements works out to your advantage. The lucky number is 6.

**Tuesday, August 26 (Moon Taurus to Gemini 8:00 p.m.)** Keep a low profile today for best results. Don't get involved when someone tries to get you involved in a borderline scheme; this is no time for intrigue. Self-discipline right now is essential if you are to keep your self-esteem. Refuse to be gullible, but do be open-minded. A realistic attitude will see you through with flying colors.

**Wednesday, August 27 (Moon in Gemini)** This is a much less tentative day then yesterday. In fact, with the moon in your sign, you can afford to take a chance or two. Your charisma will be very much in evidence and you could make some kind of "power play." Monetary success and emotional stability are potential prizes today—you could carry off one or both. Some of you will be mightily relieved when some suspicions you have had about a loved one turn out to be false.

*Thursday, August 28 (Moon in Gemini)*     Once again, the moon is in your sign and your cycle is high. It should give you the energy you need to finish what you start. It should also give some the courage to say "I won't do it anymore." You can dump that burden which is really not yours. Though there appear to be limitations, your potential is much greater than you realize. And your lucky number is 9 today.

*Friday, August 29 (Moon Gemini to Cancer 8:40 a.m.)*     Don't beat around the bush; go straight to the heart of things. An independent, forthright approach will win the day. Some may find themselves dealing with some highly creative and intelligent people; don't get overcompetitive. There is no need to. Everything you wear today should be bright, including your smile. The lucky number is 1.

*Saturday, August 30 (Moon in Cancer)*     Some inner feelings you have today can be trusted; your ESP is on high. By following your first impressions, you could actually hit the jackpot. Some will be feeling more satisfied about their financial affairs than in the recent past. Others will be trying to figure out ways to make more of their assets. It's an excellent activity today. The lucky number is 2.

*Sunday, August 31 (Moon Cancer to Leo 8:08 p.m.)* Relax! That is the key to happiness now. There may be lots of demands on your time, but you should love it if you take the right attitude. Look at it this way—you are very popular. Don't forget to keep certain of your appetites under control; remember the promises you made to yourself. Have fun with a Sagittarian or another Gemini. The lucky number is 3.

# SEPTEMBER 1986

*Monday, September 1 (Moon in Leo)*     You should be able to brush off some slight feelings of boredom and take direct action today. That is the best way out of the doldrum. Some will be finding out exactly where they stand with a very special person; others will be making it known. There is a lot of movement indicated and more than a little pleasurable activity. Don't muff this really quite unusual day. The lucky number is 1.

***Tuesday, September 2 (Moon in Leo)*** Most Geminis are great with children and young people—after all, they rarely ever grow old themselves. Set a good example now and know the satisfaction of playing teacher to someone who is less experienced. You could turn a hunch into a real prediction and amaze others; trust your first impression. A Cancer, a Capricorn, or an Aquarian could be important people in your life today.

***Wednesday, September 3 (Moon Leo to Virgo 5:06 a.m.)*** Something is nearing completion now, and you should give it the final touches. Don't get hasty and neglect to close some loopholes. You run the risk of having your attention diverted by something else. Some will have the opportunity to ask a lot of questions now; make sure you store away all the answers in a mental computer. They will come in very handy later on. The emphasis is on home and property. The lucky number is 3.

***Thursday, September 4 (Moon in Virgo)*** Something that has been rather puzzling now becomes crystal clear; someone puts in the last pieces and you can see the whole picture. Now that you are on steadier ground, you can feel free to enlarge your scope and broaden your horizons. Some should be willing to correct past mistakes and say "I was wrong."

***Friday, September 5 (Moon Virgo to Libra 11:33 a.m.)*** Don't let the romantic light blind you to reality now. Remember, no one is perfect—but they are still worthy of being loved. By defining terms you can get a better understanding of where you stand in relation to the rights of others. There are legal implications, and you should know them. Scrutinize written material carefully.

**Saturday, September 6 (Moon in Libra)**    If you refuse to let it get you down, an apparent loss can be turned into quite the opposite. Optimism is the key to victory now. You should be spurred on by people around you who indicate how important you are. Some will find themselves lucky in both money and love. It should be an antidote to some uneasy feelings caused by a minor error; be more careful next time.

**Sunday , September 7 (Moon Libra to Scorpio 4:12 p.m.)**    Someone seeks you out in private today and wants to talk turkey. Welcome the opportunity and be sure to tell all. There is no point in holding back now. Some will get back a sense of perspective and be able to put matters in focus; you should be able to see where you must revise. Children and young people could be rather prominent on the scene today. Be gentle and understanding.

**Monday, September 8 (Moon in Scorpio)**    You should have a "solid citizen" mentality today, and your sense of responsibility should be uppermost. As you deal with practical matters, you should be able to put a lot of money in your emotional bank. For some, a relationship is growing a lot stronger and could soon demand a definite commitment. It's an excellent day to do some deep thinking about the matter. A Cancer or a Capricorn could be very much on the scene. The lucky number is 8.

**Tuesday, September 9 (Moon Scorpio to Sagittarius 7:40 p.m.)**    Once more you must stick with the basics. Remember that—even if you are working for someone else—what you do well you are doing for yourself. Someone who relies on your judgment comes to you with a tale of woe—possibly concerning the end of a relationship. Listen, but don't become involved. Lovers' quarrels are best settled by themselves. The lucky number is 9.

**Wednesday, September 10 (Moon in Sagittarius)** You may have to put a big clamp on your Gemini mouth today. If you speak too soon, you will blow the whole deal. On the other hand, you will have a chance to show your own individuality; this may come as a result of conflicting ideas. Your's turns out to be the brightest and most workable. Good for you!

*Thursday, September 11 (Moon Sagittarius to Capricorn 10:28 p.m.)* Obligations to others are very much part of the day's scenario. Fulfill them without griping; remember when you have been in need. Because you may be feeling overburdened, you may be tempted to overindulge. Or, you may simply be eating on the run. Slow down or your nerves will force you to. A Cancer or an Aquarian could provide solace.

*Friday, September 12 (Moon in Capricorn)* There's a lot of coming and going today—both by you and other people. The burst of activity should chase away your temporary blues. And your natural Gemini curiosity will come into play when a new subject comes up—possibly related to your own legal rights or assets. Ask all the questions you want; the answers are there to be had. The lucky number is 3.

*Saturday, September 13 (Moon in Capricorn)* Isn't it nice to get a green light and be able to go full speed ahead? However, don't go so fast that you miss out on the enjoyment of the project itself. Some should be willing to take another look at what they've done and say "I could do it better." Others should do their homework before they make a decision.

*Sunday, September 14 (Moon Capricorn to Aquarius 1:07 a.m.)* Someone sensible articulates the sensible alternatives today; listen carefully. Also be willing to analyze your own situation and bend where you must bend. It is an excellent day to communicate clearly— perhaps you should get in touch with someone whose nose is a little out of joint. A Sagittarius or a Virgo could be an excellent companion today.

*Monday, September 15 (Moon in Aquarius)* Good news! Someone in your circle is markedly better, it should be a load off your mind. If that is not your scenario, there will be other reasons to celebrate. All those around you should be in excellent spirits, a "holiday mood." Make the most of it! The lucky number is 6.

**Tuesday, September 16 (Moon Aquarius to Pisces 4:27 a.m.)** Don't fool yourself into thinking that you are doing things the very best way; take a good look at your work and see where it can be streamlined. It doesn't much matter what your work is, it can be improved. Possibly as a result, some recognition will come your way today. It should vastly improve your mood.

**Wednesday, September 17 (Moon in Pisces)** In a dispute that erupts today, you are on the right side. Be glad of it. In another matter, your course is clear and it's obvious you must make a commitment. Or someone must make one to you. Either way, the die is cast. The lucky number today is 8.

**Thursday, September 18 (Moon Pisces to Aries 9:33 a.m.)** This full moon could be a bit unsettling for you and even touch off a touch of paranoia. Realize that many are with you and few against you. Concentrate on an important assignment and hurdle some obstacles now; it should make you feel a lot more secure. Some of you will get the opportunity to speak out and expound your views loud and clear. Make sure you have the courage of your convictions.

**Friday, September 19 (Moon in Aries)** This is a fine day for a fine romance. It needn't be a new one, but that is possible too. If it isn't love that comes your way, it will be money—possibly in the form of a promotion, career change, or business coup. On a lower key, some should realize that their powers of persuasion are particularly strong now and should put them to good use. The lucky number is 1.

**Saturday, September 20 (Moon Aries to Taurus 5:25 p.m.)** This could be a highly emotional day for Gemini. On the up side, some could receive news that brings great relief or even happiness. On the down side, you run the risk of getting bent out of shape by a minor financial matter. Realize that the difficulty is temporary. And that it is your nerves that are the problem. Get some R&R—and some advice from a Cancer or a Capricorn.

**_Sunday, September 21 (Moon in Taurus)_**     Yesterday's possibly disturbing feelings should vanish into thin air today. In fact, you should have a reason to celebrate a special occasion. If things do not work out in quite such a social manner, you will get the opportunity to satisfy your voracious curiosity. Some should remember to remember those less well off.

**_Monday, September 22 (Moon in Taurus)_**     Someone will ask you to make a plan today; you should be ready to do it if you have done your homework. Don't be afraid to totally trash something from the past; if it doesn't work, it doesn't work. You have a better way of doing it. Some are on the brink of an important discovery, and should do a bit of personal soul searching to help you make it. The lucky number today is 4.

**_Tuesday, September 23 (Moon Taurus to Gemini 4:13 a.m.)_**     It's up time again, as the moon moves into your sign. Now you have no excuse for being down—or even feeling that way. If you open up and use all your resources, you should be able to accomplish great things. Some will do it through the written word. Others will find an exciting person is drawn to them as never before. He or she will let you know it. The object of your affection could be a Virgo, a Sagittarian, or possibly another Gemini.

**_Wednesday, September 24 (Moon in Gemini)_**     Art, music, or beauty in some form is the order of the day. For some, it could be the pleasures of the palate in the form of a gourmet dinner. It's okay to go ahead and luxuriate now; leave serious work for another day. Your personal charm is great now, and you should put it to the best advantage. Without taking advantage of anyone, of course. The lucky number is 6.

**_Thursday, September 25 (Moon Gemini to Cancer 4:44 p.m.)_**   Face it, you had to make that break with the past. You should not brood over it now. Number one, it will do no good. Number two, you will shortly find yourself a lot better off. For some, a highly sensitive person provides the key that helps regain their sense of direction. Things cannot possibly be too bad, as your lunar cycle is still high.

**_Friday, September 26 (Moon in Cancer)_**   The emphasis is on power, production, and your ability to handle responsibility. You should be able to make an excellent showing now. And it should pay off where it counts. Another of the day's possible scenarios features intense emotional involvement. If that is your case, keep your wits about you and go with the flow. The deepened relationship could be an excellent stimulus to creativity. The lucky number is 8.

**_Saturday, September 27 (Moon in Cancer)_**   Even if you try, you will not be able to avoid those who seek you out today. Some may just want to show their affection; others want your advice and counsel. Give of it freely. However, don't let your popularity make you goof off from the other important things that need doing. Like bill-paying—or the search for a lost article.

**_Sunday, September 28 (Moon Cancer to Leo 5:39 a.m.)_**   Someone may try to use nostalgia to wean you away from your purpose. Resist falling back on the past when you should be moving into the future. If you observe closely, you will gain a much greater understanding of someone around you who occasionally is difficult to love. Today you may get an insight into why. And figure out what can be done about it.

**_Monday, September 29 (Moon in Leo)_**   Now that you are acting like and being seen as someone whose integrity can be relied upon, look forward to getting the kinds of offers you have almost dispaired of getting. Be alert to the conditions that come along with a request—possibly from a family member. If they are too onerous, you may have to say No. Let your intuition be your guide. The lucky number is 2.

*Tuesday, September 30 (Moon Leo to Virgo 1:57 p.m.)* Gossips will gossip as long as you give them the raw material to work with. Instead of being upset at what comes back to you, ignore the whole situation. Better yet, treat it with humor and display your ability to bounce back. On a much more important note, some will encounter a stimulating person who is the key to a whole new game plan. Listen carefully and make notes of what you hear. It could be a Sagittarian or another Gemini who lights your spark. The lucky number is 3.

# OCTOBER 1986

*Wednesday, October 1 (Moon in Virgo)* You may find yourself torn between two lovers, so to speak. Whether there are literally two people in your life—or simply two options—there is a choice you must make. If you really keep your best interests at heart, you will realize that the older and more familiar of two possibilities is the one to go with. In your domestic sphere, you could feel the ground shifting underneath your feet. However, the changes are definitely beneficial. The lucky number is 2.

*Thursday, October 2 (Moon Virgo to Libra 8:03 p.m.)* You may be feeling rather antsy today, and the reason may be that you feel your territorial rights are being threatened. Don't just wallow in your nervousness; do something about it. One productive way would be to open up the lines of communications with those in opposition to you. You will be amazed at how much a bit of frank talk can help. Some will have to renew their resolutions, diet, nutrition, and exercise. Remember—if you don't have your health, you don't have anything. The lucky number is 3.

**Friday, October 3 (Moon in Libra)**    The shaking of the foundations that you felt a few days ago now become complete. You may not be able to take anything for granted; change is the order of the day—and there is little you can do about it. One of your strongest relationships will be tested—but it can be the thing that sustains you now. Consult a Scorpio or a Taurus for some solid advice.

**Saturday, October 4 (Moon Libra to Scorpio 11:35 p.m.)**    Unlike yesterday, today you feel as if you are in charge of your own destiny. The reason is that you did not let yesterday's events shake you up unduly. It should be a good feeling to be able to dance to your own tune and call the shots—particularly with someone you love, and who loves you. He/she needs the direction, and you should be glad you are able to provide it. The lucky number today is 5.

**Sunday, October 5 (Moon in Scorpio)**    Things settle down a bit—but you could become a bit too settled. It's great to focus on practical issues and family matters, but don't get so bogged down that you fall into a "tender trap." Some may attempt to make themselves feel better by indulging in sweets and other things not good for the body—or the body image. Play it cool for best results—in all matters that come within your sphere of interest today.

**Monday, October 6 (Moon in Scorpio)**    A double-dealer could cross your path today; don't be blinded by the light of his/her personality. You can't turn people into what you want them to be; see them as they are. As the saying goes, there are plenty of other fish in the sea. Some will find themselves revved up and ready to streamline current procedures; one goal is to eliminate unnecessary expenses. Be aware that you can if you try. Others have to dig a bit to find out why they are slogging through mire. The lucky number is 7 today.

**Tuesday, October 7 (Moon Scorpio to Sagittarius 1:48 a.m.)**    No matter how you are tempted, don't flirt with danger today. Even if the danger is nothing more frightening than your financial affairs. Some may be asked for a long-range commitment and may be hesitant to give it; it is best to wait out this period and see what happens. Don't worry; the person you are involved with will give you more time if you ask for it. The lucky number is 8.

**Wednesday, October 8 (Moon in Sagittarius)** What a relief! You are able to tie up the loose end of something or get rid of a problem you never should have had in the first place. It should be an excellent feeling to have greater freedom of thought and action. Some will find that cooperative efforts are paramount today; be willing to give and take more than usual. Others will find they hit the mark with very little effort. Great going!

**Thursday, October 9 (Moon Sagittarius to Capricorn 3:52 a.m.)** You may discover the meaning of the phrase, "Money is the root of all evil." Some may actually be involved in a dispute over an inheritance. Others will feel stressed by questions like, "What's mine? What's yours?" There is really little you can do except sit back and wait for the storm to blow over. However, some who enter the fray may end up rediscovering how much they love somebody—and how much they are willing to give on his/her behalf.

**Friday, October 10 (Moon in Capricorn)** Hang on to your emotional stability today—particularly when a nitpicking individual decides to pick on you. You are not perfect, of course, but realize that this person's accusations are totally absurd. Some will find it necessary to do more than a surface job in order to complete an assignment. Others can actually hit the jackpot if they really put their shoulders into it. It's a day with a lot to gain—but some to lose. It all depends on how you play it. Listen to Capricorn.

**Saturday, October 11 (Moon Capricorn to Aquarius 7:45 a.m.)** The atmosphere is much lighter and brighter today. Many will be feeling with the positive vibes of love in bloom; others could simply fall in love with new ideas—and new possibilities. Among them are travel and continued education. It is an excellent time to consider enlarging your scope. Talk it over with a Sagittarian, an Aquarian, or possibly another Gemini. You have similar interests now. The lucky number is 3.

***Sunday, October 12 (Moon in Aquarius)*** Your mind should be so crystal clear today you should be able to see forever. Use your clarity to focus on a situation which has been clouded by emotionalism of late; you will find that there is a simple solution that will satisfy everyone. Some should reach out and touch people at a distance, there is much you haven't caught up on and you will be enlightened when the gaps are filled in for you. The lucky number today is 4.

***Monday, October 13 (Moon Aquarius to Pisces 11:03 a.m.)*** Don't get caught short when an opportunity presents itself—be ready to jump right in with both feet. You may not be totally convinced of the rightness of your move, but it is one you must make. For some, it's important to "get the message" even if it is not spelled out perfectly. If you do some reading between the lines, you should be able to figure out what is wanted of you. However, if it is more than you wish to give, don't hesitate to give a negative right away. The lucky number today is 5.

***Tuesday, October 14 (Moon in Pisces)*** There may be a lot of people trying to tell you what is good for you today; listen, but know that you cannot please everyone. In the long run, it is a superior you must look good for, and it is wise to keep that in mind. Your ambitions are your own, and no one else's. On the home scene, someone could say, "Let's get organized." Agree wholeheartedly and get on with it! Part of your remodeling scheme could include something new and beautiful that everyone will enjoy.

*Wednesday, October 15 (Moon Pisces to Aries 5:13 p.m.)*     Lucky you! It isn't often that one can recoup what seemed like a certain loss. For you, something is alive and kicking that has every right to be totally dead. Now that you have a second chance, resolve not to go off on any wild tangents—and to keep your eyes clear so that you see everything in a realistic light. Some will find romance intriguing—and possibly dangerous!

*Thursday, October 16 (Moon in Aries)*     This should be another good day, at least in general terms. Friends and relatives prove their solid support and you should bask in the glow of the knowledge that there are people who will catch you if you fall. Don't get involved in an unproductive hassle with some sort of organization or agency; it is not worth the battle. The lucky number today is 8.

*Friday, October 17 (Moon in Aries)*     More than a few Geminis will confront themselves today—and should be prepared for some kind of shock. In some way, a search is ended and you finally know exactly where you are going. Realize that this is the point of no return and that a decision must be made. For most, there are positive developments—even though there is a rather startling shake-up of the status quo. For some, the road to romance is now wide and clear.

*Saturday, October 8 (Moon Aries to Taurus 1:35 a.m.)*     The ground under your feet should seem more stable today; things are getting back to normal. For some, recent fears and doubts are totally wiped away and you can breathe a sigh of relief. Others may find they are newly independent and have some choices to make. Don't be hasty! Make it a point to socialize with some good solid citizens. A Leo or an Aquarian would be ideal.

*Sunday, October 19 (Moon in Taurus)*     This is one day you might want to curl up and pamper yourself—or let someone else do it to you. You need some emotional security and there are ways you can get it now. Encouragement comes from an unexpected source and boosts your morale. All in all, you end the day feeling more assured than you began it. The lucky number today is 2.

**Monday, October 20 (Moon Taurus to Gemini 12:15 p.m.)** It's a great way to start out the week, with the moon moving into your sign. You should feel great—and look it too! Some will have a real reason to celebrate; others may be invited to a celebratory event. Someone says, "I'm sorry," and means it. Don't gloat! If you feel lucky today, the number to try is 3.

**Tuesday, October 21 (Moon in Gemini)** Some will find themselves strolling down memory lane today—and enjoying it immensely. In fact, it's possible that you will have a reunion with someone very dear who once was near. Others will have the excellent experience of learning from experience—something Gemini does not always do. Your judgment should be keen and you should be able to promote yourself quite easily now. Look confident, and you will win the day.

**Wednesday, October 22 (Moon in Gemini)** Many will feel like kicking over the traces and doing something wild and wonderful today! Go right ahead—you can hardly lose. However, make sure your madness has some method in it, because you could make permanent gains now. A dramatic episode is in store for some—and the opposite number could be a Virgo, a Sagittarian, or another Gemini.

**Thursday, October 23 (Moon Gemini to Cancer 12:37 a.m.)** You've been living a little high lately, in every sense of the word. Come back down to earth and remember some resolutions about your budget and spending habits. If you must buy, buy only what has permanent value. Certain Geminis are facing a possible change of status, and that may include marriage or a live-in arrangement. Don't get rattled—you can handle whatever comes.

***Friday, October 24 (Moon in Cancer)*** If you stick with it and put your nose to the proverbial grindstone today, you should be able to accomplish a great deal. One reason is that your cycle is still high and your intuition is extremely sharp. However, it's important not to be vague about a rather tricky situation; the more you define your terms, the safer you will be. Be willing to get rid of something that just isn't working anymore. The lucky number is 7.

***Saturday, October 25 (Moon Cancer to Leo 1:02 p.m.)*** You may start to feel that you are on a roll; once again good things come your way with not a great deal of effort on your part. Some may have the excellent experience of having some past efforts pay off now. Remind yourself that you did it all by yourself! Some will be acutely aware of the protection they receive from others who have their best interest at heart. Be sure to show your appreciation.

***Sunday, October 26 (Moon in Leo)*** This should be a heartwarming day for many Geminis, complete with a joyous reunion. Many will find themselves in total harmony with those around them—perhaps with a special someone. Let your generosity juices flow today, but don't go overboard. That applies particularly to those who hear a hard-luck story—possibly from a member of the family. You can help others without strapping yourself. The lucky number today is 9.

***Monday, October 27 (Moon Leo to Virgo 11:20 p.m.)*** You may be forced out of a comfortable rut now and find it necessary to cut off communication or interaction with someone who no longer has meaning in your life. The arena could be business, or it could be the personal sphere. Make every attempt to practice sincerity now, and to express yourself from the heart. There is no room for equivocation or straddling fences. The lucky number today is 2.

***Tuesday, October 28 (Moon in Virgo)*** You may breathe a sigh of relief today as a nerve-wracking situation runs its course. Now you are able to turn to more practical and familiar things, and put yourself on a more solid footing. Some Geminis should look inward to their own health and nutrition. Most important—avoid brooding over the past. What's done is done, and you still have a lot of support around you. A Cancer or a Capricorn could be an excellent friend now.

*Wednesday October 29 (Moon in Virgo)* Lighten up and spread your wings now; it's important to rise above the current situation. However, realize that some restrictions are not only necessary, but also advantageous. Your sense of humor is your very best friend now, and you should spend as much time with it as possible. Relax with a Sagittarian or another Gemini. The lucky number is 3.

*Thursday, October 30 (Moon Virgo to Libra 6:04 a.m.)* Okay, the battle lines are drawn, and you're going to have to take a stand where your real convictions are concerned. You needn't worry about your image, because it remains intact. And you will gain a lot by showing how sturdy you can be. Some will find themselves very involved with children—or possibly just the young in heart. Since you belong to that constituency, it should prove enjoyable.

*Friday, October 31 (Moon in Libra)* Yesterday's slight rumble is totally over now, and you can get into the spirit of fun. It should be a relatively carefree day, but you should not miss an opportunity to change something recently important in your life by taking the first step now. It may be as simple as putting something in writing—and submitting it to the right person. The lucky number today is 5.

# N O V E M B E R   1 9 8 6

*Saturday, November 1 (Moon Libra to Scorpio 9:19 a.m.)* Step back and take a long-range view of things today. If you get bogged down in details, you will confuse yourself even more about a confusing situation. Most likely it is related to a cooperative effort—possibly even a marriage or a live-in relationship. There are currently some glitches which are disturbing the peace. They will be smoothed out by themselves; let nature take its course. Some will receive excellent news about a friend or relative at a distance.

**Sunday, November 2 (Moon in Scorpio)** Most will have some restless energy to work off today, and should find some productive ways to accomplish that. By setting something in order, you will feel on much more stable emotional ground. Someone in your circle may whisper a confidence; try not to appear surprised—even though you are. Encourage someone who is a bit down, and try to whistle while you work. The lucky number today is 4.

**Monday, November 3 (Moon Scorpio to Sagittarius 10:19 a.m.)** Don't dismiss an idea you have as a wild and wacky one; use the creative energy it gives you and you may be surprised at the outcome. For some Geminis, some very basic issues will surface today and you will not be able to ignore them. Be prepared to use all the tact you possess. Another Gemini or a Sagittarian will be the one to understand your dilemma.

**Tuesday, November 4 (Moon in Sagittarius)** Someone may demand that you put up or shut up; realize that you have come to a crossroads. For some, it may mean that basic changes are in store. For others, a clash of ideas will prove stimulating rather than upsetting. In fact, it may lead to a new grand plan for beautifying your surroundings. The lucky number today is 6.

**Wednesday, November 5 (Moon Sagittarius to Capricorn 10:49 a.m.)** If you are not careful, you could find yourself tangled in a web of circumstances that have little to do with you. The best advice is—stay out of it! In your own life, you will have to rub your eyes hard and look at someone or something more realistically. Don't commit to or sign anything at this time. And be discreet on all fronts.

**Thursday, November 6 (Moon in Capricorn)** Your temporary crisis should be over now, and you should have learned from it. The most important lesson may be not to rely so much on someone; he/she turns out to have feet of clay. On the other hand, you yourself are in a stronger position and someone rules in your favor. Some may feel like dabbling in mysteries now; it is an excellent time.

**Friday, November 7 (Moon Capricorn to Aquarius 12:29 p.m.)** Even though someone says the die is cast, continue to dig deep for information and realize that nothing is final until you say it is. Some will have their minds on money matter now, possibly even an inheritance. Others will complete a large project and feel like breathing a sigh of relief. Have some fun and celebrate with an Aries or a Libra. The lucky number is 9.

**Saturday, November 8 (Moon in Aquarius)** This is an excellent day to kick up your heels and show how independent you can be. You needn't worry about your popularity or have the problem of going out and looking for companionship. For some, it is satisfying to play tutor to a younger or less educated person. You can learn from the experience. Take a bit of time today to examine what is really important to you; your spiritual values should be easy to touch on now.

**Sunday, November 9 (Moon Aquarius to Pisces 4:30 p.m.)** This rather satisfying weekend continues on an upbeat note. Some of you may have to play Solomon today to resolve a dispute to everyone's satisfaction. You look like a hero, and you should feel like one. Some will get a pat on the back from another source—a rather surprising one. The lucky number today is 2.

**Monday, November 10 (Moon in Pisces)** The work-week starts off excellently as you find yourself dealing with higher-ups on an almost equal footing. Warning: Do not overstep your bounds. Some Geminis will experience a less positive day, and should console themselves by doing something nice—within the rules you have set for yourself for nutrition and health, however. Realize that if you are tested now, you will live up to expectations.

***Tuesday, November 11 (Moon Pisces to Aries 11:14 p.m.)*** Someone may disappoint you today—possibly rather severely. You tend to be a bit naive and should not always assume that people are loyal. Pick up the pieces and move on, protecting your interests at all times. Some may be asked to express an opinion where they have not had the opportunity to do so before. Speak up!

***Wednesday, November 12 (Moon in Aries)*** Get as familiar as possible with the rules and regulations—some of which may be new ones. That way, no one can trip you up again. Some may find themselves confronting a possible breakup—one someone else asks for. Realize the crisis is temporary, and take it with all the cool you can muster. For all, romantic interests are in the air.

***Thursday, November 13 (Moon in Aries)*** Some kind of tranquility returns today, but you still must tread lightly because the situation is still a touchy one. Your powers of persuasion are great now, however, so you should be able to further your interests with ease. Some will be surprised by a surprise gift. It could blow your mind.

***Friday, November 14 (Moon Aries to Taurus 8:24 a.m.)*** Relax and go with the flow today; no matter how you try to force the issue, you will not be able to. Things will resolve themselves in due time. On the other hand, your cycle is still high, and you should be able to get what you want in another area. Your success should make you able to stand the delay with good grace.

*Saturday, November 15 (Moon in Taurus)*    Many Geminis will find that a past experience is very valuable in helping them deal with a current situation. Be confident that it will see you through. Some may receive a special privilege today—possibly in the form of a backstage view that clears up a murky situation. For others a relationship is growing stronger but responsibilities are increasing along with it. Realize your own destiny is in your hands.

*Sunday November 16 (Moon Taurus to Gemini 7:26 p.m.)*    This could be a rather pensive day for usually gregarious Gemini. If necessary, force yourself to spend some time alone with your thoughts. The full moon is helping you gain insight into your own motives and putting you in touch with your real mission. When you do speak, however, you will be able to put your views across in a dynamic manner. The lucky number is 9.

*Monday, November 17 (Moon in Gemini)*    You should start out the week refreshed and full of energy, able to take advantage of the moon in your sign. If you work with circumstances, you will find that you are in the right place at the right time now. Some may get a rather rare second chance and the opportunity to erase past mistakes. Grab it with gratitude. A loved one tells you something that makes you more willing to strive for success.

*Tuesday, November 18 (Moon in Gemini)*    Your high spirits could lead you to act impulsively today; don't let your feelings dominate your logic. On the other hand, you should trust your intuition in a certain situation. Realize that your hunch about someone is correct. Many find that a major concession is made to them. It could be the beginning of a new direction for an important relationship. The lucky number is 2.

*Wednesday, November 19 (Moon Gemini to Cancer 7:46 a.m.)*    Once again today you should take advantage of your moon energy and apply it to the area of your finances. If there is someone you need to persuade to back you, you should approach him/her today. Be inventive and possibly even use the element of surprise to back up your attack. Some Geminis will get evidence of how much they are appreciated by their peers today. The lucky number is 3.

**Thursday, November 20 (Moon in Cancer)** Somebody may grill you today about your sources of information/authority. Be ready to give a lot of good reasons why you changed your approach. In all things, it's best to stick with the rules and regulations today. Talk things over with a stable Taurus or a logical Aquarian. More money is a distinct possibility.

**Friday, November 21 (Moon Cancer to Leo 8:25 p.m.)** Something that seems to be slipping through your hands is suddenly within reach again. Don't let it go again! A request in writing gets a favorable response, and you may find yourself with a definite financial or emotional gain. In another area, the more you know the better off you will be. That means do all the homework necessary. You might try prepping with another Gemini or a Sagittarian.

**Saturday, November 22 (Moon in Leo)** You are better off finishing rather than starting anything today. You must demonstrate your stability in order to gain someone's respect. A person with a special need may approach you now for help; be honest about what you can do and what is not possible for you. Some kind of adjustment is necessary on your home scene, and you should make it with good grace.

**Sunday, November 23 (Moon in Leo)** If you have been watching your wallet in the recent past, you will have the chance to treat yourself today—and possibly others. However, even in the midst of a lot of people and a lot of activity, you should attempt to find some time alone. Many will find that time valuable in decoding a rather garbled emotional message that someone has been sending. Others should remember someone who needs them. The lucky number is 7.

**Monday, November 24 (Moon Leo to Virgo 7:46 a.m.)**   What a comfort to know you are not alone! That becomes perfectly clear when someone says in no uncertain terms that he/she is loyal to your cause and has your best interests at heart. What's more, he/she will prove it. Team up with other creative people for best results today. You can even recoup a loss and have it boomerang in your favor.

**Tuesday, November 25 (Moon in Virgo)**   If you sell anything, your sales ability should be super now. Even if you are the product you are currently marketing, the result could be money in the bank. For all, the time is right to improve your chances for greater future security. Stick with an Aries for initiative and a Libra for a balanced perspective on the scene. The lucky number is 9.

**Wednesday, November 26 (Moon Virgo to Libra 3:59 p.m.)**   Whatever you do, do not repeat a past mistake. If that means dumping someone or something, let it go. Your future contentment depends on your rational approach now. Let new contacts give you a new outlook but also continue to cultivate a relationship that is intensifying. There appears to be a lot of perfection around you.

**Thursday, November 27 (Moon in Libra)**   A low-key but pleasant day awaits you. Be thankful that the little that does happen is on the positive side. Some may find the pleasure principle very much in force; do not overindulge! A Cancer or a Capricorn could provide a much needed and rather diverse point of view.

**Friday, November 28 (Moon Libra to Scorpio 8:13 p.m.)**   Be ready for change and variety; the more you diversify the better off you will be. It is no time to be a "Johnny one-note." A rather demanding person offers little in return; do not feel you have to comply with his/her requests. No matter how urgent they seem.

**Saturday, November 29 (Moon in Scorpio)**    A piece of information that floated into your view yesterday could prove very useful today. Be sure to apply it. A lot of basic things need doing today and will command the better part of your time and attention. Don't feel you have to go it alone; speak up and ask others to pitch in. A mutual rebuilding project could make everyone feel good.

**Sunday, November 30 (Moon Scorpio to Sagittarius 9:08 p.m.)**    Open up and listen to someone who is trying to communicate with you. You yourself may not be the voice of reason now. What's most important is to maintain your emotional balance and to be thrown off your feet by a temporarily rocky boat. Try to do something for yourself today because your self-esteem may need a shot in the arm. The lucky number is 5.

# DECEMBER 1986

**Monday, December 1 (Moon in Sagittarius)**    It appears that everyone needs more space—including you. Steer clear of close quarters today if you are to avoid an explosion. Some plans get turned upside down but you should try to take it with equinimity. The new moon in your house of relationships could cause some activity there; be willing to make a concession.

**Tuesday, December 2 (Moon Sagittarius to Capricorn 8:26 p.m.)**    Once again there may be some static between you and an important "other." If you play your cards right, it could be a productive clash of ideas rather than an open dispute. In fact, many Geminis will experience the excitement of discovery—possibly even a new relationship or partnership. The key thing is to keep talking and not let your feelings bottle up.

**Wednesday, December 3 (Moon in Capricorn)**    For many Geminis, the experience of a deepening relationship is a satisfying one. However, all should be careful not to take this for granted. It is necessary to acknowledge. For some, the recent upheavals may be resolved by a rather major change. Possibly even a change of residence or marital status. For others, the financial resources of another person may be up for scrutiny. The lucky number today is 6.

***Thursday, December 4 (Moon Capricorn to Aquarius 8:23 p.m.)*** Watch out for some tricky maneuvers; someone may be trying to manipulate you. And the scenario could include money or investment. Whatever the case, you should be absolutely clear about what you want and define your terms in no uncertain terms. At all costs, protect your interests and do not fall for a sob story. A Pisces or a Virgo could be prominent in today's activities.

***Friday, December 5 (Moon in Aquarius)*** Look before you leap now, because you could become inextricably involved. Feelings are running high—possibly romantic ones. For some, the step may involve travel or education. While these things are important, you should be very clear about your total picture before you take the plunge. The lucky number is 8.

***Saturday, December 6 (Moon Aquarius to Pisces 10:48 p.m.)*** Many will celebrate because they are able to free themselves of a losing proposition. This is no time for sentimentality. Nor for gullibility; that means, be sympathetic when someone leans on you, but do not let him/her take advantage of her. For many, it will be a very sociable weekend. And possibly a romantic one as well.

***Sunday, December 7 (Moon in Pisces)*** Make it clear that you are capable of independent action; the more direct you are, the more smoothly things will go. Some will have a pioneering spirit now and want to branch out in new directions. It is an excellent time to do so—particularly in career or community activities. A valuable contact is a distinct possibility.

***Monday, December 8 (Moon in Pisces)*** Don't try to be different just for the sake of being different. Choose

the course that is agreeable to everyone. It is probably
the most familiar one. Accept some constructive criti-
cism and realize it comes from someone who really has
your best interest at heart. He/she could be a higher-up
which makes it all the more important. A minor health
problem may disappear.

**Tuesday, December 9 (Moon Pisces 4:49 a.m.)**
Though it is not necessarily in the romantic sense,
you will be courted today. Examine the proposal carefully and realize that someone may be flattering you
deliberately. Your sense of curiosity is probably very
great now, and you should indulge it by opening the
door on some new areas of interest. Enjoy your present
popularity.

**Wednesday, December 10 (Moon in Aries)**    It's nice
to know that you've got a friend—possibly many. At
any rate, it is comforting to know that you do not have
to go it alone. Some Geminis may have to set precon-
ceived notions aside and be willing to broaden their
personal horizons. It is not like you to be narrow-
minded. A fascinating individual—possibly a Scorpio—
has invaluable information and contacts. The lucky
number today is 4.

**Thursday, December 11 (Moon Aries to Taurus 2:10
p.m.)**    Something happens today that forces you to
recognize the difference between reality and illusion;
though it may not be pleasant, you will be stronger as a
result. For many, the status quo gets a real shaking up.
However, with favorable influences in effect, the results should be excellent. Give serious thought to travel.

**Friday, December 12 (Moon in Taurus)**    Lend a
sympathetic ear and a warm shoulder to someone who
needs your help and counsel. Though you may not
regard the problem as a serious one, you should take it
seriously. Some Geminis are about to make a very important discovery and should catch glimmerings of it
now. Your cycle is moving up and you should trust
those little hunches.

ter what your scenario, you are going to have to look behind the scenes for answers. Self-reliance is the key to success now.

**Tuesday, December 23 (Moon in Virgo)**    This could be a memorable day for Gemini. For many, a commitment will be made in a relationship—or at least it will grow a lot stronger. For others, the issue may be home and property. Whatever it is, the keynote is additional responsibility but a great increase in personal satisfaction. Don't let any opportunities pass you by! The lucky number is 8.

**Wednesday, December 24 (Moon Virgo to Libra 12:05 a.m.)**    Warm feelings are the order of the day and you should be basking in the glow of affection. Possibly gratitude as well. Some long overdue thanks should come in now. Though immediate happenings are most interesting, look into the future a bit and see where the greatest potential lies. Expect a "surprise gift" from where you would least expect it.

**Thursday, December 25 (Moon in Libra)**    Many Geminis will be thinking lofty thoughts on this day of rest and recreation. You rise above immediate pleasures to an understanding of spiritual values. For some, the scenario is more mundane, but equally satisfying. A Leo or an Aquarian could add a special spark to the holiday.

**Friday, December 26 (Moon Libra to Scorpio 7:06 a.m.)**    Practical realities must be dealt with today, in spite of the season. They may cause you to make a mental review of your curent situation. Some Geminis will seek out a person who has been available for consultation in the past; he/she can offer an excellent perspective on your current dilemma.

**Saturday, December 27 (Moon in Scorpio)**    Smack in the middle of the holidays you may find yourself saddled with a lot of responsibilities—or at least an urge to get a lot done. The focus today is on work and productivity. Don't neglect your social life however, because it should be most inviting now. You can have fun and still protect yourself from overindulgence. The lucky number today is 3.

***Sunday, December 28 (Moon Scorpio to Sagittarius 8:20 a.m.)*** A change of scene is in store, and it should prove to be just what you need. You run the risk of getting bogged down in nitty-gritties when you should be looking at the overall picture. A conversation you get into today offers valuable information you should not ignore. Make notes! Dependents of all kinds—including pets—may make demands on your time today. Give yourself equal time!

***Monday, December 29 (Moon in Sagittarius)*** Moderation in all things is the watchword today. A slight of the nerves may tempt you to be rather snappish; take it slow and force yourself to be tactful. Your reward will come in the form of encouraging words from a partner or other family member. Those who have been looking for it will find the necessary funds now to bring their plans into reality.

***Tuesday, December 30 (Moon Sagittarius to Capricorn 7:54 a.m.)*** Sweet harmony should be the order of the day, in every sense of the word. In fact, you may go around humming as you review the past year with a philosophical attitude. You see that, on balance, you have made quite a bit of progress. However, you also see where you have failed to read the signals right. The accent for the coming year should be on greater objectivity.

***Wednesday, December 31 (Moon in Capricorn)*** It should be a low-key but intriguing celebration of the New Year for you. It is possible you will come into contact with an individual or individuals who open up a whole new area of interest for you—one that has been "mysterious" but very tempting for you in the past. Many Geminis will bring in the New Year with a frank and open talk with their most "significant other."

## *About the Author*

Born on August 5, 1926, in Philadelphia, Omarr was the only astrologer ever given full-time duty in the U.S. Army as an astrologer. He also is regarded as the most erudite astrologer of our time and the best-known, through his syndicated column (300 newspapers), and his radio and television programs (he is Merv Griffin's "resident astrologer"). Omarr has been called the most "knowledgeable astrologer since Evangeline Adams." His forecasts of Nixon's downfall, the end of World War II in mid-August of 1945, the assassination of John F. Kennedy, Roosevelt's election to a fourth term and his death in office . . . these and many others . . . are on record and quoted enough to be considered "legendary."

## *About This Series*

This is one of a series of
Twelve Day-by-Day Astrological Guides
for the signs in 1986
by Sydney Omarr

# COUPON

**PROF. LALLEMEND**
Dept SO-8  • POB 252
BROOKLYN, N.Y. 11204

516 Fifth Ave., N.Y., N.Y. 10036

**Dear Reader,**

You do not have to 'merely believe' Professor Lallemend, the renowned astrologer, because he will **PROVE** to you how he can help you make your life better!

Just fill out this form and mail it. Professor Lallemend will prepare **YOUR HOROSCOPE** and predict—without charge **TWO ESSENTIAL EVENTS IN YOUR LIFE.** You will be thoroughly convinced by the precision of the forecast and will also learn how you can gain success and inner contentment, as well as avoiding everything which can be an obstacle in the path of your happiness. You will receive his advice absolutely free of charge. All you have to do is, answer the questions below, and mail the coupon TODAY.

Please send me free of charge and without any obligation on my part my horoscope and two predictions in an unmarked envelope.

My Birthdate ...............

Time ........ Place ........

Please let me know as well, my lucky numbers. I enclose here a number between 0 and 9 which suddenly comes to my mind:

_______________________

NAME........................

ADD. ........................

............................

CITY .......................

STATE :.........ZIP ........

# Know in advance the changes in your life

Wouldn't it be useful to know when important events in your life are going to happen? How would you respond? What will you experience emotionally, intellectually and psychologically? And how will these experiences affect your life.

Your transits can provide valuable clues to various trends or stages of personal growth. This is especially true for the slower moving outer planets—Jupiter through Pluto. The transits for these planets are long lasting and profound in their psychological consequences. Many occur only once in a lifetime. The Astral Forecast is all about the outer planets.

This horoscope provides a reliable tool for astrological forecasting. The Astral Forecast will show you how the outer transits affect your sense of timing, that is, the times that are appropriate for you to take certain kinds of actions and inappropriate for others. This horoscope includes every significant transit to your outer planets that occurs in a twelve-month period. You can use your Astral Forecast to better understand how the outer planets affect such important life issues as career, child rearing, love, marriage and more.

For example, when Jupiter is in the first house, this transit represents a major growth cycle in your life. This is the best time for you to explore who you really are as an individual. Under this transit, you will feel more secure about yourself and the impression you make on others. Therefore, understanding yourself and your influence on others can make this transit an especially powerful and

important time in your life. This is also a time for learning and gaining new experience. All this is part of your present need for personal growth, which affects not only yourself, but also the way you deal with the world as a whole. This is one time when persons and resources are likely to be drawn to you, and you should take constructive advantage of them.

You can find out in advance what your transits are going to be. But if you do it on your own, you will have to consult several astronomical tables to find the positions of each of the transiting planets every day and then compare them mathematically to the positions of the planets at the time of your birth.

There's an easier way to learn of your transits. Our IBM System/36 computer will handle all the calculations and provide you with information on all your outer transits based on your exact time and place of birth. With the Astral Forecast you not only receive the most accurate calculation of your personal transits for the next twelve months, you will also receive an extensive printout interpreting the character and significance of your individual transits.

Your Astral Forecast is the most accurate and authoritative guide to the outer transits that you can receive. It is based on the work of Robert Hand, one of America's most famous astrologers, and the author of several astrology books.

Like all Para Research horoscopes, the Astral Forecast is inexpensive. For just $16.00 you can have the same kind of advice that would otherwise cost you hundreds of dollars. This low price is possible because the astrological data is stored in our computer, and can be easily formatted and printed. Also, the mathematical calculations can be done in a matter of minutes. Your only cost is the cost of putting your personal information into the computer, producing one copy and then mailing it.

When you order your Astral Forecast, you receive an unconditional money-back guarantee. This means you can return your Astral Forecast at any time and get a full refund of the purchase price. We take all the risk.

Order your Astral Forecast today. Discover how the transits can bring energy to each part of your personality, fulfill your potential and help you gain more control over your own life.
© 1983 Para Research, Inc.

# "Next to my mother, you have been the greatest inspiration of my life."

### You'll be amazed!

When you read what Marguerite Carter has to say about your life in the year ahead you'll be amazed. She delves into the most important areas of your life: romance, money, goals, and significant changes. You'll find out all the wonderful ways you can live a better life when you have your Unitology Forecast prepared for you by Marguerite Carter.

### She'll help you.

Marguerite Carter has counseled thousands of enthusiastic followers around the world for decades. She has been the guiding light and helping hand for people from all walks of life: business leaders, hollywood stars and just everyday folks. There is a good reason why they seek her services year after year. They get the help they need in the most important areas of their lives!

### '. . . it was amazing.'

People write all the time telling about how Marguerite Carter has helped them.

". . . it was amazing. I just can't believe it." W.C., Canada

". . . could not put it down until I read it cover to cover." M.L., Illinois.

"Without a doubt, next to my mother, you have been the greatest inspiration of my life. Many others could probably say the same thing." M.A., PA

In letter after letter people comment on the realistic guidance they've received for getting what they want from life. They've found the help they need in times of decision or resolving personal problems. These are judgments by a caring counselor, not some impersonal computer.

### Hidden Opportunities

The things you want most may not be out of reach. Marguerite Carter says, "Many people are completely unaware that the opportunities for money, love or advancement are passing them by almost daily . . ." Without knowledge of when the conditions are favorable or unfavorable, the chances for success and happiness are greatly diminished.

Get your Unitology Forecast with special notations by Marguerite Carter. It will be prepared to your specific birthdate information. Remember that you will receive a full year of guidance, regardless of when your request is received, and you'll know that your forecast has come from one of the world's most highly respected astrologer-counselors.

MARGUERITE CARTER

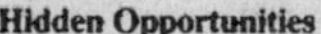

O-6

Marguerite Carter • P.O. Box 807 • Indianapolis, Indiana 46206

☐ Yes Miss Carter, Please send me my Unitology Forecast for the year ahead. Enclosed is my remittance of $9.95 plus $1.00 for postage and handling. (First Class $1.30) Make all checks payable in U.S. funds. Allow 4 weeks for delivery.

Name ___________________________________________________

Address _________________________________________________

City _______________________________ State __________ Zip Code __________

Birthplace _______________________________________________

Month _________________ Day _________________ Year _________________

Place _________________________________ Hour _________________

# ASTROLOGY QUESTIONNAIRE

Help us bring you even better astrology guides by filling out this survey and mailing it today.

A.  Book Title (Sign): ___________________________

B.  Using the scale below how would you rate this astrological guide? (Place one rating from 0–10 in the space provided.)

| Poor | Not So Good | O.K. | Good | Excellent |
|------|-------------|------|------|-----------|
| 0  1 | 2  3 | 4  5  6 | 7  8 | 9  10 |

Rating

Overall Opinion of book

Essay On:
1. Defining Terms _______
2. Your House of The Sun _______
3. The Geometry of Relationships _______
4. Twelve Places at the Table _______
5. Moods of the Moon _______
6. Venus and Mars _______
7. Venus Sign Position Chart _______
8. Mars Sign Position Chart _______
9. The Planets as "Stars" _______
10. Astrotrivia _______
11. Sun Sign Changes _______
12. Your Sign: The Big Picture _______
13. Your Sign: Objectives and Obstacles _______
14. Pairing Off With Your Sign _______
15. Your Sign's Sex Role Dilemma _______
16. Your Sign: Female _______
17. Your Sign: Male _______
18. Your Sign: Help Wanted _______
19. How "Pure" a __________ are you? _______
20. Find Your Rising Sign _______
21. Your Sign: Astro-Outlook for '86 _______
22. 15 Months of Day-By-Day Predictions _______

C. In total about how many astrology guides have you purchased for yourself in the past 12 months?
# of books _______________

D. What topics would you be interested in having Sydney Omarr write about in the 1987 Astrology Guide?

_______________________________________

_______________________________________

E. What is your education?

1( ) High School    3( ) 4 yrs college
2( ) 2 yrs college    4( ) Postgraduate

F. What is your occupation? _______________

G. What is your marital status?

1( ) Single    3( ) Divorced    5( ) Widowed
2( ) Married   4( ) Separated

H. Age: _______        I. Sex: 1( ) Male
                               2( ) Female

---

**Please Print Name:**_______________________________

**Address**_______________________________________

**City**_____________**State**____________**Zip**__________

**Phone # (    )**_______________

**Thank you. Please send to New American Library, Research Dept., 1633 Broadway, New York, NY 10019**